Conflict and Cohesion
in Western European
Social Democratic Parties

This Book is dedicated
to F.W. Bealey

Conflict and Cohesion in Western European Social Democratic Parties

Edited by
David S. Bell and Eric Shaw

P I N T E R
PUBLISHERS
LONDON, NEW YORK

Distributed in the United States and Canada by St. Martin's Press

Pinter Publishers Ltd.
25 Floral Street, London WC2E 9DS, United Kingdom

First published in 1994

Distributed exclusively in the USA and Canada by St. Martin's Press, Inc., Room 400, 175 Fifth Avenue, New York, NY10010, USA

British Library Cataloguing in Publication Data

A CIP catalogue record for this book is available from the British Library

ISBN 1 85567 127 1

Library of Congress Cataloging-in-Publication Data

Conflict and cohesion in the west European social democratic parties /
    edited by David S. Bell and Eric Shaw.
        p.   cm.
    Includes bibliographical references and index.
    ISBN 1–85567–127–1
    1. Political parties – Europe.   2. Socialism – Europe.   I. Bell,
David S., 1949–   .   II. Shaw, Eric, 1949–   .
JN94.A979C647   1994
324.24'072–dc20   94–15116
                                                                                      CIP

Typeset by Mayhew Typesetting, Rhayader, Powys
Printed and bound in Great Britain by Biddles Ltd., Guildford and King's Lynn

Contents

List of contributors

David Arter is Professor of European Integration at Leeds Metropolitan University

David S. Bell is Lecturer in Political Studies at the University of Leeds

Martin Bull is Lecturer in Politics at the University of Salford

Byron Criddle is Senior Lecturer in Politics at the University of Aberdeen

Richard Gillespie is Professor, School of Languages and Area Studies, at the University of Portsmouth

Knut Heidar is a Lecturer at the Institute of Political Science in the University of Oslo

Stephen Padgett is Senior Lecturer in European Politics at the University of Essex

Philip van Praag Jr is Lecturer in Political Science at the University of Amsterdam

Eric Shaw is Lecturer in Politics at the University of Stirling

Preface

This book is a series of case studies on the internal politics of social democracy. We are aware of the substantial theoretical and taxonomic work done in this domain but the authors have neither stuck to any one approach nor chosen particular definitions (of social democracy, for example). Our aim has been to lay out the factual groundwork on the inner life of these parties in a comparative framework – something which has not been attempted before.

Many people have participated in the preparation of this research and of this book at various stages. The planning took place at a conference funded by the Friedrich Ebert Foundation to which our thanks are due. In addition, we would like to thank the participants at the conference in the University of Leeds, whose comments were well taken: Dr Abse, Dr Hine, Prof Paterson, Dr Ware, Dr Coates and Dr Schwarzmantel. We are particularly grateful to Dr Peter Schulz for his advice and encouragement. Finally we would like to thank our long-suffering publishers (Nicola Viinikka, in particular) for their patience.

D.S. Bell
Eric Shaw
November 1993

List of abbreviations

AfA	Arbeitsgemeinschaft für Arbeitnhemerfragen (Germany)
AP	Alianza Popular (Spain)
APO	Ausserparlamentarische Opposition (Germany)
ARP	Anti-Revolutionaire Partij (Netherlands)
ASF	Arbeitsgemeinschaft Sozialdemokratischer Frauen (Germany)
ATP	Allmän Tillaggspension (Sweden)
AUEW	Amalgamated Union of Engineering Workers (UK)
CCOO	Comisiones Obreras (Spain)
CDA	Christen Democratisch Appel (Netherlands)
CEPES	Centro de Estudios Políticos y Sociales (Spain)
CERES	Centre d'Etudes, de Recherches et d'Education Socialiste (France)
CFDT	Confédération Française Democratique du Travail (France)
CGIL	Confederazione Generale del Lavoro (Italy)
CHU	Christelijk Historische Unie (Netherlands)
CLPD	Campaign for Labour Party Democracy (UK)
CPSU	Communist Party of the Soviet Union
D'66/D66	Democraten 66 (Netherlands)
DC	Democrazia Cristiana (Italy)
DGB	Deutscher Gewerkschaftsbund (Germany)
DNA	Det Norske Arbeiderparti (Norway)
DS '70	Democratisch Socialisten '70 (Netherlands)
EEA	European Economic Area
EETPU	Electrical, Electronic, Telecommunications and Plumbing Union (UK)
ENA	Ecole Nationale d'Administration (France)
FEN	Fédération de l'Education Nationale (France)
FNV	Federatie Nederlandse Vakbeweging (Netherlands)
GMWU	General and Municipal Workers' Union (UK)
IG	Industrie Gewerkschaft (Germany)
IS	Izquierda Socialista (Spain)
IO	Izquierda Unida (Spain)
JUSO	Jungsozialisten (Germany)
KAS	Kristendemokratisk Samhällsparteit
KdS	Kristen demokratisk Samling (Sweden)

KVP	Katholieke Volkspartij (Netherlands)
LCC	Labour Coordinating Committee (UK)
LO	Landsorganisationen (Sweden)
NEC	National Executive Committee (UK)
NUPE	National Union of Public Employees (UK)
PCF	Parti Communiste Français (France)
PCI	Partito Comunista Italiano (Italy)
PDS	Partito Democratico della Sinistra (Italy)
PdUP	Partito di Unità Proletaria (Italy)
PLP	Parliamentary Labour Party (UK)
PPR	Politieke Partij Radikalen (Netherlands)
PS	Parti Socialiste (France)
PSI	Partito Socialista Italiano (Italy)
PSOE	Partido Socialista Obrero Español (Spain)
PSP	Pasifistisch Socialistische Partij (Netherlands)
PSU	Parti Socialiste Unifié (France)
PvdA	Partij van de Arbeid (Netherlands)
SAFE	Socialdemokratiska arbetsgruppen för en alternativ energipolitik
SAP	Sveriges Socialdemokratiska Arbetareparti (Sweden)
SDS	Sozialistischer Deutscher Studentenbund (Germany)
SF	Sosialistisk Folkeparti (Norway)
SFIO	Section Française de l'Internationale Ouvrière (France)
SHB	Sozialdemocratischer Hochschulbund (Germany)
SIFO	Svenska Institutet för Opinionsundersökningar (Sweden)
SPD	Sozialdemokratische Partei Deutschlands (Germany)
SNES	Syndicat National de l'Enseignement Secondaire (France)
SSU	Sveriges Socialdemokratiska Ungdomsorganisationen (Sweden)
SV	Socialistisk Venstreparti (Norway)
TCO	Tjänstemännens Centralorganisation (Sweden)
TGWU	Transport and General Workers' Union (UK)
TUC	Trades Union Congress (UK)
UCD	Unión del Centro Democrático (Spain)
UDE	Unión Democrática Española (Spain)
UGCS	Union des Groupes et Clubs Socialistes (France)
UGT	Unión General de Trabajadores (Spain)
VpK	Vänsterparteit Komunisterna (Sweden)
VVD	Volkspartij voor Vrijheid en Democratie (Netherlands)
WAO	Wet op de Arbeidsongeschiktheidsverzekering (Netherlands)
WBS	Wiardi Beckman Stichting (Netherlands)

Introduction
David S. Bell and Eric Shaw

Modern political theory has not yet caught up with the fragmented nature of political parties. Although obvious to participants and to commentators, there has been a distinct tendency to portray political parties as unitary actors. Whereas the analysis of parties and party systems will refer to internal party power structures, for the most part these are discounted in subsequent analysis.

Parties are not monolithic and the actors, politicians, activists and institutions are involved in 'games' at several levels. Party actions cannot be understood if these internal conflicts are ignored and the nature of internal alliances and coalitions has to be understood to make any sense of party behaviour. Within parties there is political competition, and this competition can spill over into the struggle for power within the national party system. Sometimes the inner party struggle can result in a split, but less dramatic conflicts also have an impact on party behaviour.

In America inner party competition is legitimised and a working part of the system – for example, through the many primaries – but in Europe it is not so well regarded. To some extent the public perception of party unity is important: it is a commonplace that party discord will be punished at the polls and politicians (possibly wrongly) strive to demonstrate solidarity within the party. To some extent, therefore, party factionalism tends to be hidden where possible (better in some parties than in others) but the nature of the modern media makes this increasingly difficult. It remains that the cohesion, or otherwise, of political parties is important and is a key variable in the explanation of party behaviour.

We have therefore taken the principal social democratic parties in Europe and looked at the factional situation in each one. There is good reason for adopting their approach, although it is unusual, and the parties chosen are the main 'northern' European ones plus the Spanish PSOE and the Italian PDS (former Italian Communist Party and now in the Second International). The similarity of political family cannot disguise the differences of political situation but they all display a marked factionalism distinguishable by national characteristics. There is no comparative study of these parties' factionalism, although it is a well-recognised feature of party life, and the nature of factionalism has to be related to the individual party. Nevertheless, we attempt here a systematic study.

In this study we start with the German Social Democratic Party (SPD) which, for a long time after the war, was held up as a paradigm 'non-factional' socialist party. However, as Stephen Padgett points out, the 1980s saw the rise of new dimensions of conflict which the SPD was unable to contain, and there was a 'loss of cohesion' at all levels.

Stephen Padgett locates the relative post-war cohesion of the SPD in the general party consensus about the aims of social democracy (which margin-alised the left) and the autonomy of the party leadership. In the German party power lay with the leadership which had a powerful machine at its disposal, so that the party 'resembled a pyramid' with the Bonn elite at the apex. In addition, the external constraints in the party, the centripetal force of the German political system in particular, helped enforce a high degree of discipline. These pillars of party unity were increasingly weakened in the 1980s.

First the SPD was challenged by the rise of the New Left and became 'infected' through the Young Socialists (JUSO), an organisation which itself became resistant to party discipline. This '1968 generation' was inte-grated into the party and emerged in the 1980s as a left-wing challenge to the party's organisation and values. In the 1970s, under Helmut Schmidt's chancellorship, the government's autonomy from the party began to diminish and by the SPD Congress of 1982 the government no longer commanded a majority in the party. Likewise, although Helmut Schmidt was on good terms with the German union leadership, relations with ordinary activists deteriorated to the extent that a clash was almost inevitable (the government fell before the collision). The third component of the change was the rise of the external challenge of the Greens, which repeated many of the themes which the 1968 generation within the party was using.

The SPD was further split in the 1980s by conflicts over tradition and modernity and then made a confused response to German reunification. Despite this background the intensity of factional conflict has declined. The explanation of this apparent paradox lies in the SPD's movement away from the extra-parliamentary movements where conflict was generated, and the loss of the Bad Godesberg value system led not to in-fighting, but to demobilisation. German social democracy has thus come a full circle from disunity to unity since the 1970s, but with the difference that the ferment and motivation evident then are now missing.

The creation of the PDS in Italy provides a case study of a move from a totalitarian organisation – the Italian Communist Party – to a social demo-cratic one. The change was both a cultural and organisational one and factionalism is at the heart of the matter. Italian communism, like other communist parties, outlawed any contacts not specifically endorsed by the leadership, and these were termed 'factional'. The implication of members in 'factional activity' was grounds for immediate expulsion. The 'democratic centralism' of the old Communist Party made it distinctively disciplined in a notably conflictual Italian political system, but was also a reminder of its Leninist origins and Soviet loyalties. In order to manage a transition to social democracy, democratic centralism, the extreme suppression of intra-party conflict, had to be abandoned. (The PCI had been relatively tolerant before its recomposition.)

Martin Bull analyses the transition and the new PDS party. The peculiarity of the Italian Communist Party's position was that 'democratic centralism' was the disciplinary weapon which the party most needed to manage a successful transformation, but no transformation could be complete without a formal factional system flourishing within the party. The dismantling of democratic centralism strengthened the opponents of reform and helped put the leadership under the power of competing factions, much as in other Italian parties. As Martin Bull describes it the PCI, the 'most highly disciplined and organised political party in Italy', has been replaced by the PDS which has gone to the other extreme. The PDS is decentralised and has a new local structure and its tutelage over satellite organisations has been reduced. The result has been a paralysis as an outcome of factional dispute and the representation of factions on governing bodies (plus a split). The new party has yet to find an antidote to factionalism, and the sudden outburst of factional in-fighting has been blamed for the directionless drift of the PDS. However, as Martin Bull argues, every fresh defeat for the new party (and its birth was not accompanied by immediate success) worsened the internal turmoil. The experiment with social democracy cannot now be reversed, but the author's conclusion is that the PDS has embraced the principle of 'unity in diversity' and has both been accepted by the social democratic world and retained some of its past with it.

The Spanish PSOE, discussed by Richard Gillespie, is burdened with a long history of intense rivalry which could have led to intense factionalism within the party. To some extent this did occur, with a short period of rivalry between fundamentalists and moderates from legalisation (in 1977) to the Congress of 1979. At the extraordinary Congress of 1979, however, Felipe González triumphed over opponents and a period of near-monolithic unity was ushered in. Richard Gillespie examines this extraordinary period of unity and attributes it to the PSOE's success in government, but a big part of the reason for the discipline of the PSOE from 1979 to 1988 was the unifying personality of González himself, though it also depended on the control of the party by Alfonso Guerra.

Since 1988, however, the PSOE has begun to show symptoms of the old malaise. The economic growth achieved in the 1980s has begun to falter as external pressures from the unions and pressure groups began to have their effects. Alfonso Guerra was removed from the government in January 1991 after a financial scandal and divisions reasserted themselves. If the PSOE had been modernised by González and Guerra, and the ideological dimensions to conflict were accordingly weak, there was a continual argument between traditional social democrats and the New Left and between the technocratic free market 'managers' and the market sceptics. In the first phase of PSOE government the left, the unions and Guerra's supporters had all accepted the restructuring of the Spanish industrial system in the name of modernisation. However the PSOE's persistence with the same policies led to a clash with the unions and, eventually, to criticism by Guerra's supporters. At the end of the 1980s other 'oppositional' factions appeared, based on personalities rather than issues or ideology, but these had a lesser impact (they did, however, draw attention to the continuing personal nature of party alignments in the PSOE) although the regional federations began to make their presence felt in intra-party battles. PSOE factionalism began to reappear, and was fuelled by the González government's decline in the polls and the prospect of a victory by the revamped conservative right. The PSOE therefore stood, in 1993, at a crucial juncture, and whether it can manage fruitful, non-destructive debate during electoral decline is a question as much about the nature of the Spanish party as about its future in Spanish democracy.

The Swedish Social Democratic Party (SAP) has, like the German SDP, been held up as a model of what a socialist party should be, but it, too, underwent change as its astonishing 40 years in power began to falter. Swedish social democracy was from the start a coalition. The end of the 1945–75 *trente glorieuse* years of postwar economic expansion imposed strains on the party and its crucial relationship with the unions and this, combined with structural and ideological changes (such as the collapse of communism and the rise of the Greens), was expressed as internal friction within the SAP.

David Arter recalls that if Swedish social democracy always was a forum for the cooperative resolution of competing interests, in the second half of the 1980s the forces making for cohesion were significantly weakened. In particular, two potential cleavages, those between 'ecological socialists' and others (over nuclear energy) and those between the pro- and anti-marketeers (over European Community membership) became salient. The SAP was split by a change in its composition – as middle-class interests began to expand and ruling-class cohesion to decline – and in the problems (particularly spending) which have hit Sweden's elaborate welfare state.

All the same the SAP, so David Arter shows, has not suffered the splits inflicted on the Labour parties of Finland, Denmark and Britain, and the intense political personal factionalism has been absent from Swedish social democracy. The splits have been issue-based, but have not resulted in the debilitating internal struggles characteristic of, say, the French Socialist Party. The source of this unity could be the party's ideology, but more likely contributing factors are the unity arising from government discipline and the conciliatory style of the party's leader, Ingvar Carlsson. David Arter also points out that the 'structural distance' resulting from the change in relationship between SAP and the unions has loosened the link to one of its most hawkish elements.

Swedish social democracy, however, was in 1993 not over its crisis and it had not, any more than other socialist parties, overcome the problems of the welfare state and the challenge from the New Right. Swedish social democracy was still seeking its mobilising issue for the 1990s, and still had not found it, as the decline in membership seems to indicate. However, the sources of cohesion in the Swedish party probably indicate that issue cleavages will not result in the intense factionalism triggered off by the same crisis in its sister parties.

Knut Heidar, in a study of the Norwegian Labour Party (DNA), examines the paradoxical decline in both conflict and cohesion in the party and the institutional context of the political evolution of the party. The problem, as Knut Heidar identifies it, is that during the 1960s the DNA went through a period of open and quite intense conflict but that during the 1980s the party became a site of relatively muted conflict and poor cohesion.

The immediate postwar years, despite some opposition from the left to Nato membership, were years of great party solidarity no doubt further cemented by attacks from the Communist Party. This period ended in the 1960s with the eruption of the issue of EC membership which caused a split (with one group moving to the left-wing Socialist Party) and internal opposition rising fast. The membership resented the high-handed, not to say crude, manner in which the European issue was handled. Party areas which were clearly opposed to membership of the EC voted for the leadership's policy of joining. An organisational battle opened, which has its equivalent in other parties of the social democratic left, as activists on the left struggled to wrest the levers of power from the Old Guard, generally right-wing, figures. The 1980s saw a familiar addition to the dimension of conflict as the anti-Nato 'peace movement' rose and as environmental issues came to the forefront.

These conflictual years changed the culture of the DNA, and the diminution of the ideological conflicts did not lead to a new feeling of party solidarity. The activism of the party declined, the old working class also diminished and a generational 'modernisation' process was under way. By the same token the old oligarchical leadership was not restored and the comparison of the leaders' handling of the first and second Norwegian applications to join the EC is instructive. The first was old-style machine politics and touched off a 20-year crisis, the second was more deftly (and delicately) handled by party archons. The DNA, in the outcome, is not so faction-ridden but still faces potential conflict even if this is no longer, in Heidar's view, the ideological, mobilising struggle of the past.

The French Socialist Party, both in its old (SFIO) form and its newer form as the Parti Socialiste (PS), has been prone to factionalism and has split on several occasions. The factionalism pre-dates the creation of the

French Communist Party (PCF) in a split in 1920, but the PS has seen its factional in-fighting fuelled by the difficulties of dealing with a large communist party to its left. The Fifth Republic did not eliminate the PCF and it added one further dimension to faction politics: presidentialism. The personalisation of factions around potential presidential figures added a further intensity, and bitterness, to factional rivalries within the French Socialist Party.

The history of the French Socialist Party from its refoundation (as the PS) in 1969 and its takeover by François Mitterrand in 1971, can be seen as a history of factional interplay. This was both a strength and a weakness. It was a strength because, masterfully manipulated by Mitterrand, the pluralism of the party was both enlivening and yet not exclusive, allowing, as it did, for many contributions to be made to the questions of the day and for newcomers to enter the debate without difficulty. It was a weakness because the factionalism was played on by the PCF and presented an incomprehensible and bafflingly divided front to public opinion.

The factionalism of the 1970s revolved around the self-styled CERES left, the Mitterrand leadership, and a challenge from the 'social democratic' wing (a label they repudiate) led by Michel Rocard. Both of these wings were structured around their attitudes to the PCF (in particular on how to deal with it), but the challenge from Rocard was the more dangerous because Rocard was himself a presidential aspirant with strong support in the opinion polls.

The collapse of the PCF did not end the factional disputes inside the PS although the removal of a revolutionary Marxist party on the left did transform the ideological landscape. The continuing personal rivalries, however, intensified with the prospect of the presidential nomination fuelling the principal disputes. This erupted in the 1990 Rennes Party Congress, from which the PS never recovered. One aim of Rocard's new leadership of 1993 was somehow to refashion a party in which factional rivalry would be controlled, if not eliminated, but to facilitate pluralism.

The Partij van de Arbeid (PvdA, the Netherlands Labour Party) is a social democratic party which has known various fortunes but which is forced to deal with the dominant religious parties and has in consequence not been able to develop the extensive electoral base of other socialist parties. The PvdA's relationship with the confessional parties was, argues Philip van Praag, one of the sources of internal factionism in the party but it also experienced many of the problems of its sister parties, including the arrival of the New Left and the mid-1980s ecological surge. The New Left changed the PvdA's organisation to decentralise candidate selection and reduce the power of the parliamentary party. The left-leaning party in the early 1970s moved to confront the confessional parties but the activists distorted the party leadership to the extent that, in 1977, a coalition deal was rejected with a traumatic outcome.

A gap opened up between the party leadership and the activists and between activists and voters. This was confirmed by the election of Max van den Berg and campaigns against nuclear power plants and Nato. Van den Berg supported activist pressure which forced PvdA ministers out of the government after only a year. On leaving government the PvdA became one of the leading forces in the campaign against the deployment of Cruise missiles in the Netherlands.

The result of this and the confrontational strategy was a series of electoral defeats and a recognition that the voters' loyalties had been taken for granted. A change of policy was instituted in 1981 and this met little resistance. The PvdA participated in the October 1989 government but by 1991 it was in deep crisis because it had seemingly had no impact on the confessional–conservative coalition. Having operated a strategic change it found itself facing a crisis of the welfare state and having to meet expectations, and it had no answer to either. A series of factional battles for key posts was expected as the old certainties about the welfare state were examined, but none was forthcoming. As Philip van Praag notes, the history of the PvdA does not support the proposition that frequent and intense conflict are necessarily debilitating nor that unity and solidarity are either necessary or sufficient factors in an election victory.

The British Labour Party, which is the subject of Eric Shaw's analysis, hardly needs to be underlined as the site of a virtually uninterrupted factionalism from the 1950s to the 1980s. This process reached its apotheosis in the late 1970s and early 1980s when the party split under the impact of a grassroots insurgency. Eric Shaw looks at this factionalism through the nature and composition of power in the party and its evolution. The emergence of the factionalism which so characterised the Labour Party was a result of the dissipation of the unusual concentration of power in the hands of the leadership of the parliamentary party. This power was, however, based on institutional control and the cohesion of the dominant coalition and both of these centripetal forces began to weaken during the decade 1970–79. The unions, which traditionally supported the leadership, shifted markedly to the left and there was a rising left-wing tide which, among other things, gave the party left a majority in its National Executive Committee. A rift gradually widened between the predominantly right-wing parliamentary leadership and the wider party (although this was masked by Wilson's conciliatory tactics for some years, this gulf between leaders and led steadily widened after the advent of the Labour government in 1964).

In consequence of the widening split, the Labour Party spiralled down into its 1979–1983 'civil war', one major element of which was a constitutional reform which shifted power away from the parliamentary leadership to the extent that the power of the leader touched its nadir. By the end of this time factions had become very well organised, skilled at manoeuvre (famously exploiting, for example, the AUEW's ineptitude) and the factions sharply reduced the leadership's freedom. But in the 1983 general election Labour was badly defeated, the eirenic Michael Foot resigned and Neil

Kinnock took over as leader, endorsed by a handsome majority. Over the decade Neil Kinnock virtually reversed the gains made by the factions by using the strength of the unions against the left in a more or less traditional leadership manner. However, factional alignments had at the same time become much more fluid and the left itself fragmented and this, too, was exploited by the leadership to discipline the party. One further factor, argues Eric Shaw, was that the changes were made and accepted because they were perceived as the necessary minimum for a recovery of electoral fortunes. This explains the union and activist acceptance of the reversal of changes which had been made only a few years before. The party wanted a victory after three severe drubbings at the polls. The victory did not come and this leaves open the question of how secure the new balance of power in the Labour Party really was even in the light of Neil Kinnock's reforms.

What our brief survey shows is that western European social democratic parties all had a similar political culture and faced similar organisational and ideological challenges during the period under review. Most adapted to rising factionalism in similar, sometimes identical ways (the PCI/PDS excepted).

The starting point was the solidarity of the generally right-wing leadership around cold war and 'welfare state' issues. Thus they supported Nato, the Atlantic alliance (in which many were prime movers), and anti-Soviet positions while at the same time promoting both welfare state building and Keynesian economic stances. These came under challenge from largely ineffectual left wings and were handled in a heavy-handed organisational manner – in the last resort the leadership could call in 'big battalions' on its side (though not necessarily so obviously as the British Labour Party's card votes). The leaders, voters and unions mutually reinforced each other's political positions.

However, this consensus was challenged by the left and, later, by the right (which came to doubt the old social democratic values of welfare state Keynesianism). The left, broadly speaking, was the 1968 generation and the rise of this left was associated with factional strife in most parties. Unlike the postwar left the 'New Left' refused to accept the old rules and set about changing the organisational structures to deprive the parliamentary leadership of its dominant position. In most parties there was a challenge from the 1968 generation and in most parties this group had some success in changing structures. The 'northern' social democratic parties (once seen as the right-wing sheet-anchors of the movement) were most affected, the 'southern' parties (once seen as the most ideologically volatile) were less prone to left-wing factionalised challenge. Thus the Norwegian, Swedish, German, Dutch and British parties were all hit by the rise of the 1968 generation although in slightly different ways. If it could be argued that the French party was taken over by the new generation around François Mitterrand (although Mitterrand remained in control at all times), the Spanish party, as Richard Gillespie shows, dealt with factional dissidence in an 'old-fashioned' organisational response (orchestrated by Guerra).

The rise of the ecological and peace movements also fuelled factionalism in the social democratic parties of the 1970s and 1980s. The principle issues here were the deployment of Cruise and Pershing 'Euromissiles' and the response to the superpower arms race. Ecological issues had a generally more intricate impact on the left–right factional balance but also provided further fuel for ideological and factional mobilisation within the social democratic parties.

The social democratic parties were open to the rise of factionalism because, even when they were not prone to factional fighting, they espoused debate and dispute as legitimate activities with the parties. The history of the German SPD is instructive as it virtually invited the 1968 generation of *contestataires* to enter the SPD and engage the debate inside the party itself. This they did, in large numbers, and with consequences for factionalism which are still being worked through. Unity in diversity had always been a social democratic value, but then the leadership had also had the cards stacked in its own interests (though not unchallengeably, it must be said).

The upshot of the intense factionalism of the 1970s and early 1980s was that most parties concluded that this warring was self-destructive. Leaving aside the issue of whether that was true, the absence of the parties from office (and they are parties with a reformist, hence governmental, vocation) led to a re-examination of their positions and in most cases a reversal of some or all of the organisational and programme changes of the recent past. Factionalism became subdued in the interest of the general good of the party which was widely thought to mean unity, solidarity and leadership cohesion. The parties which diverged from this pattern at the end of the 1980s, the French PS, the Spanish PSOE and the Italian PDS, had mixed fortunes.

The late 1980s saw the collapse of communism but also the rise of the New Right and the individualistic challenge to the values of the welfare state. These challenges have yet to be met by any of the western parties and may yet give rise to other factional debates (or splits) and there have been hints of this development in a number of parties. However, for the moment the general impression is of (to use Heidar's depiction) both less cohesion and a lesser factional activity.

It is difficult to say that these contributions add up to an overall conclusion. The contexts are diverse and the personalities and structures are very different. However, van Praag's view that factional conflict is not necessarily an electoral handicap and that the absence of strife not necessarily an attribute is worth further discussion. Likewise, the position of the party activists, mobilised by ideological debate within the party, is not the same as that of the average voter who is widely thought to dislike factionalism. But what the various conclusions do demonstrate is that models of party behaviour that assume the party, or indeed, the leadership and the rank and file to be homogeneous single actors are not substantiated by the evidence. The interplay of forces within a party, as much as the interaction of a party with its environment, offers important clues to its conduct.

1 The German Social Democratic Party: between old and New Left

Stephen Padgett

The Sozialdemokratische Partei Deutschlands (SPD) represents a paradigm case of the loss of cohesion experienced by social democratic parties in the last decade. It has undergone a transformation from a highly centralised and relatively disciplined *Volkspartei* (catch-all or people's party) to a party characterised increasingly by 'loosely coupled anarchy'.[1] This concept denotes a process of decomposition in the party's organisational structure with its roots in the social and cultural heterogeneity of the party. Social diversity is not in itself a new feature of the SPD; indeed, it is one of the defining characteristics of the social democratic *Volkspartei*. During the social–liberal coalition era, however, its effects were counteracted by a relatively cohesive leadership elite, bound by the traditional behavioural precepts of the social democratic party. This elite exploited the hierarchical structure of the party to deflect challenges from below, particularly from New Left elements which had entered the SPD in the late 1960s and early 1970s. This began to change after the fall of the coalition of the SPD and Freie Demokratische Partei (FDP) in 1982, and the permeation of the New Left into the upper echelons of the party bureaucracy and the parliamentary party. Social and cultural diversity, combined with the highly developed individualism of the New Left generation, eroded the cohesion and discipline of the leadership elite, giving free play to the forces of organisational disintegration within the SPD.

The forces of cohesion in the social democratic *Volkspartei*

Up to and including the era of the social–liberal coalition (1969–82), the SPD was relatively free from internal conflict. The explanation of this lies with the ideological and organisational character of the party. At the ideological level, the very strong allegiance of the party mainstream to the core values of social democracy meant that the dissident left was almost entirely marginalised. Organisationally, the structure of the party enabled the leadership to absorb and neutralise the challenge from the Extra-Parliamentary Opposition (APO) in the late 1960s and that of the party's youth wing (JUSO) in the early 1970s, deploying a strategy which steered between demarcation and integration.[2] The SPD distanced itself from extra-parliamentary movements of the left, at the same time trying to draw their adherents into the party mainstream. For the first three decades of the postwar period, this strategy met with a considerable degree of success. Moreover, although the SPD experienced some factional activity, this served to regulate rather than exacerbate internal conflict.

IDEOLOGICAL COHESION

The forces of ideological cohesion within the SPD were heavily conditioned by the social structure and political culture of the early postwar Federal Republic. The weakening of party ideology experienced in other western European countries was especially marked in western Germany. Some have identified a double 'ideological trauma' arising from the experience of the Third Reich on the one hand and the installation of a repressive communist regime in eastern Germany on the other. A recoil from ideology was the reflex response, accentuating the effects of those social trends – increasing affluence, social mobility, and the consequent weakening of social networks – that served to weaken class politics and ideological conflict in all western democracies. Moreover, the early success of the Christian Union parties (CDU and CSU) in forming and maintaining a broad catch-all alliance of voters enabled them to become the prototype of Kirchheimer's model of the *Volkspartei*.[3] The logic of the model was that the electoral success of the *Volkspartei* would force opposition parties to emulate them, de-emphasising class politics and overt party ideology. These factors combined to bring about a very rapid and thorough social democratisation of the western German left in the postwar period.

The core ideological values of the SPD were defined by the Bad Godesberg programme of 1959 in terms of the triad of principles: freedom, justice, and solidarity. Explicitly disavowing the party's Marxist past, the programme emphasised the eclectic philosophical sources of democratic socialism in the Christian ethic, classical philosophy and the humanist tradition. It went on to endorse the liberal pluralism of the West German state and the market economy, calling for an extension of democratic principles into the social and economic spheres. Thus the Bad Godesberg programme combined an acceptance of the postwar order with an appeal for reform in a formula with which all sections of the party could identify. The ideological overhaul which the SPD undertook at Bad Godesberg was in reality merely the culmination and formalisation of a progressive policy reorientation which had taken place over the previous decade. By 1959, the new orientation was virtually uncontested, as indicated by the ease with which programme reform was accomplished. Opposition was restricted to academic circles on the margins of the party.

The Godesberg consensus did not preclude political debate. The precepts set out in the programme were deliberately open-ended and capable of different interpretations, particularly between those who placed an emphasis on support for the existing economic order and those who emphasised the reform vocation which the programme proclaimed. At times, this conflict of interpretations became quite acute, but all sections of the party mainstream took the Bad Godesberg programme as their reference point. Thus the left's critique of the party in the 1960s was often put in terms of the failure to realise the reform components of the programme. For its part the right focused on the programme's affirmation of allegiance to the liberal market economy: competition as far as possible; planning as far as necessary. For them, the acceptance of this axiom was the touchstone of party loyalty. The pervasiveness and persistence of the Bad Godesberg consensus can be adduced from the absence of any serious challenge to the central principles of the programme. All subsequent programmatic activity has had as its objective the augmentation, elaboration or updating of the Bad Godesberg principles.[4]

ORGANISATIONAL COHESION

The organisational structure of the SPD provided a near-optimal framework for conflict management. It allowed the top party leadership a high degree of autonomy and freedom to manoeuvre in the face of adverse circumstances. The formal and informal structuring of the leadership elite fosters compromise and facilitates conflict resolution. In the party at large, organisational structures enable the central party apparatus to coordinate and direct, negating the influence of oppositional elements.

Effective power in the SPD centred on an elite of decision-makers and managers occupying positions on the Praesidium, the Executive, the parliamentary party leadership, and when in power, the members of Federal and *Land* governments. This elite was neither homogeneous in its political composition, nor hermetically sealed from the party at large. However, the balance of power was heavily stacked in favour of the elite. It had at its disposal the formidable resources of the central party machine. Despite some policy differences, it was extremely cohesive, especially at the top of the hierarchy.[5] It could normally invoke the backing of the powerful Deutscher Gewerkschaftsbund (DGB) trade union leadership, and in government it was able to rely also on the wider public prestige of the Chancellor. The tightly knit triad of chancellor, party chairman and Bundestag *Fraktion* leader was the focus of power.

The structure of the SPD in the country also contributed to elite domination.[6] The hierarchy of the party organisation resembled a pyramid, with the Bonn elite at the apex. A high degree of top-down power was inbuilt, through the axis between the central party apparatus and the 22 *Bezirk* (district) organisations. The role of the districts in electing delegates to the national party congress and in selecting candidates for Bundestag elections gave them pivotal importance. Although the JUSO-led left was successful in capturing control of the party in cities like Berlin, Frankfurt and Munich in the 1970s, its support was not sufficiently widespread to enable it to control the district level of party organisation. The inability of the left to gain control of the districts explains its underrepresentation in party congresses, and in the parliamentary arena. The parliamentary party was hierarchically structured, and geared to consensus building and the maintenance of discipline. Although the left began to mobilise in the parliamentary arena in the 1970s, its numerical strength was relatively modest, and its members rarely took their opposition to the point of voting against parliamentary party leadership or government.

FACTIONAL ACTIVITY

For the first two postwar decades, factional organisation was virtually absent from the SPD. The parliamentary party was dominated by a group of right-wing trade union members known as the *Kanalarbeiter*, 'parliamentary navvies' serving as 'voting fodder' and performing all the necessary but dull groundwork of politics. Initially little more than a social club, this group became more tightly organised in the late 1960s. In the face of the challenge from the left, the *Kanalarbeiter* made common cause with the H-J Vogel Circle, a new parliamentary group comprising middle-class professionals and academics on the right of the party. In the extra-parliamentary party, the right was organised in the Godesberger Circle.

The organisation of the left in the SPD was prompted by the compromises made by the SPD in the Grand Coalition (1966–69) and the stirrings of the extra-parliamentary opposition. A round of discussions was convened in Frankfurt in 1966 with the aim of providing a forum for the left, and strengthening its representation in the party at federal level. SPD success in the federal election of 1972 brought an influx of left-oriented deputies into the Bundestag. They formed the Group of the 16th Floor (named after their location in the parliament building), later to become known as the Leverkusen Circle.

Initially the right and the party leadership resisted the attempt of the left to bolster its position in the party by mobilising to form a cohesive block aimed at keeping the left in check. With the attempt to integrate the extra-parliamentary left into the party, however, a more accommodating attitude was adopted. For its part the left adopted a pragmatic strategy. Careful not to alienate the centre, they were flexible and undoctrinaire on most issues, rarely taking opposition to the point of divisiveness. However, they were concerned with promoting discussion and sometimes challenging aspects of government policy, not least because the leadership gave them a role in policy formulation and coopted them to positions of responsibility. Indeed, some, like Wolfgang Roth, Karsten Voigt, Volker Hauff and Gerhard Schröder rose to junior ministerial posts. Horst Ehmke, Research and Technology Minister, played a not inconsiderable part in the placement of the left in positions of responsibility.

Thus instead of acting as a source of conflict and instability, factional mobilisation served as a source of strength and cohesion. 'Internal party groupings have been a stabilising element in the internal structural development of the party . . . a dysfunctional element is nowhere to be seen'.[7] In particular, the structural and behavioural characteristics of factionalism at the parliamentary level facilitated the integration of the JUSO leadership into the party mainstream.

Challenges to stability

THE CHALLENGE OF THE APO

For the first two postwar decades the left was no more than a minor irritant to the SPD leadership. It was easily held in check through disciplinary action. Unrepresented in the parliamentary party, its principal forum was the party's auxiliary student organisation, the *Sozialistischer Deutscher Studentenbund* (SDS, Socialist German Student Federation). This previously quiescent organisation was radicalised in the late 1950s. Many of its members espoused the Marxist theory of the Frankfurt school, and conceived of the SDS as an organisation of socialist intellectuals independent of the SPD. Sections of the SDS had opposed the Bad Godesberg Programme, and were critical of the SPD's post-Godesberg strategy of working towards a Grand Coalition with the party's main rival, the CDU/CSU. For its part, the SPD leadership regarded the SDS as a Trojan horse of communism in the party and a threat to its new image. Attempts were therefore made to split the SDS in order to retain control of its moderate faction. When this strategy failed, the SPD leadership withdrew financial support and established an alternative body, the Sozialdemokratischer Hochschulbund (SHB, Social Democratic University Federation) to act as an auxiliary organisation of students and academics. Shortly thereafter in 1961, it was established that membership of the SDS was incompatible with SPD membership, and a number of its leading figures were expelled from the party.[8] With this action the SPD succeeded for a time in distancing itself from the left.

The rise of the APO movement posed a much more serious challenge to the SPD. The German form of the New Left student movement which emerged across western Europe, the APO movement was characterised by its extreme political diversity, and by its lack of formal organisational structure.[9] The main channel through which the SPD became 'infected' by the APO movement was the party's youth wing, JUSO. Although it did not conceive of itself as a constituent part of the student revolt,[10] many of its members participated in APO demonstrations. Moreover, JUSO now began to attract members who were not members of the SPD, making it harder to subject to party discipline and control. It adopted policy positions sharply divergent from those of the party. At its 1969 Munich Congress, for instance, it proclaimed as its goal the transformation of the capitalist system into socialism through state ownership of the big banks and key industries. Moreover, its communist STAMOKAP (state monopoly capitalism) faction attempted to colonise groups on the orthodox left of the SPD. A second enclave of the APO movement in the SPD was the SHB. With the entry of the party into the Grand Coalition the SHB had emerged as a force for inner-party opposition, formulating a critique of the SPD's new course. The identification of the SHB with the APO movement intensified its estrangement from the parent party.

Initially the attitude of the SPD leadership towards the APO movement was one of undisguised hostility: 'the gulf between the extra-parliamentary opposition and the policy of the SPD in the Bundestag was greater than that between the SPD and the CDU/CSU parliamentary parties'.[11] The SPD city government in Berlin imposed a total ban on demonstrations and the Berlin party leadership expelled prominent figures for defying the ban.[12] At federal level, SPD leaders attempted to demarcate the party from the APO movement, warning against participation in mass action which involved the extra-party left. Nevertheless many SPD members did participate, often proclaiming their party affiliation on placards.

The failure of this strategy, along with the unexpectedly poor performance of the SPD in Landtag elections in 1968, brought about a radical change of perspective. The new strategy of opening up the SPD to the APO generation has been subsequently associated with Willy Brandt, but it had the support also of the party Executive and was endorsed by leading figures on the SPD right.[13] After some initial hesitancy and mistrust the SPD's invitation to APO participants to enter the party *'mit allen Euren Methoden'* ('with all your methods') was widely accepted. The impact was considerable.[14] Membership had been static during the Grand Coalition. Between 1969 and 1972 it rose from 778,945 to 954,394, an increase of 22.5%.

The incorporation of the APO generation into the SPD temporarily defused the challenge of the New Left. However, it had important implications for three areas of internal party life. Firstly, the influx of the radical youth of the APO generation precipitated ideological conflict over the party's political orientation which was to continue into the 1970s. Secondly, it substantially increased the representation of the left in the SPD, and led to organisational initiatives aimed at increasing the left's influence in both the extra-parliamentary and parliamentary arenas. As the right responded, this led in turn to a general increase in factional mobilisation in the party. Thirdly, the influx of the APO generation into the SPD meant a very significant change in the social composition of the party, and a corresponding change in the quality of internal party life. In particular, the activism of the new recruits precipitated a conflict between representative and participatory democracy, and challenged the hierarchical organisational structures of the SPD.

THE CHALLENGE OF THE JUSOS

The experience of the APO movement, and the entry of many of its participants into the JUSO organisation had the effect of radicalising the SPD's youth wing. Thereafter it became the vehicle for many of the issues which the APO movement had raised. Conflict between JUSO and the parent party took place on both the ideological and organisational dimensions. JUSO strategy included an ideological offensive in which it sought to reverse what it saw as the renunciation of socialism in the SPD. Parallel to this, it sought to permeate the organisational structure of the party, in order to realise its optimistic claim to be 'the SPD of the eighties'.[15] The intention was to infuse new life into the participatory structures of the party organisation, and to introduce the doctrine of the imperative mandate whereby representatives would be bound by the views of members.

The response of the party leadership was characteristically ambivalent, steering between discipline and concession. Holding the threat of expulsion in the background, the leadership encouraged JUSO members to become functionaries in the party. An attempt was also made to involve JUSO in the preparation of the draft for a new medium-term programme under the chairmanship of Helmut Schmidt. The involvement of JUSOs in the programme drafting was marked by acrimony, which surfaced at Hanover Congress of 1973. In the face of JUSO criticism of the pragmatism of the Schmidt draft, it was dropped, and a new Commission appointed under the chairmanship of Peter von Oertzen, a figure identified with the SPD left. JUSO representation on the new Commission was increased, but while the new draft (adopted in 1975) was somewhat more reform-oriented, it could not be said to have been a victory for the left. Thereafter, the force of the JUSO movement was dissipated by its own sectarian fragmentation.

It was at the municipal level of SPD politics that JUSO was most successful, particularly in Berlin, Munich and Frankfurt.[16] With their demands for a more participatory role, the left came into conflict with the party machine. Conflict often centred on the attempt to invoke the imperative mandate and the resistance of the old guard to this challenge to their autonomy. The organisational structures of the party, however, meant that at federal level the organisational offensive of the JUSO had no significant impact, resulting in frustration and disillusionment. The fast growing *Bürgerinitiativen* (citizens' initiative movements) represented a more congenial political home for many JUSO activists and many abandoned the SPD for this form of action. The JUSO leaders of the late 1960s and early 1970s were assimilated into the parliamentary party (Wolfgang Roth and Karsten Voigt), the party group in the European Parliament (Heidi Wieczorek-Zeul) or into *Land* party leadership (Gerhard Schröder).

Under Helmut Schmidt's chancellorship after 1974, the marginalisation of the JUSO was completed. As architect of the integration strategy, Willy Brandt had granted its members a legitimate role in inner-party discussion, although their influence on party and government policy was negligible. Schmidt scarcely concealed his contempt for the organisation, and quickly set about reducing the financial resources available to it. Ultimately, however, the failure of JUSO to make any significant impact on the SPD was due to the inclination of its members towards abstract theory and their tendency towards sectarianism which prevented them from mobilising support in the party at large.

PARTY–GOVERNMENT CONFLICTS

The influx of the APO generation into the party and the mobilisation of the JUSO coincided with the entry of the SPD into government as leading partner in the social–liberal coalition with the FDP in 1969. The formation of the first SPD-led government in the Federal Republic was accompanied by a rhetoric of 'the social democratic revolution', serving to create a 'myth of a new *Stunde Null*', or new beginning.[17] Although the new Brandt government was initially very successful (particularly in foreign policy), the expectations which this rhetoric fostered ultimately became an increasingly heavy burden upon Brandt in his relations with the party.

The Brandt government was effectively insulated from direct pressures from below by the hierarchical structure of the party. The Praesidium was dominated by members of the federal government, and while the left was represented on the Executive, it represented an insignificant minority. In the *Bundestagsfraktion* discipline was maintained by the astute management of the *Fraktion* leader, Herbert Wehner. Challenges to the government were restricted to the Party Congress. The Saarbrücken and Hanover Congresses of 1971 and 1973 expressed dissatisfaction over the slow pace and limited scope of the government's promised reform programme, passing resolutions which went well beyond government proposals. Brandt's response to these challenges was twofold. On the one hand he emphasised his autonomy from the party. Congress resolutions could have an effect upon it but were in no sense binding upon it. On the other hand Brandt – the 'listening Chancellor' – recognised the legitimacy of policy formulation and programmatic activity in the party.[18] Thus while successfully maintaining his autonomy as chancellor, Brandt sought neither to dominate nor to distance himself from the party. Brandt's fall in 1974 is in no sense attributable to forces in the party at large. Rather it came about as a consequence of a loss of confidence in the chancellor in the upper echelons of the SPD, which stemmed in large part from the feeling that Brandt was too indulgent towards the government's critics on the left.

Helmut Schmidt's relationship with his party can best be described as one of uneasy coexistence: 'I am not wholly satisfied with my party, nor it with me . . . But I can find no better party and it has no substitute for me. So we must get along with one another.'[19] Schmidt's successes in economic crisis management, and in the fields of internal and external security, brought him widespread acclaim in the electorate and yet brought him into frequent conflict with SPD left. However, the receding influence of the left in the mid-1970s meant that in the early years of the Schmidt government the chancellor was able to dismiss criticism from this quarter with a disdain which approached arrogance.

This situation began to change from the election of 1976, in which the SPD majority in the Bundestag was reduced to ten. The management of the parliamentary party became more problematical, and on a number of occasions Wehner was hard pressed to provide the government with a majority. Although outright dissent was confined to a handful of deputies, there was a larger number who were not prepared to give unconditional support to the government, and the chancellor or his ministers were sometimes obliged to justify their policies to the *Fraktion* or even defer policies for which Wehner could not guarantee a majority. Nevertheless, at the parliamentary level, it was usually possible to contain conflict between party and government within safe limits.

The containment of conflict in party congresses was more problematical. In the later years of the Schmidt chancellorship, the government's autonomy from the party congress was steadily eroded. This process began with the congresses of 1977 and 1979, and centred on the contentious issue of nuclear energy. While continuing to assert his government's autonomy from congress decisions, Schmidt was nevertheless obliged to undertake an exercise in persuasion and conciliation. On each occasion he won majorities only through compromise resolutions which left the government's energy options open, but made gestures towards the anti-nuclear position. In defence and security issues, which focused on the upgrading of NATO weapons systems and the deployment in the Federal Republic of intermediate range nuclear weapons, it was even more difficult to bridge the widening gulf between government and party congress. At the Munich Congress of 1982 confrontation was side-stepped by a compromise resolution in which the peace politics of the SPD were given full expression, while the issue of missile deployment was postponed.[20] The 1982 Congress was a watershed for the SPD, underlining the fact that on major issues of policy the government no longer commanded a majority in the party.

LABOUR MOVEMENT CONFLICTS

An essential component in the capacity of SPD governments to assert their autonomy from the party was their close relationship with the leaders of the labour movement. Schmidt had quickly established a relationship of mutual trust with DGB trade union leaders, assisted by a shift to the right in the leadership of the large chemical workers' union, IG Chemie. In the early years of the Schmidt chancellorship, key union leaders formed a close political alliance with the right wing of the SPD, giving unconditional support to the government. Schmidt fostered this axis by repudiating his predecessor's strategy of cultivating the radical young, and reasserting the SPD's traditional identity as the party of organised labour. The demands of economic crisis management, however, placed an intolerable strain on the relationship.

While the DGB leadership had striven to maintain the 'stability pact' with government, the rank and file grew increasingly unwilling to submit to wage discipline and to tolerate rising levels of unemployment. The metalworkers' union, IG Metall, led mass protests against the terms of the 1981 budget, and the following year's proposals aroused even greater unrest. IG Metall leader Eugen Loderer warned that 'even trade unionists loyal to the chancellor have reached the limits of their endurance',[21] and DGB General Secretary Heinz Oskar Vetter expressed regrets that he had helped in the past to 'carry' the coalition.[22] The large industrial unions became more aggressive in their wage negotiations. In the face of mounting union pressure, the Munich Party Congress rejected the Executive's resolution on economic policy, substituting a text more sympathetic to union demands. Full-scale conflict between the trade unions and government was only averted by the break-up of the social–liberal coalition in autumn 1982, for which the inability of the government to command authority in the party and labour movement was partially responsible.

The breakdown of cohesion and the 'Balkanisation' of the SPD

The breakdown of ideological cohesion and organisational discipline experienced by the SPD since the early 1980s has its roots in the changing social and cultural profile of the party. In particular, it stems from the increasingly heterogeneous social composition of the party, and a fragmentation of its organisational structure. The social transformation of the SPD is the culmination of long-term secular trends: the decline in the party's traditional working-class membership; the rise of the new middle class; and a tendency towards social differentiation along the lines of generation, gender, educational attainment and lifestyle. Social and cultural heterogeneity is reflected in organisational fragmentation. The internal life of the party has been characterised as 'loosely coupled anarchy' in which a disparate variety of cliques, factions, patronage groups and interest organisations form temporary and unstable coalitions and alliances.[23]

ORGANISATIONAL PLURALISM

The role of *Arbeitsgemeinschaften* (working groups) increased dramatically over the 1980s and early 1990s as these groups progressively acquired an institutional identity within the party. Prominent among them are the *Arbeitsgemeinschaft für Arbeitnehmerfragen* (AfA, Working Group for Labour Affairs), formed as a defensive response to the rise of the New Left, and the *Arbeitsgemeinschaft Sozialdemokratischer Frauen* (ASF, Working Group for Social Democratic Women). The role of women in the SPD has been formalised further by the introduction of a quota system; by 1994 women should constitute 40 per cent of the party's office holders and elected representatives. Working groups have recently been permitted to accept members from outside the party, and there are proposals to formalise their status further by granting them the right to submit congress resolutions.[24] Another internal party grouping, though less formally organised, is the *Sozialdemokratische Wählerinitiative* (SWI, Social Democratic Voter Initiative). Initially formed as an electoral campaign group of leading figures in intellectual and cultural life, the SWI now serves as a forum for the left intelligentsia in the party, running cultural events and participating energetically in programmatic debate. The institutionalisation of social and cultural milieux within the SPD has led to a fragmentation of the internal life of the SPD.

Tendencies towards social heterogeneity and organisational pluralism are not new to the SPD. Previously, however, they were contained within a tightly disciplined and centralised party apparatus, under the control of a relatively cohesive party elite which remained bound to the principles of orthodox social democracy. With the emergence of a new generation of office holders and elected representatives since the fall of the social–liberal coalition, the New Left has permeated the upper echelons of the party. The result has been an increase in the intensity of conflict between the old and the New Left. Moreover, the New Left generation of SPD leaders lacks the cohesion of its predecessors. Characterised by social and cultural diversity, and by an individualism bordering on the egotistical, the new SPD elite is particularly susceptible to conflicts of both a political and personal nature.

NEW POLITICS/OLD POLITICS CONFLICTS

The Federal Republic was in the vanguard of the 'new politics' movement which accompanied postwar affluence and the transition to a post-industrial society.

As a society makes substantial progress in addressing traditional economic and security needs, a growing share of the public shifts their attention to post-material goals that are still in short supply, such as the quality of life, self expression and personal freedom.[25]

For the SPD the conflict between these new political currents and orthodox social democracy had two distinct dimensions. On the one hand the social democrats faced an external challenge from the Greens, a new party of the post-materialist left which robbed the SPD of its electoral monopoly of the left. On the other hand the new politics had penetrated deep into the SPD itself, creating a dualism between the old left and the New.

In the initial period after the fall of the social–liberal coalition there was more continuity than change in the composition of the SPD leadership elite, with old-guard figures like Hans-Jochen Vogel and Johannes Rau retaining their authority. The most significant change was the emergence of relatively young up-and-coming minister-presidents in the *Länder*. Protégés of Brandt, this circle was known as his *Enkel* (grandchildren). The most prominent representatives of the *Enkel* were the charismatic and mercurial Oskar Lafontaine (Saarland), Bjorn Engholm (Schleswig-Holstein), Gerhard Schröder (Lower Saxony) and Rudolf Scharping (Rhineland Palatinate). Broadly speaking of the 1968 generation, a number had been leaders of the radical JUSO movement of the 1970s. However, their affinity with the left was tempered with a strong streak of pragmatism and strategic flexibility. In comparison to the SPD elite of the Brandt, Schmidt, Wehner generation the *Enkel* have been characterised as

made of a quite different, less robust material; they are more spontaneous and independent; they confess their doubts more readily in public; they are bon viveurs, and enjoy cultural events; they prefer an evening at the opera to laborious reports and discussion at a regional party congress.[26]

During the 1980s the New Left made steady inroads into the party hierarchy. Its advance at district level increased its weight in party congresses and in 1986 a number of prominent old-guard figures were displaced from the party executive in favour of the New Left. It was at the *mittlere Basis* of intermediate-level party functionaries, however, that the New Left advanced furthest. This group is marked by its predisposition towards what has been termed 'the politics of self actualisation – a tendency to adopt rigid utopian positions placing self-gratification before party objectives.'[27] These tendencies in the SPD elite have had the effect of reducing the internal cohesion of the party, giving freer reign to policy differences.

The conflict between the old and New Left in the SPD was graphically illustrated in the campaign for the federal election of 1987. Chancellorship candidate Johannes Rau, emphatically identified with the old left in terms of values, style and image, was required to represent an incongruous New Left platform, nevertheless rejecting any possibility of cooperation with the

Greens. Conflicting styles and strategies culminated in the resignation of Rau's campaign manager midway through the campaign, and to deteriorating relations inside the party's leadership corps: 'the once harmonious relationship between Brandt and Rau has deteriorated into a purely formal, businesslike affair – and that only for the sake of maintaining appearances'.[28]

PROGRAMMATIC CONFLICT

The fragmentation of internal party life was very evident in the exercise in programmatic renewal which the SPD undertook between 1984 and 1989. Programme review was conceived in very ambitious terms as the reappraisal and reformulation of the basic values contained in the Bad Godesberg programme. An attempt to regain the ideological hegemony which the party had lost at the beginning of the decade, it was a recognition of the collapse of the Bad Godesberg conception of social democracy. A central objective of the programme review was the reconciliation of the conflicting values of the old and the New Left. A step in this direction was the formula for 'the ecological modernisation of the economy' conceived in the review. Significantly, the formula was readily endorsed by trade unions which had previously displayed an open scepticism towards the endeavour of reconciling the old left preoccupation with employment and New Left concerns for environmental protection.

For the most part, however, the programme drafting exercise merely served to underline the social and cultural fragmentations of the SPD. The first draft of the programme was heavily marked by the predisposition of the New Left intelligentsia towards abstract theoretical formulations, and by their hostility towards market capitalism and technological development. In the finalised programme, these tendencies were redressed, after interventions by the party's labour wing, and by the economics ministers of the SPD-governed *Länder*. In the sections on economics, the Berlin programme did little more than reiterate the orthodoxies of Bad Godesberg social democracy. On to these were grafted the new politics issues of environment, the humanisation of the workplace, gender equality, and commitments to a 'critical dialogue between elected representatives and citizens'.[29]

The new Basic Programme symbolised the social and political fragmentation of the SPD. Programme drafting was marked by the mobilisation of internal party groupings intent on leaving their mark upon the new programme. Incorporating the concerns of all these diverse groups, the programme resembled a 'department store catalogue . . . contradictory in style and argumentation . . . more of an internal party scorecard than a statement of party policy'.[30]

The attempt to synthesise diverse values was personified by Lafontaine, SPD chancellorship candidate in the 1990 election, who combined a New

Left image with an appeal to the manual worker constituency in his home state. However, Lafontaine's eclecticism was widely perceived as opportunism.[31] His campaign and its failure were interwoven with conflicts over German unification, but it exemplified also the disorientation of the SPD in the face of the conflict between the New Left and the old. Bjorn Engholm, party chairman from 1991 to 1993, was more closely associated with mainstream social democracy, but his leadership was undermined by the need to satisfy the diverse social and political currents in the SPD.

THE CONFLICT BETWEEN TRADITION AND MODERNITY

In common with other social democratic parties, the SPD experienced considerable difficulty in coming to terms with socio-economic and political changes in the 1980s and early 1990s. Change occurred on a broad front. On the sociological level it involved the progressive disintegration of the historic social formations which gave rise to social democracy. In the economy, the globalisation of markets and the advance of new technologies meant the ascendancy of economics over politics often expressed in the drive for liberalisation and deregulation. The SPD was alert to these changes, but the formula for a coherent strategic response proved elusive, particularly since there was no common understanding of the nature of change or where it was leading. In the face of this dilemma, the party was divided between the advocates of a rather vague conception of modernisation and the guardians of tradition. This was a conflict which cut directly across conventional left–right cleavages.

A central theme in the conflict between modernity and tradition was the perceived gulf between the historic social democratic ethos of social solidarity, and the individualist, achievement orientation of large and growing sections of German society. The issue was brought to a point by the election of 1987, in which the unevenness of the party's performance suggested that while the values of social solidarity still commanded a resonance among the socially deprived, it was alien to the achievement orientation of the 'affluent majority'. The most radical attempt to address this question took the form of an attack on party and labour movement orthodoxy by Lafontaine and the *Enkel*.

The initiative broke from the tradition of left politics in the SPD. Indeed, the debate which it precipitated cut across orthodox left–right divisions. Beginning from the premise that in economic and social policy many of the SPD's prescriptions were antiquated, the *Enkel* argued that more attention had to be given to economic success. In particular, they advocated a more positive approach towards technological development and structural economic change. The centrepiece of their agenda, however, was a new order in working practices, combining a reduced working week with labour market deregulation. It was presented in very ambitious terms as 'a concrete Utopia which can move millions . . . a human idea capable of binding together different strata in society'.[31]

These proposals for labour market deregulation encountered bitter opposition from the trade unions. Indeed, the attempt to modernise party policy in defiance of labour movement orthodoxy was met by an heterogeneous coalition of the SPD's labour wing, the conventional left and the right, which was largely successful in repulsing this attack upon tradition. In the new programme, the ideas of the modernisers were severely attenuated, and were hedged around with qualifications designed to render them acceptable to labour movement orthodoxy.

The conflict between tradition and modernity also has an organisational dimension. The modernisers criticised the closed character of the party organisation and the '*unter uns gesagt*' (between ourselves) style of decision-making. In his acceptance speech upon election as party chairman on 29 May 1991, Engholm expressed a determination to open up the SPD:

Open societies do not tolerate closed parties. . . . The SPD is neither a closed shop, nor a party of dogmatic beliefs . . . the less we formulate our intentions behind closed doors, the more successful we will be as a party.

The sterility of the top leadership bodies attracted criticism in the party press, which was itself accused of conformity with party orthodoxy.[33] Some critics advocated a decentralisation of the party structure and a greater measure of autonomy at the base. However, it was hard to see how a meaningful decentralisation could be made compatible with the discipline inherent in a party geared to government office.

UNIFICATION CONFLICTS

A number of explanations have been offered to account for the ambivalence which the SPD displayed towards German unification. One of these centres on the left's 'inadequate understanding of nationalism as a major force and powerful agent of collective identity'.[34] According to this explanation, 'Socialist, social democratic and left libertarian political discourse has difficulties conceiving of particularistic and naturalistic conceptions of collective identity, whether based on religion, ethnicity, language, or territory'.[35] Another explanation focuses on the SPD's *Ostpolitik* of the 1970s, in which attempts to persuade GDR governments to improve the condition of their people, especially in terms of human rights and freedom of movement, were combined with a recognition of the status quo. This policy had been extended in the 1980s in a second *Ostpolitik* of active engagement with GDR government in pursuit of *détente*. Having led the way in *rapprochement* with the GDR, elements of the SPD were slow to accept the total collapse of its legitimacy and viability.[36] A third source of misgivings was a residual ambivalence in the SPD to the political and social character of the

Federal Republic itself. This was expressed in opposition in some quarters to the chosen instrument of unification – the extension of the constitutional framework of the Federal Republic to the whole of Germany under the provisions of Article 23 of the Constitution. The alternative was a new constitution, drafted by a convention composed of representatives of both German states, to be ratified by referendum. Implicit in this procedure was the conception, vaguely formulated on the left, of a 'Third Way' between east and west.

Ambivalence towards German unification was expressed most emphatically by Lafontaine. This brought him into conflict, not only with the newly formed east German SPD, which favoured rapid unification, but also with other sections of the leadership of the party in the west. In particular, Willy Brandt (elected honorary president of the east German SPD) wholeheartedly embraced German unity and pleaded with the party to do likewise. However, although the Berlin Congress of December 1989 accepted the principle, the party's position in the 1990 election campaign was indelibly stamped by that of its chancellorship candidate. Emphasising the economic burden of unification for the west, and criticising the terms of Economic and Monetary Union, Lafontaine advocated opposing the unification treaties in the West German parliament. This issue publicly divided the SPD, with party and parliamentary group chairman Vogel, the majority of the parliamentary party and most of the SPD's minister-presidents in the *Länder* combining to overrule the chancellorship candidate. In view of the historic importance of unification, conflict between the main body of the party leadership and its chancellorship candidate was electorally damaging, especially in the east.

POST-UNIFICATION CONFLICTS

The susceptibility of the SPD to conflict was graphically illustrated by its response to the contentious issues arising out of Germany's post-unification traumas. Indeed, the inability of the SPD to exploit deepening economic recession and successive political crises in the governing coalition, was due in large part to its own internal disunity. By 1993, unemployment had risen to 3.3 million (7.1% in the west, 14.7% in the east), the economy was contracting by around 2% per annum and the budget deficit was spiralling out of control. Moreover, there was a growing perception that the downturn was neither a temporary effect of unification, nor part of the international economic cycle, but reflected the structural condition of the new German economy. Pessimism over economic prospects was compounded by disarray in the governing coalition and the perception of a power vacuum at the centre of government. Far from being able to capitalise on these uniquely favourable circumstances, however, the SPD was itself tainted by the syndrome of *Parteiverdrossenheit* – a profound disaffection towards the entire 'political class'.

In addition to economic recession and government unpopularity, the Social Democrats might also have been expected to derive an advantage from its structural majority in the Bundesrat (upper house). This placed the SPD in a strategic position in the legislative process, especially in relation to constitutional amendments and financial legislation in which the Bundesrat has a key role. However, Kohl was able to counter the SPD's hold on the Bundesrat by offering incentives for Social Democratic *Länder* to break ranks and vote with the government. Thus in 1992, Brandenburg secured additional revenues by voting for government measures to increase VAT, undermining the SPD's *Steuerlüge* (tax lie) campaign against the chancellor.

Participatory opposition also meant that the SPD was obliged to acquiesce in policy compromise, thereby shouldering responsibility in a quasi-coalition with the government.[37] This was particularly evident in the 'Solidarity Pact' for financial stabilisation, negotiated between the governing parties, the federal SPD, and state governments in spring 1993. For some Social Democrats the formalisation of cooperation through a Grand Coalition represented an attractive route towards government power. Signalling its readiness for coalition, the SPD undertook a *Schmusekurs* (soft-soap approach) towards Kohl, at the expense of effective opposition. Thus, despite his unpopularity, Kohl was consistently able to outmanoeuvre the SPD.

His ability to do so was greatly enhanced by the internal schisms in the SPD over the contentious issues arising out of Germany's post-unification traumas. The chancellor was able to turn his reliance on opposition consent to his own advantage by deflecting attention away from the divisions in the government and towards the disunity and indiscipline in the SPD.[38] This was graphically illustrated by the SPD's response to the emotionally charged issue of constitutional amendment to restrict legal rights to political asylum following the explosion of racially inspired violence in a number of German cities in 1992. The issue precipitated a bitter and debilitating internal conflict at all levels of the party.

Conflict was rather diffuse, and did not correspond to very clearly defined ideological communities of left and right. Opposition to the proposed constitutional amendment was strongest in the so-called *mittlere Basis* of intermediate-level party functionaries, permeated by the New Left. The parliamentary *Fraktion* and party Executive were both divided on the issue. The strongest advocates of constitutional change were the state and city administrators with responsibility for the reception and accommodation of asylum-seekers. This convoluted spectrum of conflict placed the party chairman in an unenviable position.

Initially Engholm remained somewhat detached from the debate, reluctant to commit himself to measures for which he was uncertain of winning majority party support. With his leadership under critical scrutiny, however, and with the SPD driven into an untenable corner, he reversed his personal position, urging the party to accept the need for more restrictive asylum laws. At a special congress in November 1992 the SPD endorsed the principle of constitutional change, subject to a number of qualifications. The obscurity of the resolution, however, was indicative of the continuing ambivalence and disunity of the party on this issue. A similar disarray was also exposed in the debate over Germany's new security role, and constitutional amendments to enable German forces to participate in UN operations.

These issues are very sharply illustrative of the SPD's loss of internal cohesion. Within the leadership elite, decisions which were previously taken on the basis of informal mutual understanding among like-minded individuals are now subject to acrimonious public discussion.[39] Political differences are compounded by rivalries and conflicts of a personal nature. These surfaced in the hard-fought election of Hans-Ulrich Klose as chairman of the parliamentary *Fraktion* early in 1992, and the jockeying for position between party leaders at federal and *Land* level.

The political and personal differences evident in the SPD in the west are even more pronounced in the east. Indeed, in its advocacy of participatory democracy, its pursuit of ethical issues, and its tendency towards in-fighting, the SPD in the east bears a very strong resemblance to the Greens.[40] Relations between the eastern and western wings of the SPD have been strained. The ambivalence of the SPD to unification was reflected in a lack of commitment to strengthening the party's organisation in the east.

Disunity in the SPD almost certainly contributed to Engholm's decision to resign as party chairman and chancellorship candidate in May 1993, following revelations of a relatively trivial impropriety in his conduct before a parliamentary commission of inquiry into the scandal surrounding his opponent in the Schleswig-Holstein election of 1987. Frustrated in his attempts to lead the SPD towards the political centre, and undermined by the fractiousness of the party, Engholm lacked the will to withstand the affair. His resignation intensified the instability of the SPD, especially since the principal contenders for the party chairmanship and chancellorship candidacy represented conflicting strategic objectives. While Gerhard Schröder, state premier of Lower Saxony, stood for a strategy of coalition with the Greens, Rudolf Scharping, his counterpart in Rhineland Palatinate, advocated a much greater readiness for coalition with the centre-right parties. In addition to underlining the internal disunity in the party, this shows that after a decade, the SPD has yet to resolve its coalition dilemma.

Conclusion

It is possible to identify four cross-cutting conflict dimensions in the contemporary SPD. Firstly, although the traditional left–right conflict has weakened, it is not yet a spent force. It was evident, for instance, in the programme review in the conflict over the relationship between state and the market in the economy. Secondly, the conflict between orthodox social democracy and new politics currents corresponds to a deep-rooted cleavage between the competing social and cultural milieux of the old and the New Left. In large part the milieux are constituted along generational lines. This conflict theme pervades all aspects of party life in the 1980s and early 1990s. It can be clearly discerned in the SPD's response to unification, in which the party's ambivalence can be traced to the New Left generation.[41] Thirdly, the tension between tradition and modernity is acutely divisive. It centres on the tension between the values of social solidarity at the core of the social democratic tradition, and the individualism and achievement orientation of modern society. Engholm's very strong emphasis on modernity was slow to coalesce into a definite project. Translating rhetoric into action in this area will inevitably challenge party orthodoxy. Finally, these conflicts are overlaid by a new east–west conflict dimension. Moreover, the SPD in the east is itself prone to in-fighting.

Arguably, political conflict is endemic to the contemporary SPD, due to the quasi-institutionalisation of competing social and cultural milieux. This is well advanced in the case of the labour wing of the party (AfA) and the social democratic women's organisation (ASF). The New Left is less formally organised, but has a stronghold in the *mittlere Basis* or intermediate levels of the party's functionary corps. The increasingly pluralistic character of internal party life may be seen as leading to a progressive Balkanisation of the SPD.

Notes

1. Lösche, P. and Walter, F., *Die SPD: Klassenpartei, Volkspartei, Quotenpartei: Zur Entwicklung der Sozialdemokratie von Weimar bis zur deutsche Vereinigung* (Darmstadt: Wissenschaftliche Buchgesellschaft), 1992, p. 380.
2. Gorol, S., 'Zwischen Integration und Abgrenzung; SPD und studentische Protestbewegung', *Die neue Gesellschaft/Frankfurter Heft*, No. 9, 7, 1988, pp. 597–615.
3. See Kirchheimer, O., 'The Transformation of the Western European Party Systems', in J. La Palombara and M. Wiener (eds), *Political Parties and Political Development* (Princeton, NJ: Princeton University Press), 1966.
4. Herz, J.H., 'Social Democracy versus Democratic Socialism; an Analysis of SPD Attempts to Develop a Party doctrine', in B.E. Brown (ed.), *Eurocommunism and Eurosocialism* (New York, Cyrco Press), 1979.
5. Klotzbach, K. *Der Weg zur Staatspartei: Programmatik, praktische Politik und Organisation der deutschen Sozialdemokratie 1945 bis 1965*, (Berlin and Bonn: Dietz), 1983, pp. 575–6.
6. Padgett, S.A. and Burkett, A.J., *Political Parties and Elections in West Germany: the Search for a New Stability* (London: Hurst), 1986, pp. 70–72.

7. Müller-Rommel, F., *Innerparteiliche Gruppierungen in der SPD; eine empirische Studie über informell-organisierte Gruppierungen von 1969–1980* (Opladen: Westdeutscher Verlag), 1982, p. 267.

8. Fichter, T., 'Vier SDS Generationen', *Die neue Gesellschaft/Frankfurter Heft*, No. 9, 1987, pp. 799–804.

9. Shell, K.L., 'Extra-Parliamentary Opposition in Post War Germany', *Comparative Politics*, Vol. 21, No. 2, July 1970, pp. 653–80.

10. Gorol, op. cit., p. 604.

11. Padgett, S.A. and Paterson, W.E., *A History of Social Democracy in Postwar Europe* (London: Longman), 1991, p. 76.

12. Fichter, op. cit., p. 376.

13. Baring, A., *Machtwechsel; die Ära Brandt Scheel* (Stuttgart: Deutsche Verlags Anstalt), 1982, pp. 90–93.

14. Gorol, op. cit., p. 606.

15. Braunthal, G., *The West German Social Democrats. 1969–1982 Profile of a Party in Power* (Boulder, CO.: Westview Press), 1983, p. 89.

16. Braunthal, G., 'The West German Social Democrats: Factionalism at the Local Level', *West European Politics*, Vol. 7, No. 1, pp. 47–64.

17. Bracher, K.-D., Jäger, W. and Link, W.R., *Republik in Wandel 1969–74; die Ära Brandt; Geschichte der Bundesrepublik Deutschland*, Vol. V (Stuttgart: Deutsche Verlags Anstalt), 1986, p. 439.

18. Mayntz, R., 'Executive Leadership in Germany; Dispersion of Power or Kanzlerdemokratie', in R. Rose and E. Suleiman (eds), *Presidents and Prime Ministers* (Washington, DC: American Enterprise Institute), 1980, p. 169.

19. Carr, J., *Helmut Schmidt; Helmsman of Germany* (London: Weidenfeld and Nicolson), 1985, p. 101 (quoting Helmut Schmidt).

20. SPD Pareivorstand, *Protokoll SPD Parteitag; München April 1982* (Bonn: SPD), 1982, pp. 907–11.

21. Kastendiek, H., 'Struktur und Organisationprobleme einer staatstragenden Arbeitnehmerpartei; zum Verhältnis von SPD und Gewerkschaften seit 1966', in R. Ebighausen and F. Tiemann (eds), *Das Ende der Arbeiterbewegung in Deutschland?* (Opladen: Westdeutscher Verlag), 1984, p. 436.

22. *Stuttgarter Machrichten*, 14 April 1982.

23. Lösche, P., 'Zur Metamorphose der politischen Parteien in Deutschland', *Gewerkschaftliche Monatshefte*, Vol. 43, No. 9, 1992, pp. 531–9; Lösche, P. and Walter, F., op. cit., pp. 380–86.

24. Silvia, S.J., 'Loosely Coupled Anarchy; the Fragmentation of the Left', in S.A. Padgett (ed.), *Parties and Party Systems in the New Germany* (Aldershot (Dartmouth): Association for the Study of German Politics, 1993), p. 174.

25. Dalton, R.J., 'The German Voter', in W.E. Paterson, G. Smith and P. Merkl (eds), *Developments in West German Politics* (London: Longman), 1989, p. 113.

26. Lösche and Walter, op. cit., p. 383.

27. *Der Spiegel*, 14 September 1992.

28. *Der Spiegel*, 5 January 1987.

29. Padgett, S.A., 'The German Social Democrats; A redefinition of Social Democracy or Bad Godesberg Mark II?', *West European Politics*, Vol. 16, No. 1, January 1993, p. 33.

30. Lösche, op. cit., p. 535; and Silvia, op. cit., p. 175.

31. Fichter, T., 'Political Generations in the Federal Republic', *New Left Review*, No. 186, March/April 1991, pp. 78–88.

32. *Wirtschaftswoche*, 29 April 1988.
33. Conradi, P., 'Wie wird die SPD geführt?', *Vorwärts*, 22, 1987, pp. 16–17.
34. Markovits, A., 'The West German 68-ers Encounter the Events of 1989; More than a Numerical Reversal', *German Politics*, Vol. 1, No. 1, April 1992, pp. 13–30.
35. Kitschelt, H., 'The 1990 German Federal Election and the National Unification', *West European Politics*, Vol. 14, No. 4, October 1991, p. 131.
36. Padgett, S.A. and Paterson, W.E., 'The Rise and Fall of the West German Left', *New Left Review*, No. 186, March/April 1991, pp. 46–77.
37. Sturm, R., 'The Territorial Dimension of the New German Party System', in Padgett, *Parties and Party Systems in the New Germany*, 1993, pp. 120–22.
38. Perger, W.A., 'Ein Winter der Ohnmacht', *Die Zeit*, No. 6, 5 February 1993, p. 6.
39. Weege, W., 'Zwei Generationen im SPD-Parteivorstand. Eine empirische Analyse', in T. Leif, H.-J. Legrand and A. Klein (eds), *Die Politische Klasse in Deutschland; Eliten auf dem Prüfstand* (Bonn: Bouvier), 1992, pp. 196–220; Silvia, op. cit., p. 173.
40. Silvia, op. cit., p. 174.
41. Markovits, op. cit.

2 Social democracy's newest recruit?: conflict and cohesion in the Italian Democratic Party of the Left

Martin J. Bull

A case study of the nascent Italian Democratic Party of the Left (Partito Democratico della Sinistra, PDS) provides an excellent example of the themes of this book specifically through highlighting the differences in those themes between social democracy and a more radical Marxist tradition to its left (west European communism): the elements and the maintenance of cohesion; the nature of internal conflict and its management; the value placed on conflict; and, finally, the degree of problems conflict causes. The PDS originates in the Marxist tradition to social democracy's left, specifically in the form of the Italian Communist Party (Partito Comunista Italiano, PCI). Five days after the collapse of the Berlin Wall in the autumn of 1989, Achille Occhetto, the leader of the PCI, proposed the dissolution of the party and its rebirth as a non-communist party of the left. Approximately 15 months later, on 3 February 1991, delegates at the PCI's Twentieth (and final) Congress approved their leader's proposal. It is impossible to understand the nature of cohesion and conflict inside such a short-lived party without understanding the nature of cohesion and conflict in the PDS's predecessor and in the transition period by which the PCI crossed the Rubicon. The reason is that, despite the attempt of the leadership to enact a radical break, the PDS's current internal life is indelibly marked with the past. The new party, it could be argued, in its nascent state, remains the product of two traditions, and specifically of an attempted transition between them, and the completion of this transition will require more than the decisions made at the 1991 Congress. Indeed, these probably represent little more than a starting point.[1] This chapter, therefore, is divided into three parts, each of which analyses cohesion and conflict in the PCI, the PCI/PDS transformation, and the PDS.

Conflict and cohesion in the PCI

The PCI had the distinction of being the largest and, many argued, the most successful communist party in western Europe. Its vote consistently increased in the postwar period to reach a peak of 34.4 per cent, and, despite its decline thereafter, the party was able to avoid the severity of the decline experienced by its neighbouring parties, particularly the French Communist Party (PCF). Yet, despite this success in electoral terms, the PCI never saw office. Its status as a permanent opposition party was a product of its apparent 'anti-system' nature: the other political parties regarded the PCI as an unacceptable coalition partner in government because it represented a threat to Italian democracy itself. The paradoxical effect of this combination of electoral strength and delegitimisation on the stability of Italian democracy is not the concern here. The important point to emphasise is that the PCI's 'anti-systemness' was equivocal, and became increasingly so from the 1960s onwards. Many observers found the party difficult to classify either as an orthodox Marxist party or as a social democratic party. On the one hand, the PCI declared that, in the event of gaining power, it would respect those rights and institutions characteristic of bourgeois democracy, and which were present in the Italian constitution which the party had helped to draft in the immediate postwar period. On the other hand, for most of the postwar period the party refused to renounce its goal of building a socialist society; it maintained a privileged link with the Soviet Communist Party (CPSU); it continued to affirm the validity of its seventy-year national and international Marxist heritage; and it continued to govern itself through democratic centralism which all non-communists regarded as fundamentally undemocratic. This ambiguity was epitomised in the party's claim to have found a 'third way' to socialism, one which would respect those rights, traditions and institutions which were characteristic of western political systems. The ambiguity surrounding the exact nature of the PCI and the party's problems of operating in two environments – a national capitalist environment and an international communist environment – resulted in a party characterised by a curious mixture of conflict and cohesion.

COHESION: DEMOCRATIC CENTRALISM, IDEOLOGY AND A COMMUNIST CULTURE

Leninist theory does not deny that conflict exists in communist parties, but it does argue that it should be managed effectively. It is important, therefore, to begin with the sources of cohesion in the PCI and those factors which inhibited conflict. Two sources of cohesion (ideology – or a belief system – and democratic centralism) can be identified, and one factor (democratic centralism) which operated to inhibit conflict.[2] Both the idea of a belief system and the organisational principle of democratic centralism were inherited from Marxist-Leninist theory.[3] The idea of the belief system was that it should be hostile to the prevailing political and social cultural order, or it should, as Pellicani (1979: 497) has noted, constitute 'the *counter-society*, making the revolutionary party a form of prefiguration, on a reduced scale, of future communist society'. In orthodox communist parties this prefiguration was embodied in democratic centralism. The PCI's belief system embodied democratic centralism as a core component, but it was reinforced by other, closely linked, factors: a continual reaffirmation of the teleological nature of the party, an ideological link with the 'motherland of socialism', and a national Marxist heritage (which was developed to reinforce a belief system which became problematic with the degeneration of the Soviet Union). These constituted the core components of the PCI's belief system. However 'fictitious' or real, together they made up the PCI's *diversità* ('distinctiveness'), which allowed communist activists to distinguish it from other political parties and claim moral authority over them.

This distinctiveness was cultivated and maintained by two mechanisms. The first was democratic centralism, which provided: centralised control in the hands of the elite over the formulation of the party line; removal of dissent with the party line through expulsion of recalcitrant party members; and mobilisation of the party base through 'contained' discussion on the party line. The second was a more outward-looking method of promoting cohesion which originated in Gramsci's writings and specifically his theory of hegemony (Gramsci 1978: 235ff.). This involved the building of a 'communist culture' in society through the *presenza* ('presence') of party activity at all levels of society. This was attempted through the mobilisation of communist cultural instruments such as newspapers, journals, the mass media, youth organisations, trade unions, in addition to active participation in local government.

What emerges from this brief analysis is the fundamental role of democratic centralism in the cohesion of the PCI. On the one hand, it constituted the core of the ideological belief system. On the other hand, it was the essential means by which the binding effect of ideology and the belief system within the party was maintained. Paradoxically, the dynamics of conflict were also located inside democratic centralism, and specifically in the manner of its operation when pressures impinged from the external environment.

CONFLICT AND ITS MANAGEMENT

The PCI became more susceptible to the growth of internal conflict in the postwar period for three reasons: first, because the party moved away from the traditional cadre party towards being a 'mass party' which attracted members from different strata of society; second, because the party had inserted a 'democratic phase' into the struggle for socialism; and third, because Italian capitalism was undergoing major changes. These three factors increased the pressure of the external environment on the party's internal environment, specifically through increasing the distance between the nature of the party's 'belief system' and the external behaviour of the party. The operation of democratic centralism was aimed to manage the potential conflict arising from this *doppiezza* (literally 'duplicity'), epitomised both in the failure of the party membership to perceive the changes in party line as anything more than tactical, and in the emergence of 'revisionist' or 'sectarian' tendencies. The attempt to bridge the increasing divorce between external behaviour and the internal belief system was made through greater work by party intellectuals (to justify the gap) and by the promotion of contained discussion on the party line. As Rossana Rossanda (1976) (a member of the PCI expelled in the late 1960s) commented, the PCI

is a party which facilitates discussion, because it knows that discussion can be a powerful factor of cohesion. It is a party which seeks to be all embracing and to accommodate all dissent within the party line, so that the leadership can retain overall control. This method requires a real capacity for compromise and works quite naturally as long as that consensus is possible.

In short, if pressures from the external environment demanded change, the internal environment demanded continuity, and the two were made compatible if democratic centralism functioned efficiently. This allowed debate to stay within the parameters of the party's external environment and not focus on key issues of the party's internal environment, that is, the nature or identity of the party itself. Yet, this policy carried dangers with it. The capacity for achieving a consensus became more difficult the greater the pressures from the outside world and the more the party attempted to establish a closer relation with it. Consequently, the postwar history of the party saw the dimensions of internal conflict become ever larger and more profound.

THE DIMENSIONS OF CONFLICT AND ITS IMPACT

Conflict in the PCI rarely focused on issues of public policy or concrete issues of the day. This was due not only to the manner in which the party operated (as outlined above), but also to two other factors: the party's status as an 'irresponsible' opposition (that is, it could not be considered as a candidate for government); and the fact that public policy programmes have never featured highly in Italian political parties because of the unlikelihood of them being carried through (due to the unstable coalitional nature of Italian governments). Conflict arose over the more grandiose theme of party strategy.

Strategic conflict can be dated back to the early postwar years, but it became most apparent in the 1960s through the Amendola–Ingrao dispute which surfaced as a result of irresistible pressures arising from the external environment, in the shape both of the Italian 'economic miracle' and the prospect, and later realisation, of an 'opening to the left' through the incorporation of the PSI into the Christian Democratic governing alliance.[4] The right of the party, led by Giorgio Amendola, argued that the centre-left experiment should be supported because its reforms would go some way towards alleviating the conditions of the working class and would lay the groundwork for a future entry of the PCI into government. The left of the party, led by Pietro Ingrao, argued that the opening to the left amounted to a neo-capitalist plan designed to rationalise Italian capitalism and split the working class in the process; it should, therefore, be opposed.

The Amendola–Ingrao dispute set the pattern of conflict inside the party for the next twenty years. On all issues which arose there was a continual tension between those favouring a radicalisation of the party line and those favouring a moderation of it. The significant point about this conflict was the role played by the centre based around the leadership. Using the party's mechanisms to manage conflict it mediated between the two camps, while leaning clearly towards the right. This continual bridging manoeuvre was symbolised in the lengthy congressional theses which achieved the type of synthesis referred to by Rossanda above. The divisions were contained within the parameters governing debate inside the party, and, where those parameters *were* broken by a recalcitrant minority, democratic centralism's ultimate mechanism could be deployed (as was done with the expulsion of the Manifesto group in the late 1960s). Conflict, then, became an important element of the internal nature of the PCI, but it was conflict of a particular type in so far as it was contained within certain parameters beyond which lay questions which went to the heart of the party's identity. This explained the PCI's reputation for continuity with the past and thus maintenance of its distinctiveness (which provided cohesion) and compromise among its factions (which contained conflict). But there was a cost involved.

The curious mixture of cohesion and conflict inhibited the degree to which the PCI could adapt to the changing demands of Italian politics and society. The value of change was, to a large extent, sacrificed on the altar of continuity. The costs of this commitment became apparent in the 1980s, when the sources of cohesion began to crumble and the potential for more fundamental conflict increased. The party's strategic alternatives appeared to be exhausted with the failure of the Historic Compromise; its votes and members were in inexorable decline; links with the Soviet motherland had been officially severed over Poland; and debate inside the party had shifted openly to internal questions concerning the party's very identity, thus stretching democratic centralism almost to breaking point. By the mid-1980s genuine action to reverse the decline could not be taken without confronting internal divisions which went to the heart of the party's identity. Ingrao and the left attributed the decline to the party's virtual abandonment of a radical anti-capitalist programme of reform in favour of a strategy that involved simply overseeing or monitoring the contemporary process of capitalistic modernisation. They proposed a shift to a clear anti-capitalist stance. The moderate right wing, led (after Amendola's death) by Giorgio Napolitano, argued that it was the very ambivalence of the PCI that was at the root of its problems: the party should abandon unequivocally its socialist rhetoric and formulate a clear programme limited to 'improving' capitalist society (hence their name, the *miglioristi*, 'improvers'). Finally, there was a small pro-Soviet group to the left of the *ingraiani* led by Armando Cossutta, which demanded a return to a much closer relationship with the Soviet Union. These factions had become so well entrenched that they had their own journals and institutes despite remaining officially unrecognised by the party.[5]

The resignation of the party leader, Alessandro Natta, after defeat in the local elections of 1988 proved to be the watershed (see Bull 1989b). The resignation of a leader after an electoral defeat was unprecedented in the history of the party, and confirmed not only that the party had reached a strategic impasse but that its internal dysfunctioning had reached a critical point. The new leader, Achille Occhetto, had little option but to embark on a programme of internal reform. Besides the effects of the programme of reform, the very act of attempting to carry it through was to change irrevocably the internal life of the party.

Conflict and cohesion in the PCI/PDS transformation

It seems that Occhetto wished formally to dismantle the core elements of the PCI's ideological belief system, while not having a clear idea of what exactly should replace these elements. His objective focused more on removing the party's old identity than on tackling the specifics of a possible new one. He aimed to do this through a gradual process which maintained the party's unity intact. The transformation period illustrates the problems of a party attempting to pass between two traditions of cohesion and conflict.[6]

CONFLICT CONTAINED: DEMOCRATIC CENTRALISM'S SWAN SONG

The specially-convened Eighteenth Congress in March 1989 represented the culmination of a first wave of internal reforms put together since the previous autumn. Altering several of the operational rules of the congress to ensure that genuine change could not be prevented by the traditional need for unanimity, Occhetto guided through several important changes to the party's ideological belief system (including its teleological nature, its national Marxist heritage and its organisational structure) while apparently retaining the unity of the party intact.[7] Yet, if this was a success, it was one which paradoxically removed the very element (democratic centralism) which would have been essential to weather the unseen gathering storm. The Eighteenth Congress completely dismantled the party's organisational principle through the drafting of a new party statute, inspired (according to the chairman of the commission which drafted it, former leader Natta) by the 'democratic rule of law'. The new statute, among other things, allowed members of the party publicly to criticise the political action of the leadership and to use party facilities for the 'free expression and circulation of ideas'. The rights of minorities were to be protected through guaranteed representation on the Central Committee. The membership of the three central organs (Central Committee, *direzione* and *segretaria*) was increased, giving the Central Committee in particular the appearance of a national assembly rather than party organ in the Leninist mould.

That the leadership was fearful of the implications of removing the chains of democratic centralism was evident in two ways. Firstly, organised factions – which were defined by reference to external financing and the support of internal groupings – were still banned. The disingenuous nature of this trace of the old system was exposed by an amendment introduced by Cossutta which pointed out that, if operative, the article forbade the existence of not only his own journal, *Marxismo Oggi*, but also those supported by Ingrao's and Napolitano's institutes. That the article was to have no impact was seen shortly after the congress (see below). Secondly, a large proportion of the leadership was reluctant to be elected by secret ballot. Openly divided on the issue, it came up with a compromise whereby election would be by an open vote unless a tenth of the voters requested otherwise. The congress rejected this compromise and eventually approved a motion requiring election of the leadership by secret ballot. The Eighteenth Congress, then, besides giving formal recognition to certain practices which had already developed in the PCI, went further in delivering a fatal blow to the organisational principle which had, to varying degrees, shaped the internal life of the party since its birth.

CONFLICT EXPOSED: THE TWILIGHT OF THE PCI

The significance of the dismantling of democratic centralism became apparent shortly after the congress, when the Central Committee elected the top organs of the party (the *direzione* of 49 members and the *segretaria* of six members), by secret ballot. The *miglioristi*, to the fury of Napolitano, found themselves marginalised, the product of an evident backroom deal to vote against particular candidates. (Napolitano, as head of the *miglioristi* faction, rather ironically accused the party of 'factional practices'.) But the vote was also a rejection of Occhetto's recommended list of candidates (which, following tradition, had attempted to maintain the balance between left and right inside the party). The vote provided the first evidence that dismantling democratic centralism reduced the leader's power and left him at the mercy of different factions, as in other Italian parties. Moreover, and paradoxically, its removal had the effect of strengthening the very forces (the left) which were to oppose the completion of internal changes.

In the course of the summer of 1989 conflict inside the PCI reached unprecedented proportions for three reasons. First, when the leadership attempted to complete its internal reforms (specifically through tackling the issues of the party's heritage and international alignment), the differences in perception (by the different factions) of the scale of the reform programme became quickly apparent. Members of the left and the old guard put up a spirited resistance to any further changes, which caused the leadership to hesitate, if not retreat, on these issues. Second, the dilemma of hesitating on the reform programme was made acute by rapid changes in the external environment in the form of the eastern European revolutions. These suddenly made Occhetto's reforms appear to be moderate, if not conservative, by comparison with the changes taking place in the communist regimes, at the same time as having the effect of deeply dividing the party. The left and the old guard rejected the idea that Occhetto's reforms should be speeded up as a result of the changes taking place in eastern Europe. Third, when the above two factors registered their impact the party had already renounced the mechanisms of control which had traditionally allowed it to enact changes without a totally unrestrained and damaging debate. As a consequence, the party began visibly to fragment as the left and the old guard exploited the new democratic procedures available to them to oppose the proposals of the centre and the right.

This situation prompted Occhetto to attempt to short-cut the traditional channels of party change, and he unexpectedly launched his proposal to dissolve the party and form a non-communist party of the left, which would be an integral member of the Socialist International and the European Left.[8] This threw the party into its deepest crisis since its inception. The proposal split the party and demolished not only the (precarious) centre-left axis which had been established at the Eighteenth Congress, but the centre itself as a long-standing supporting component of the party leadership. Opposition to the proposal prompted an unholy alliance of *cossuttiani*, some *ingraiani*, members of the 'old guard' such as Pajetta and key members of the centre such as former leader Natta. The left was also split, few *ingraiani* following their mentor. The *miglioristi*, meanwhile, gave their full support to the proposal. The proposal, in short, broke up the party's internal alliances in an unprecedented manner. This was confirmed when, in a historic vote on 24 November 1989 (which was made subject to confirmation by the Nineteenth Congress in March 1990), the proposal was approved by the Central Committee with 219 members voting for it, 73 against, and with 34 abstentions. A third of the representatives, then, voted against the proposal, including key members such as Ingrao, Natta and Pajetta.

The run up to the Nineteenth and Twentieth Congresses, and the congresses themselves, saw, for the first time, the disintegration of all elements of cohesion and the mechanisms of conflict management inside the party. What occurred was a bitter struggle between publicly warring factions fighting for a particular conception – or dissolution – of the communist identity. The PCI's 'distinctiveness', and the mechanisms upholding it, went asunder.

THE DIMENSIONS OF CONFLICT AND ITS IMPACT

The period between the historic Central Committee vote in November 1989 and the official birth of the new party in January 1991 saw the party's norms, values, belief system, strategies, assumptions and structures laid bare. Symptomatic of this was the dubbing of the party as *la cosa* ('the thing') after the Nineteenth Congress. In the absence of any elements of cohesion, the conflict was unrestrained and had three dimensions which became mercilessly entangled with each other: first, the merits of the proposal to dissolve the party and the possible alternatives to it; second, how to proceed at each successive stage, and the exact meaning and implication of each decision taken; and third, public policy issues which intruded from the external environment at critical stages in the transition period (and most particularly the issue of the Gulf War). The majority of those supporting the motion were continually influenced by the awareness that a full third of the party opposed the proposal and that the dangers of a schism were very real. They therefore attempted to do all they could to reach a compromise to ensure the minority stayed in the party. The opposition, aware of this, employed every tactic possible to delay or obstruct the transition of the party. The divisions became rapidly crystallised into specific factions, but these were not to remain completely unchanged.

In the run up to the Nineteenth Congress the party was divided into three factions, two of which (the *cossuttiani* and *ingraiani*, making up the so-called *no* faction) attempted to galvanise enough votes to overturn the *si* faction's proposal. They failed to do this and the Nineteenth Congress (held in March 1990) officially dissolved the PCI and instituted a 'constituent phase'. Occhetto's motion obtained the support of 726 delegates, while 322 supported the Tortorella–Natta–Ingrao motion proposing reform without the party's name and symbols and 37 voted for Cossutta's motion, a more radical variant of Tortorella's.[9] The 'constituent phase' was meant to mark *il nuovo inizio* ('the new beginning'): a new party would be constructed which then had to be ratified at the party's Twentieth Congress. The only precondition set by the Nineteenth Congress was that the new party would not be communist. Formally speaking, then, the PCI, as an autonomous organisation with control over its own destiny, no longer existed. The party appeared to have a predetermined and transient existence which would end with the Twentieth Congress. But this did not stop the minority attempting to reverse the decision of the Nineteenth Congress. This was made possible primarily due to Occhetto's decision to give the minority representation on the new Central Committee (which was to guide the constituent phase) in proportion to its strength at the congress. This resulted in 236 *occhettiani*, 12 *cossuttiani* and 105 supporters of the Tortorella–Natta–Ingrao position. This decision tended to institutionalise the divisions in the party. Moreover, disappointing results in the local elections in May 1990 (the PCI's vote dropped by 6 per cent compared with the previous elections in 1985), confirmed the minority's view that the Nineteenth Congress's decision was a wrong one, and they decided to continue their struggle to reverse it.

Consequently, the constituent phase, instead of concentrating on the shape of the new party, quickly became bogged down in a discussion over the old one: specifically, whether the decision of the Nineteenth Congress permitted the possibility of delegates voting for a 'refounded' PCI at the final congress. The majority faction argued that the congress had been convened precisely to make a decision on this and had ruled against it. The minority faction, on the other hand, argued that the congress had left completely open the question of what type of party should be built. Moreover, the convening of a further congress was, for them, confirmation that the PCI was effectively still in existence. It followed that since the congress was the sovereign body of the party, the Twentieth Congress could overturn any decisions made by the Nineteenth Congress (or previous congresses). The majority faction was effectively ensnared in its own rules: no congress could bind its successor. The two minority factions, therefore, developed a united position around the *rifondazione* ('refounding') of the PCI. The majority faction, meanwhile, developed a project for the Democratic Party of the Left (PDS). A third project was constructed by Antonio Bassolino as a bridging manoeuvre between the two camps, with the result that the party arrived at its final congress with three separate motions: for a *Partito Democratico della Sinistra* (Occhetto), a *Rifondazione Comunista* (Tortorella–Natta–Ingrao) and a *Partito Antagonista e Riformatore* (Bassolino). The divisions were exacerbated by further pressures from the external environment: the Gulf crisis saw the PCI, for the first time in its sixty-year history, divided in parliament in August 1990, with the symbolic leader of the left, Pietro Ingrao, leading other rebels in a public display of defiance of the party line.

The minority failed to achieve its objective. Indeed, at the Twentieth Congress (January 1991) Occhetto's faction obtained an *increase* of nearly 2 per cent compared with the previous congress (from 65.8 to 67.69 per cent), while Tortorella's motion declined by over 5 per cent compared with the combined vote for the two motions at the previous congress (from 34.1 to 26.85 per cent), and Bassolino's motion obtained 5.4 per cent.[10] For the majority, however, numerical victory was less important than a victory which at the same time convinced the minority to stay in the party. The radicalisation of the PCI's position on the Gulf crisis, when the allied bombardment began only two weeks before the Twentieth Congress, appeared to be a tactical manoeuvre on the part of Occhetto to do precisely that. If so, it was only partially successful. Armando Cossutta led a small number of delegates out of the new party to 'refound' the PCI as *Rifondazione Comunista*. Most of those supporting the two minority motions, however, including influential figures such as Tortorella, Ingrao and Bassolino, stayed on. Whether the shift in foreign policy was the only factor behind their decision to stay in the party remains unclear, but it was certainly an indication to the left that it would probably continue to retain influence over the leadership in formulating party policy in the future.

The shift in the party's foreign policy, however, alienated the *riformisti* (the old *miglioristi* led by Napolitano), who, while not rejecting the new party, would not vote for its foreign policy. This division over an issue of public policy was a telling beginning for the new party. It also gave the PDS's nascent identity a far more radical tinge than would otherwise have been the case. Welcome or not to Occhetto, the image ensured an unequivocal rejection of the PDS by the other Italian political parties and, in particular, by the Socialist Party (Partito Socialista Italiano, PSI), which argued that the PDS was continuing the old PCI's 'irresponsible' ways, with no evidence that it was ready to take on the responsibilities of government.

The new party, in short, was born as the product of a deep internal conflict, one which had its origins in the PCI of the 1960s, and which had been contained for two decades but finally brought to a head in the late 1980s through irresistible pressures arising from the external environment. It is hardly surprising, therefore, that the new party's early life should bear the marks of that struggle.

Conflict and cohesion in the PDS

The PDS is too young for any definitive judgements to be passed on its new internal life. Nevertheless, it is possible to make a tentative identification of the new elements of cohesion, the patterns of conflict and its management and the impact so far of that conflict on the party's fortunes.

COHESION IN A WORLD WITHOUT IDEOLOGY AND DEMOCRATIC CENTRALISM

If the fundamental advantage of the maintenance of the PCI's 'distinctiveness' had been the source of cohesion it provided for the party membership, this is something the PDS is having to learn to do without. Uncomfortable to wear at times, the ideological coat had nevertheless provided a feeling of security about the *raison d'être* of the party and its objectives. The ideological binding has disappeared, and the new party – coming from a deeply ideological tradition – has struggled to find a replacement for it. The deep-rooted opposition from the left to the birth of a party which they feared might simply be 'absorbed' by the PSI led to Occhetto's idea that the words 'democracy' and 'the left' should be contained in the name of the new party. The lack of reference to socialism enraged the left, just as the lack of reference to social democracy raised murmurs from Napolitano and the right. In his speech to the Twentieth Congress, Occhetto argued that the goal of socialism was not being renounced, but socialism was defined as meaning simply 'a process of the comprehensive democratisation of society'. Hence, the new party arose from the two guiding principles ('democracy' and 'the left') which united the forces of renovation across the world. The objective was not to abolish the market in order to install socialism but rather to govern the market to develop a society which placed joint emphasis on the values of liberty and equality. This, Occhetto claimed, would allow the new party to house the ideals and experiences of *all* the progressive Italian traditions, symbolised in the roots of the oak tree (which is the new party's symbol): communism, liberal and socialist reformism, and democratic Catholicism.

This rather loose-fitting coat has been made tighter by padding it with a programme around which, it is hoped, the party will eventually unite. Indeed, to reinforce the non-ideological nature of the PDS, it was made clear from the outset that the PDS's *raison d'être* was a programmatic one (because of the failure of successive governing coalitions to carry through major reforms), which accepted that a future social order had to be constructed inside the contradictions of the old. The programmatic *raison d'être*, as outlined by Occhetto at the congress, has three fundamental objectives: to resolve the long-standing underdevelopment of the south of Italy; to introduce a modern system of economic and industrial relations which would see an effective end to unemployment; and to 'refound the democratic state' through major institutional reforms.

With the removal of the belief system has gone much of the structure which helped to uphold it. The PCI was the most highly disciplined and organised political party in Italy; its successor is a rather different animal. The PDS's organisational structures are based on two principles which aim at reducing conflict, rather than suppressing it. The first is decentralisation. The structures mark an irrevocable break with the PCI's traditional centralism (which was still present even after the Eighteenth Congress). The PCI's old structure, consisting of sections and cells, has not, as yet, been discarded (the minority succeeded in preventing this) but coexisting alongside it are new *unioni comunali* ('communal unions'), which have a large degree of independence from the centre (a truly federalist structure, demanded by the *cossuttiani*, was rejected, for fear of creating 'parties within the party'). The expectation (or aspiration) is that the strength of the sub-national elements will prevent the crystallisation of different positions at the centre. At the centre, the old triarchy of *comitato centrale* (357 members), *direzione* (48) and *segretaria* (9) has been replaced with a large *consiglio nazionale* (547 members) and an expanded *direzione* (about 100). Alongside decentralisation, the other guiding principle of the new organisation is overcoming the division of the sexes. The PDS aims to be a genuine 'party of men and women', ensured through the creation of a number of party units reserved to women, and through quotas (40 per cent minimum and 60 per cent maximum) for both sexes in the new party.[11]

Finally, other organisational changes confirm the overall abandonment of the other elements which, as noted earlier, reinforced the ideological and organisational cohesion of the PCI, through establishing the 'presence' of a 'communist culture' in Italian society. The PCI's newspapers, journals, radio and television have been given independence from the new party, and are now run by professional journalists. The communist component of the socialist-communist trade union, the Confederazione Generale del Lavoro (CGIL) has been dissolved, and the party's youth organisation has re-organised itself simply as the 'Youth of the Left'. The new culture, then, will be a generic one of the left.

The weakness both of the new binding elements and the mechanisms to inhibit conflict, particularly in a party born through intense conflict, has been evident in the PDS's early life.

CONFLICT: OLD WINE IN A NEW BOTTLE?

The PDS's early life has shown that in removing the chains of democratic centralism the new party has followed the tradition of other Italian political parties: intense factional rivalry which paralyses party activity. Indeed, the PDS's president, Stefano Rodotà, has described the new party statute as 'an entrenched encampment of the factions', meaning that little influence can be obtained in the new party but through an organized grouping (cited in Hellman 1992: 84). The rather bloated National Council reproduces faithfully the strengths of each of the factions according to the results of the Twentieth Congress: the 'centre' (Occhetto, 53 per cent), the 'reformists' (Napolitano, 15 per cent), the 'left' (Tortorella, 27 per cent) and the 'Bassolino' faction (5 per cent). These factions receive party funding for their activities and their political initiatives do not have to be approved by the leadership. In May 1991 a new 'liberal' faction (which claims not to be a faction) surfaced, which is primarily made up of the non-PCI members who participated in the constituent phase. In March of the same year Lucio Magri and other former PdUP members of the 'left' announced their resignation from the party and joined Cossutta's Rifondazione Comunista.[12] The 'left', meanwhile, has been active in setting up an autonomous cultural association, named after former leader Berlinguer, inside the party, an obvious attempt to protect and cultivate the radical element of the party. The adoption of the name 'Democratic Communists' by many of them is symptomatic of the gulf dividing the two extremes in the party. Indeed, the left of the party is still seeking a thorough evaluation by the party of Occhetto's entire project.

The general impression (even publicly expressed by party members) is that the party has become directionless because of the intensity of its internal divisions. The abolition of the *segretaria* has exacerbated the fragmentation and lack of coordination. In recognition of this the leadership in May 1991 revived the institution, albeit in a different and informal guise (the leadership refers to a 'coordinating executive'). Conflict has also been intense between some of the party's local units and the centre, particularly over alliance strategies to be adopted and whether to enter local and regional governments. The leadership has, at times, seemed reluctant to provide its sub-national units with the autonomy which the new party statutes allow them.

These tensions have been exacerbated by a failure, thus far, of the new elements of cohesion (which, as noted above, are rather amorphous) to have an effect on a large proportion of the membership. The purpose of dissolving the PCI (rather than simply changing its name) was to bring to an end the idea of the dedicated communist activist who had a monopoly on the truth and who therefore 'stood apart' from the system of western democracy (which was the psychological attribute underlying the PCI's 'distinctiveness' from other political forces), thereby opening the party to new members. Many observers argue that this has failed. Massimo Salvadori (1991), for example, argues that, due to internal divisions, and to Occhetto's desire to compromise with the forces opposing the transformation of the PCI and to welcome into the party social and protest movements, the confusion between 'opposition within the system' and 'opposition to the system' has been carried into the new party. It cannot be denied that continuity, in terms of attitudes and behaviour, is deeply ingrained. It is perhaps best symbolised in the PDS leadership's ironic claim – in a court case with Rifondazione Comunista over which party is the rightful owner of the PCI's name and symbol – that the PCI's heritage, name and symbol is owned by the PDS and cannot, therefore, be used by other organisations; this, despite the concomitant attempt by the leadership to convince other political forces, and its own membership, that a clean break with the past has, in fact, been enacted. There is a sense, then, in which, because of the disparate nature of the new elements of cohesion, party members have a tendency to fall back on the security offered by the old. Giuliano Zincone (1991), for example, argues that the former communists have become a 'sponge party', happy to accept a range of new ideas and movements:

But they cannot give up their forefathers, the structures, the organisation, the bureaucracy, the places of work, the glue that holds them together. They cannot give up their culture, their *raison d'être*, their group language. This all creates solidarity, complicity, identity, power. It is a *mélange* which we might want to call neo-communism, post-communism or the new party. The essential thing, though, is that the adherents identify with each other, know they are the best, the most honest, the ones who are right.

The continued dependence of many ex-communists on the old reference points increases the friction with other members, and particularly new members, of the PDS who regard the past as definitively liquidated. The 'liberal' faction, for example, was formed partly as a result of a disillusionment with the entire process of building the new party which they felt had been hijacked by the factional activities of the old PCI. The old elements of cohesion have, paradoxically, become elements of conflict: the party's identity is in a malleable state and the continual tension between the factions is a product of their different designs to mould or remould it. Despite the rhetorical claims about the PDS's credentials as a 'new type' of party, then, its early life has indicated that it has failed to escape the stranglehold of its old divisions. This paralysis has impaired the party's performance in the external arena.

THE IMPACT OF CONFLICT: THE PDS AND ITS EXTERNAL ENVIRONMENT

Electorally, Occhetto had evidently hoped that the PDS would attract disillusioned socialist voters, progressive Catholics, newly enfranchised voters and the so-called 'lost left' (which had been disillusioned with both the socialists and the communists). This has not occurred. On the contrary, the first major electoral test (the April 1992 national elections) witnessed an effective collapse in the old communist vote.[13] The PDS polled 16.1 per cent, a decline from 26.6 per cent polled by the PCI in the 1987 national elections. This represented an unprecedented haemorrhage of votes, and even if one adds to the PDS vote the percentage obtained by Rifondazione Comunista (5.6 per cent), the 'political space' previously occupied by the PCI shrank by 4.9 per cent, not an inconsiderable amount in the Italian party system. Its most marked losses were in the industrialised belts of the north with high concentrations of manual workers and in parts of the south where its vote was halved compared with 1987 (Bull and Newell 1993: 216–17). Electoral defeat has exacerbated further the party's internal problems, and has not endeared it to potential new members. Membership is approximately a million (compared with just under 1½ million in 1988, the year before Occhetto launched his proposal) and the vast majority of these have been inherited from the PCI – that is to say, the party is thus far failing to attract any new recruits.

Strategically and tactically the party has also floundered, faced with fierce competition to its left (from Rifondazione Comunista) and to its right (from the PSI). Rifondazione has made a much more telling impact than was envisaged by the PDS leadership. It has not only absorbed the former PdUP members from the PDS but also the Democrazia Proletaria which dissolved itself at its Seventh Congress in June 1991. With over 140,000 members, including 11 senators, seven deputies and hundreds of local politicians, Rifondazione launched its own 'constituent phase' and moulded *la cosa comunista* ('the communist thing') into a formal political party. Its attempt to steal the PCI's mantle (not just literally, by claiming the name and symbol, but by continually taking up oppositional stands reminiscent of the old party) has squeezed the political space which the PDS has attempted to carve out for itself. The PSI, meanwhile, at least under the leadership of Craxi, has done little to further the prospect of a political alliance between the two parties, deemed essential to ousting the Christian Democratic Party (Democrazia Cristiana, DC) from its 45-year hold on power.

The PDS's prospects, however, are not necessarily as gloomy as the above analysis suggests, because of dramatic changes which are currently taking place in the party's external environment. Parties should not be viewed as simply *adapting* to their external environment but also as attempting to *dominate* or *shape* that environment (Panebianco 1988: chs 1 and 11). In this respect it is worth recalling Occhetto's rationale for transforming the PCI into a non-communist party of the left. He had portrayed the transformation as the beginning of renewal of the party system *tout court* through the birth of a new type of party and the ending of the 'communist question'. Whether or not a new type of party has been achieved is open to question, as this analysis has indicated. But what is undeniable is that Italian politics is currently undergoing a sea change of such dimensions that it threatens to transform the Italian political system itself.[14] True, the transformation of the PCI has not been the sole origin of this sea change, but it has been the most significant one. The cement of Italian politics in the postwar period was a coalition of parties bent on keeping the PCI out of office at all costs. With the end of the cold war and the transformation of the PCI the supports of this model were suddenly removed. This factor, combined with others, led to a destabilisation of Italian politics in the late 1980s which culminated in the April 1992 elections. These elections produced some of the most significant changes in individual party strengths since the Second World War, the most striking of these being the fall in votes for the DC and the PDS and the dramatic rise of the Lombard League, a protest party based in the north. The elections acted as a catalyst for further change, and Italy is currently witnessing an inexorable advance towards major institutional reform (through both referenda and government action), and towards the possible wholesale removal of a large sector of the old political class (through the unfolding of a massive corruption scandal involving virtually all the major parties). For the first time in 45 years there is a very real search under way to replace the old governing formula (currently under a socialist leader, Amato) with an alternative involving the PDS.

These changes in the PDS's external environment present the party with new opportunities which, if properly exploited, could help to overcome the historic divisions persisting in its internal life. The other political parties' unequivocal acceptance, since the elections, of the PDS's credentials for government has helped to dull the old ideological-strategic debate inside the party. This factor, combined with the party's recent acceptance into the Socialist International, suggests that the profound divisions over the party's identity may not be destined to last. The type of conflict engendered by this historical factor may well decline in importance next to the growing importance of new factors which tend to prevail in traditional social democratic parties – for example, public policies, governmental alliances, institutional changes. These factors were always important in the PCI, but were habitually shaped and distorted by the more fundamental ideological-strategic debate. This is not to suggest that the PDS will quickly rid itself of its past divisions. On the contrary, they will always figure in the party's make up simply because a party's 'genetic model' is one of the most influential forces in a party's subsequent evolution (Panebianco 1988: ch. 4). But the continued presence (in attenuated form) of the 'ghost' of the PCI does not mean that the PDS will always remain 'apart' from the other parties in the Socialist International. Those parties also carry their past with them, which is one of the reasons why European social democracy's hallmark in the postwar period has been 'unity in diversity'. This, moreover, is a tradition which is close to the heart of the PDS: it was, after all, former PCI leader Togliatti's principle for the western European communist movement.

Acknowledgements

The author would like to thank the participants (and particularly the discussant, Tobias Abse) in the conference 'Contemporary Social Democracy: Unity in Diversity', for their comments and suggestions on an earlier draft of this chapter; and the British Academy and the University of Salford for financial assistance during the preparation of the chapter. Responsibility for the final text rests with the author.

Notes

1. This, of course, raises the question of whether the PDS *can* be described as 'social democratic'. There are also, of course, some observers who believe that the PCI itself was social democratic from the 1970s onwards, or at least would argue that the PCI remained closer to the idea of European social democracy than the Italian Socialist Party (e.g. Padgett and Paterson 1991: 48). This question, while relevant to this analysis (as will be seen), is part of a much wider debate which goes beyond the overall scope of this chapter (for this author's view see Bull 1991b: esp. 96–106). As a starting point for this chapter's analysis, it can be noted that the PDS is officially a non-communist party and in 1992 became a member of the Socialist International.

2. For reasons of space this chapter does not deal with a third source of cohesion, that of 'selective incentives' (for a theoretical treatment of this point, see Panebianco 1988: ch. 2). As a highly disciplined organisation with a strong membership, selective incentives (primarily that of the prospect of promotion through the party hierarchy) were an important source of cohesion (with the leadership's line). Yet, because the PCI was a party of 'permanent opposition' it did not have the scope of state (politicized) appointments to offer party officials (as did the governing parties, and particularly the

Christian Democrats). This, therefore, increased the dependence of the party on the 'belief system' (or what Panebianco would define as 'collective incentives').
3. For a more detailed treatment of the following themes see Bull (1989a). For a general treatment of the inheritance of democratic centralism see Waller (1988: 17ff.).
4. See Amyot (1982) for a detailed account of the origins of the dispute.
5. For example, *Marxismo Oggi* (Cosutta); *Centro per la Riforma dello Stato* (Ingrao); *Cespi* (Napolitano).
6. The course and outcome of Occhetto's reform programme is best documented in the pages of *Italian Politics: A Review* (1989–92), and Ignazi (1992).
7. See Bull (1991a: 25–9) for a detailed analysis of these achievements.
8. See Bull (1991b) for an attempt to explain the reasons behind Occhetto's decision.
9. For an analysis of the Nineteenth Congress see Bull and Daniels (1990: 34–7).
10. For a more detailed analysis of the Twentieth Congress, see Bull (1991c) and Hellman (1992).
11. For a comprehensive analysis of the formal structures and rules of the PCI and the PDS see Bardi and Morlino (1992).
12. The PdUP was the (now dissolved) party created from the Manifesto group which was expelled from the PCI in the late 1960s.
13. In fact, the Sicilian regional elections in June 1991 were the first significant test: the PDS's vote fell by 7.5 per cent compared with the PCI's performance in the 1986 regional elections (Bull 1992). These gave the clearest indicator of what was likely to occur in the national elections.
14. For a detailed elaboration of this change see Bull and Newell (1993).

References

Amyot, G. Grant (1982) *The Italian Communist Party – The Crisis of the Popular Front Strategy* (London: Croom Helm).

Bardi, Luciano and Leonardo Morlino (1992) 'Italy', in Richard S. Katz and Peter Mair (eds), *Party Organizations. A Data Handbook on Party Organizations in Western Democracies, 1960–1990* (London: Sage).

Bull, Martin (1989a) 'Strategy, Identity and Democratic Centralism in the Functioning of West European Communist Parties', Paper presented to the *European Consortium of Political Research* Joint Sessions, 10–15 April, Paris (Workshop: 'The Organisation of the West European Communist Parties).

Bull, Martin (1989b) '*Perestroika* is Catching: the Italian Communist Party Elects a New Leader', *Journal of Communist Studies*, Vol. 5, No. 1, March.

Bull, Martin (1991a) 'The Unremarkable Death of the Italian Communist Party', in Filippo Sabetti and Raimondo Catanzaro (eds), *Italian Politics. A Review*, Vol. 5 (London: Pinter).

Bull, Martin (1991b) 'Whatever Happened to Italian Communism? Explaining the Dissolution of the Largest Communist Party in the West', *West European Politics*, Vol. 14, No. 4, Oct.

Bull, Martin (1991c) 'The Italian Communist Party's Twentieth Congress and the Painful Birth of the Democratic Party of the Left', *Journal of Communist Studies*, Vol. 7, No. 2, June.

Bull, Martin (1992) 'Distant Thunder at a Picnic: the Sicilian Regional Elections of June 1991', *Regional Politics and Policy*, Vol. 2, No. 3 (Summer).

Bull, Martin and Philip Daniels (1990) 'The "New Beginning": the Italian Communist Party under the Leadership of Achille Occhetto', *Journal of Communist Studies*, Vol. 6, No. 3, Sept.

Bull, Martin and James Newell (1993) 'Italian Politics and the 1992 Elections: From "Stable Instability" to Instability and Change', *Parliamentary Affairs*, April.

Gramsci, Antonio (1978) *Selections from the Prison Notebooks of Antonia Gramsci*, (London: Lawrence & Wishart).

Hellman, Stephen (1992) 'The Difficult Birth of the Democratic Party of the Left', in Stephen Hellman and Gianfranco Pasquino (eds), *Italian Politics. A Review* (London: Pinter).

Ignazi, Piero (1992) *Dal PCI al PDS* (Bologna: Mulino).

Italian Politics. A Review (1989–92), Volumes 4–7, chs by Amyot, Bull, Belloni and Hellman (London: Pinter).

Padgett, Stephen and William E. Paterson (1991) *A History of Social Democracy in Post-War Europe* (London: Longman).

Panebianco, Angelo (1988) *Political Parties: Organisation and Power* (Cambridge: Cambridge University Press).

Pellicani, Luciano (1979) 'Il Partito "Diverso"', *Rivista di Scienza Politica*.

Rossanda, Rossana (1976) 'The Khrushchev Speech, the PCF and the PCI'. Interviewed by *Politique Hebdo*, in Ralph Miliband and John Saville (eds), *The Socialist Register* (London: Merlin Press).

Salvadori, Massimo (1991) 'Il PDS e l'eredità del "Migliore"', *Avanti!*, 11 March.

Waller, Michael (1988) 'Democratic Centralism: The Costs of Discipline', in Michael Waller and Meindert Fennema (eds), *Communist Parties in Western Europe: Decline or Adaptation* (Oxford: Blackwell).

Zincone, Giuliano (1991), 'Sui postcomunisti il macigno della storia', *Corriere della Sera*, 15 November.

3 The resurgence of factionalism in the Spanish Socialist Workers' Party

Richard Gillespie

The reappearance of conflict within the Spanish Socialist Workers' Party (Partido Socialista Obrero Español, PSOE) in the late 1980s showed once again in the history of this party its propensity to behave differently from other European socialist parties. Two contemporary factors seem particularly relevant in explaining the PSOE's relative factiousness at a time when factionalism appeared to be in decline elsewhere. There was, first, the extremely privileged position that the Spanish socialists enjoyed in their national party system during the 1980s, which according to Sartori should lead us to expect strong factionalism.[1] And second, there was an unusually strong divergence in Spain between the PSOE and its erstwhile trade union supporters, provoked primarily by the market-oriented economic policies pursued by the PSOE in office.[2] The PSOE's relatively long and often bitter tradition of factional dispute may also be relevant, in spite of very substantial party renewal during the 1970s.[3]

However, it is not our aim here to account for the PSOE's peculiarity in a comparative analysis but rather to provide a national case study in which to explain why conflict re-emerged in the PSOE after Felipe González had united his party so successfully in the early 1980s.

Founded in 1879, the PSOE experienced very little internal conflict during its early decades, when the struggle for organisational survival was the prime concern of the party builders. Yet factionalism and fragmentation featured prominently during and after the First World War and again during the country's first attempt at genuine democratisation in the 1930s. The failure of the Second Republic of 1931–36 amidst growing social polarisation led to the creation of several PSOE factions with radically different views on the Spanish crisis and the appropriate solutions. Given that the party was the only republican force organised throughout Spain, its fragmentation contributed decisively to the institutional crisis of the republic. During the ensuing civil war, the PSOE's divisions were such that it ceased to be an effective, single party and the bitter rivalry between its components helped undermine the republican war effort.[4]

Defeat in the civil war served to reunify the anti-communist PSOE sectors, and both in Spain and in exile defeat led to strong collaboration with the socialist General Workers' Union (Unión General de Trabajadores, UGT). Nevertheless, the rhetorical refighting of old battles persisted for several years before new lines of factional conflict appeared in the 1950s. From then until the early 1970s, the fundamental division was between a sector of the party that supported the ageing exiled leadership based in Toulouse, whose outlook was still formed by the experience of the 1930s, and another sector that struggled to re-establish a party leadership in Spain, and whose politics was much more receptive to the changing realities of their country. The PSOE also experienced the influence of new left radicalism, especially Trotskyism, in the early 1970s, and the effects persisted into the early years of post-Francoism.

Since the death of Franco in 1975, the internal political life of the PSOE has undergone considerable variation in its cohesiveness. After returning to legality on 18 February 1977, there was rivalry between moderates and left-wing socialists while the party served as the main opposition to governments formed by the Union of the Democratic Centre (Unión del Centro Democrático, UCD). This period lasted until September 1979 when González finally triumphed over the left at an extraordinary party congress and, as its general secretary, went on to lead a much more united party to national victory and office in 1982.

With some dissidents leaving, others falling silent and new González supporters entering the party, the PSOE then became almost monolithic, leading some commentators to question the usefulness of factionally focused analysis of its internal life.[5] Since 1988, however, the party has experienced a resurgence of factional tension which for a while even undermined the effectiveness of the socialist government. Though constrained by a common socialist desire to remain a governing party, factionalism seems likely to remain a feature of PSOE politics in the foreseeable future.

In seeking to identify the sources of cohesion and division and the nature of intra-party conflict, this study will focus on the period from 1979 to the eve of the general election in 1993. The assumption made is that, even in the event of electoral defeat, there is unlikely to be a return to the level of internal party democracy that existed in 1976–79, when grassroots sections (*agrupaciones*) had a significant input into party decision-making and factionalism was permitted to develop virtually unhindered. Strong party management and internal authoritarianism are now the norm among European socialist parties;[6] and the obstacles to a reversion to the status quo ante in Spain include the highly restrictive party organisational rules adopted since 1979, the clientelist nature of much party recruitment (which has grown with electoral success) and the broad public antipathy to activism in political parties.

Sources of unity

For much of the 1980s, unity rather than disunity was the dominant feature of the PSOE. Open warfare within the party was rare. Although there were individual defections, there were no large-scale desertions by PSOE dissidents; indeed, the party was a net importer of members.

The party's cohesiveness can be attributed to both external and internal factors. It was enhanced by the early successes of the socialist government, the most trumpeted of these being Spanish entry into the European Community in 1986 and impressive rates of economic growth in 1986–89. The government disappointed left-wingers by emphasising growth at the expense of redistribution and by performing a volte-face over the question of NATO membership, but it was difficult for critical members to condemn government shortcomings while the party kept winning elections. Although the fall in the socialist share of the vote from a peak of 48.4 per cent in 1982 to 39.6 per cent in 1989 provoked internal recriminations, the PSOE remained dominant in parliament while also recording some notable electoral triumphs at regional and local level. The United Left (Izquierda Unida, IU), created in 1986, was seen as an attractive alternative by only a handful of socialist dissidents: for most, its appeal was undermined by its communist leadership.

González's own charismatic appeal is a major source of party unity. His personal leadership qualities impress party members through direct experience of them and also indirectly due to the good impression they make on the electorate and on other European leaders. Whatever their own political differences and personal rivalries, for the great majority of PSOE members González's leadership was sacrosanct throughout this period.

González has been a tremendous electoral asset to the PSOE. He remained Spain's most respected politician throughout the socialists' first ten years in office, even when obliged to acknowledge a serious economic recession in 1992.[7] This enduring popularity has given him immense personal authority in his party, as was demonstrated in 1991 when he removed the powerful deputy prime minister and deputy party leader, Alfonso Guerra, from the government. Guerra felt totally unable to criticise González directly; instead he claimed that an innocent 'Felipe' had been 'kidnapped' by bankers and entrepreneurs, and needed to be 'rescued'.[8] The importance of the González factor has been underlined also by PSOE left-winger Antonio García Santesmases, who described the timing and circumstances of González's future departure from the leadership as crucial variables in any perspective on the future of the party and the outcome of its internal struggles.[9]

In opposition and from 1982 to 1991, González's relationship with Guerra was also crucial to the party's cohesion. The involvement in the government of Guerra who *de facto* controlled the party meant that the PSOE and its parliamentary group would (until the relationship started to break down) loyally echo government messages. Guerra's presence in the Moncloa governmental complex strengthened the intelligence network that was a source of his power: he concerned himself personally with masses of reports coming in from the provinces via government delegates, local leaders and PSOE stalwarts. Information on opponents was carefully stored up for later use.[10]

Large numbers of non-compliant socialists suffered for their defiance of Guerra by their being discredited within the party, replaced in public office, dropped from election lists or suspended from membership. A Malagá veteran, 75-year-old José Fernández Gálvez, was suspended for criticising Guerra and other party members, after no less than 55 years of service to the PSOE.[11]

Guerra's grip on the PSOE proved problematic for González in the long run, but for much of the 1980s the arrangement suited González: it released the general secretary from potentially heavy party commitments and enabled him to concentrate principally on the international political work that appealed to him so much more. The post of deputy prime minister gave Guerra great influence upon policy-making, especially as chairman of the committee of under-secretaries which every Thursday prepared the business for the cabinet meeting the following day. At the end of the day, though, González always had the option of removing the *guerristas* from his government, as he did effectively in March 1991.

Of course, the authoritarian internal regime would not have worked if the rewards for loyalty had not been so great. However, there were ample opportunities for rewarding political loyalty with public office as a result of the process of regional devolution in the 1980s and due to doubts about the reliability of Franco-era state appointees. The proportion of public office-holders in the PSOE has varied but what has remained steady over the last three party congresses (1984, 1988 and 1990) has been the proportion of delegates who are on the government payroll: over 70 per cent. González has voiced the ambition to increase this percentage to 100 per cent.[12]

It is really this combination of effective discipline and patronage, together with the personal leadership factors, that provided the internal sources of party cohesion in the 1980s. Ideology has not been a strong binding force in a party that deliberately set out to 'de-ideologise' itself in 1979. 'Modernisation' may be a theme unifying most PSOE members, but it is by no means exclusive to the socialists. However, most party members do tend to 'internalise' and echo the official party discourse,[13] and the traditional party culture has been resistant to the public airing of disputes, from which rivals may benefit.

In the long term, the weakness of ideological and normative integration may present problems for the pragmatic PSOE's coherence, especially if economic growth fails to return to the levels of 1986–89, if the party continues to lose votes and the resultant need for coalitions or loss of governmental power provokes intra-party dissension. Also, of course, there will be a problem when González decides to call it a day. Given his relative youth, there is no great risk of his demise threatening to unleash internal conflict, but he has always been rumoured to have ambitions to move on to fresh pastures, such as the presidency of the Socialist International or of the European Commission. Moreover, it is unlikely that González would be prepared to continue as prime minister in the event of his party having to deal with the IU in order to stay in office after a future election. There is no heir apparent waiting in the wings, but there is a series of candidates among whom there might be a struggle over the leadership succession when the time comes.

The renewal of conflict

The repeated spectacle of anodyne PSOE congresses in the 1980s, designed to present an image of party coherence to the Spanish electorate, did not mean that disagreement was non-existent: rather that it was extremely difficult to manifest dissidence volubly in a party whose leaders were not only politically successful, but also able to make or break political careers and exclude dissentient voices.

In the circumstances, anti-government sentiment found vocal expression mainly outside the party, both on the streets, when workers, school students or peace campaigners mobilised, and through the traditionally fraternal but organisationally autonomous socialist union federation, the UGT. Indeed, it was the general strike of December 1988, called by the union leaders of the UGT and Workers' Commission (Comisiones Obreras, CCOO), partly to protest over the employment policies of González's government,[14] that really cracked open the edifice of PSOE coherence. In its wake came widespread internal concern about the party's loss of labour support, whose electoral implications were confirmed during 1989 as the party vote fell from 43.4 per cent (in 1986) to 39.6 per cent. The fall was most striking in working-class districts. The strike helped to 'loosen up' the PSOE and to provoke a more questioning attitude among its members, some of whom began to form groups to lobby for democratic debate in the party and for policy changes in the government.

Equally important was the national and international context of economic downturn, which put an end to the aura of success that the government had acquired from economic buoyancy and admission to the EC. The loss of unity also derived from the adverse publicity provoked by corruption within the party. The PSOE had been able to withstand exposés of high living and corrupt dealings on the part of some of its officials, and it had survived earlier questioning about the origins of party finances, but destabilisation was sure to ensue when the exposure of corruption undermined the standing of party boss Alfonso Guerra through the 'Juan Guerra scandal' (named after his brother), which came to light in January 1990. In a case involving the use of government offices in Seville by Juan Guerra for illegitimate party and private money-making purposes, it seemed inconceivable to many Spaniards that his brother had no knowledge of what was going on. The weakening of the iron man of the party apparatus through this scandal encouraged his critics to challenge the distribution of power within the socialist hierarchy, especially after González removed him from the government in January 1991. The start of the 1990s thus saw the PSOE more internally divided than at any time during the previous decade.

The bases of disunity

Analysis of this resurgence of intra-party divisions shows conflict within the PSOE to be far more concerned with 'power, careers, spoils and rewards' than with 'strategy, policy or ideology',[15] and what appears to be ideological confrontation is often little more than a façade for battles designed to redefine the internal distribution of power between different groups. To the limited extent that ideology is relevant, the divergence is twofold. One can differentiate both between traditional social democrats and New Left elements, and between those who believe in the efficiency of the market economy and those who remain sceptical about it.

During the 1980s the classical social democrats (José Maravall, Javier Solana, Joaquín Almunia, José Barrionuevo) formed a minority group among González's ministers, which was also identified by the media as a 'clan' (an informal group of like-minded associates) within the Madrid federation of the party. Although highly pragmatic, these social democrats were generally to the right of the New Left elements that constituted the party's 'Socialist Left' current, Izquierda Socialista (IS), which had no representation in the government. IS was founded by neo-Marxist intellectuals after the defeat of the left-wing *sector crítico* in 1979 and it functioned as the party's only officially tolerated 'current of opinion' during the 1980s, its main support coming from Madrid, Catalonia and Valencia. It was not fundamentally at odds with social democracy but was distinguished by its post-materialist emphasis upon pacifist and ecological themes. Unlike the rest of the party, the left took part in campaigns against NATO membership and US military bases.

The other ideological cleavage dates from the early years of PSOE government. Notwithstanding a 1982 election manifesto that raised hopes of radical change, the socialists' economic policies, first under Miguel Boyer and later under Carlos Solchaga, were consistently inspired by orthodox market-oriented economic ideas, with little regard for their social consequences.[16] The successive finance ministers were constrained by a lack of support in the party, which helps explain why the role of the state was enhanced rather than rolled back during the 1980s; but they became clearly distinguished from other party members by their persisting commitment to monetarism, to greater 'flexibility' in the labour market and to privatisation. A lot of observers referred to their supporters, somewhat loosely, as 'neo-liberals', while Solchaga used the term 'liberal social democrat' to describe himself. (For the sake of brevity, the more market-oriented PSOE sector will henceforth be described as 'liberals' in this chapter.) Although the economic policies devised by these liberals were often accepted by traditional social democrats and other moderates as the necessary means of achieving Spain's modernisation, sooner or later they provoked criticism from the weak IS current, the UGT, and the *guerristas*.

It must be emphasised, however, that initially both the UGT and the *guerristas* went along with the liberals' economic policies, accepting that industrial restructuring, lay-offs and wage restraint were necessary for economic recovery. For the UGT it was the government's *persisting* subordination of redistribution to growth even after economic recovery had been achieved that led to tension from 1985. The UGT was particularly sensitive to the steep rise in unemployment that industrial restructuring and monetarist policy brought: this not only affected the lives of ordinary trade unionists, but also had serious implications for UGT affiliation and bargaining power.[17]

Guerrista opposition to market-oriented policies was even less a matter of principle. Opposition came about in the course of a government power struggle in 1985. After Finance Minister Boyer had sought (unsuccessfully) to increase his influence at the expense of the *guerristas*, Guerra cynically responded by repeating complaints made by the UGT about government economic policy. The power struggle continued after Boyer's replacement by Solchaga, in part because after 1986 the economic policies were helping to erode the PSOE's electoral support. Since they controlled the party, masterminded its electoral strategy and actually organised and ran its election campaigns, the *guerristas* were much more sensitive than the successive finance ministers to the effects of government policies on public opinion. Largely because of this sensitivity, and because Guerra has a populist discourse among others in his repertoire, the *guerristas* are often characterised as 'populists'.

Theirs is not just the standard behaviour of modern party managers, duly concerned with opinion polls and the party image. Electoral reverses are setbacks for the *guerristas*, not simply as party officials but as the builders of a clientelistic empire for which electoral success provides further opportunities to expand influence, and electoral decline involves the possible alienation of political clients whose careers are disrupted. At the peak of his success, Guerra's empire was reported to include the party executive and apparatus, the Socialist Parliamentary Group, some key positions in the Moncloa, seven ministries, three regional governments, two universities and growing influence in the judiciary; while in its principal regional fief of Andalusia, the empire extended to the regional government, seven of the eight provincial councils (*diputaciones*), 80 per cent of the municipal councils, the regional television channel, cultural and sporting associations, and several state savings banks.[18]

Guerrismo is a clientelistic network that has thrived in the Spanish political culture and through the power that the electoral list system gives to party elites. This faction has manipulated ideology in an instrumental way, for example by using Programa 2000, ostensibly an exercise in programmatic renewal, as a means of attacking and isolating liberals like Solchaga in the government.[19] One of the real complaints of the *guerristas* is that the party has been denied opportunities for patronage in liberal-controlled domains: for example, Guerra is reported to have lamented the fact that in the Treasury there was only one PSOE appointee among 36 senior officials.[20] There is an element here of tension between party politicians and liberal technocrats, over whether political criteria or expertise should prevail in appointments, but both sides sponsor candidates for posts in the administration and public sector.

Consistency has never been a hallmark of the *guerristas*. They have defended PSOE collaboration with the IU in Asturias, when in that region PSOE–IU cooperation served as an obstacle to the liberals' plans to close coalmines, while in Madrid, where their rival Joaquín Leguina has survived as regional president with IU support, they have opposed such collaboration. In comparison,[21] the liberals have been more consistent: they have been prepared to take unpopular economic decisions, safe in the knowledge that in the event of electoral defeat they can resume former careers in the world of banking or business. Their problem has been that most members of the party consider their market-oriented principles to lie either beyond the frontiers of socialism or at least on the perimeter of what social democracy can embrace. They have thus functioned as a small group of ministers, officials and public sector managers, commended by bankers and foreign investors but lacking organised support in the party; as such they have been crucially dependent upon González's support.

Besides ideology and the pursuit of power and position, the party rules themselves provide a further basis for conflict within the PSOE, although usually there are other dimensions of conflict mixed in with any disputation over the contents and applications of the statutes. Especially in the hands of the *guerristas*, who have never seen pluralism as a particularly positive party feature, the post-1979 party statutes have imposed great limits on the tolerance of democratic debate and especially public disagreement with the party line: *monolitismso* has been the main charge levelled against the Guerra camp by liberals and social democrats alike.

Democratic representation within the party is undermined by the way in which central and regional officials intervene to influence the composition of congress delegations, and by federal congress decision-making often being based on open voting by just the heads of regional delegations. In the case of the 1988 Congress, when regional filtering mechanisms helped keep IS representation to just 7 per cent of the delegates, it is revealing that IS did well only in the election to the large Federal Committee (which in theory controls the PSOE executive): it won 22.5 per cent of the delegates' votes in what was the only congress vote carried out on the basis of a secret, individual ballot.[22]

IS has been the most consistent agitator for party democracy, but two other groups also deserve mention. Since the start of 1987, party democracy, combined with opposition to neo-liberalism, has served to inspire a group known as the Centro de Estudios Políticos y Sociales (CEPES); and internal democracy, together with social democracy and solidarity with the UGT, were the banners of Democracia Socialista, a group led by the PSOE leader in the Basque province of Vizcaya, Ricardo García Damborenea, which tried unsuccessfully to develop semi-autonomously within the PSOE in 1989–90. However, in both cases internal democracy was campaigned for only when socialist officials suffered personally from a loss of patronage or became victims of party disciplinary procedures.

CEPES was founded by former socialist minister Julián Campo and three former politically appointed ministerial under-secretaries, all of whom felt they had been dismissed from their posts because they were to the left of the government.[23] The democratic credentials of Democracia Socialista were even more suspect. Vizcaya had been the only provincial federation of the PSOE to sympathise openly with UGT complaints about government policy, but as a small federation it had only 14 delegates (2 per cent at the 1988 Party Congress). On that occasion it alienated party democrats by being the only province not to respect a norm whereby minority lists in congress delegation elections are given 25 per cent of the places if they receive a minimum of 20 per cent of the votes.[24] Minority groups can be particularly intolerant of their own minorities' rights.

The case of Democracia Socialista, which García Damborenea subsequently attempted to register as a party current, provides an illustration of the extent of group toleration within the PSOE. Initially, registration was deemed impossible because the existence of a coordinating committee, founding documents, meetings to which provincial groups were invited, the discussion of political resolutions and the adoption of its own symbols were all seen as evidence of the existence of an organised 'tendency' (proscribed under the party statutes). García Damborenea was subjected to party disciplinary proceedings both for factional activity and for publicly comparing a meeting addressed by Alfonso Guerra with Francoist rallies; in the end he decided to form an independent party rather than accept a long suspension. As soon as he had announced the launch of the new party, however, the PSOE decided that it could, after all, see its way to registering a current with the new name of Democracia Socialista. The remarkable elasticity of the party statutes on this occasion served an apparent party objective to confuse potential supporters of the new party or to deny it its name.[25]

Although there were rumours of UGT financial support for Democracia

Socialista, the socialist union took a deliberate decision not to try to change government policy by urging members to intervene *en masse* in the PSOE in the late 1980s. Here it was mindful of the close subordination of the party to the government, the limited size and influence of the party's rank and file, and the pretext that intervention would give for pro-government PSOE 'entryism' in the UGT. There is not, then, an *organised* basis for conflict between economically oriented 'workerist' elements and social groups with post-materialist values within the PSOE. Nor has there been a generational basis for conflict in recent years. The veterans of the 1930s have in some cases been coopted, and in many others have ceased to be active due to old age or political disgust. At the other end of the age span, the party has lost support among young people and maintains only a small, obedient youth organization. The bulk of the party is middle-aged and forms part of the González generation.[26]

There is, however, one remaining cleavage underlying party factionalism: that between central and regional interests. What has helped prevent the emergence of French Parti Socialiste-type factionalism in Spain is the strength of regionalism, and its reflection in the territorial structure of the party. Conflict within the party's regional federations is rarely about ideology and nearly always about power.[27] Where the regional government presidency and the post of regional party general secretary are in separate hands, there is often a struggle to unite the two power bases; and where power is concentrated in one set of hands, there is often a struggle to put an end to this situation. The 1980s saw tension between regional power-holders and the central party apparatus, often when the latter was sponsoring a local offensive against a non-*guerrista* leader.

In the case of the PSOE's Catalan federation, there has been tension with the centre because of the strength of regionally based nationalism and the existence before 1977 of a strong independent Catalan socialist party which merged with a weaker official PSOE federation. Well aware that they pay an electoral price, especially in regional contests, for accepting the PSOE's rejection of full-blooded federalism, the Catalan socialists have pressed for regional power to be developed to the full under the existing Spanish constitution, and for regional federations to enjoy more meaningful autonomy within the PSOE.[28] Elsewhere, regional leaders often find it frustrating to wield considerable power in their own bailiwicks and then find that they lack weight in the party nationally.

The term 'baron' is often applied to regional leaders, especially those heading both the party federation and the regional government simultaneously. During the 1980s, the central party apparatus tried to manipulate these men. In Madrid, Andalusia and Castilla-La Mancha, however, local barons who were helped into office by the *guerristas* subsequently asserted their autonomy. Barons are able to exploit their own command of patronage and sometimes of large congress delegations in order to assert some autonomy from the centre. But, initially at least, due to the difficulty of joining forces, they proved vulnerable to *guerrista* counter-attacks, which in Madrid and Andalusia deprived regional presidents of their general secretaryships before threatening their presidencies. Only after Guerra had been weakened by the Juan Guerra scandal did opposition to the central party apparatus become widespread among the regional leaders, whose ideal is a more federal party in which they would be more influential.[29] Rather too late, perhaps, did Guerra begin sponsoring the municipal cause of PSOE mayors demanding a larger proportion of public funds; they were courted in 1991 as a potential counter-weight to baronial power.[30] By this time González himself had started holding regular meetings with the regional leaders. Although such meetings had no status in the party statutes, they seem to have played a part in persuading key figures to abandon *guerrismo* as it became openly critical of the González government.[31]

Variables affecting party conflict

In order to appreciate the dynamics of conflict within the PSOE, it is not sufficient to simply identify where the antagonisms and the sources of coherence lie; it is necessary also to identify variables that facilitate or inhibit conflict. The party's statutes seem to have engendered conflict at some times and helped ensure coherence at others. In the early 1980s there was fairly broad internal acceptance of the PSOE's quasi-Leninist discipline, it having helped give the party a unified image in the 1982 election, while rival parties were being rent by their own factionalism. The party had benefited electorally; moreover, González's ambition to make the PSOE 'as solid as a rock' was shared by many while the military coup attempt of 1981 remained a fresh memory. Only in the second half of the decade, with democracy more consolidated and the PSOE's continuing electoral success now inspiring self-confidence, did the demands for internal democratisation become more insistent.

Electoral performance has been a crucial variable governing PSOE cohesiveness. Not only can national victories disarm leadership critics, and setbacks give them ammunition; regional and local election results have been important too. The *guerristas* were pushed on to the defensive by the Juan Guerra scandal at the start of 1990 but the following June their strength was restored by the regional election in Andalusia, where the PSOE list was headed by the *guerrista* Manuel Chaves and Guerra's identification with the campaign was so strong that many saw the poll as a plebiscite on whether the *vicepresidente* (deputy prime minister) should remain in office. The increase in the PSOE's vote, from 47.2 per cent to 49.6 per cent,[32] encouraged the *guerristas* to stage a fresh offensive against the liberals, and to resist stubbornly any power-sharing with them at the following party congress. Conversely, after they had already suffered reverses as a result of González's government reorganisation in March 1991, the *guerristas* lost further ground in the south in May as a result of the electoral failure of their candidate, on this occasion Luis Yáñez, when heading the PSOE list in the municipal elections in Seville in May. Defeat in what had been a heartland of Spanish socialism since the 1970s immediately led to intra-PSOE conflict in the provincial federation, as a result of which the *guerristas* lost positions.[33]

In the case of the PSOE's liberal ministers, the state of the economy seems to have influenced the extent to which they have been prepared to compromise with other groups in the party. Within considerable limits, Solchaga was willing to tolerate moderately inflationary pay settlements as a means of buying industrial peace in his very early period as finance minister, yet later he became more intransigent over pay and public expenditure. Not only had economic growth become sluggish; there was also a greater liberal determination to push through their policies because of the pressure to adapt to the challenge posed by the EC Single Market of 1993, and subsequently to achieve adequate 'convergence' with the EC's more successful economies in the aftermath of the Maastricht Treaty. This inevitably helped stir conflict within the government between the liberals and their critics, and it was expressed in the party too.

Finally, individual gestures by leaders, or changes in their circumstances, may also have a bearing on the internal harmony of socialist parties. To paraphrase Adolfo Suárez, González 'destabilised his own party' by suggesting in October 1989 that the previous general election campaign had probably been his last; this immediately triggered a battle over the succession, which González halted only with some difficulty, through a subsequent retraction.[34] Conversely, González's initial solidarity with his deputy when the Juan Guerra scandal broke – he declared that he would resign if Guerra did – mitigated the effects of the event on party cohesion for several months. A year later, however, when González decided finally to dispense with Guerra, this gave rise to internal party instability because it broke a partnership on which the party hierarchy had been based for over a decade, and particular bitterness was added to the ensuing struggle because many socialists who hitherto had been loyal to Guerra now turned against him.

Those committed to ending *guerrista* control of the party apparatus became known as *renovadores* (renovators). Early in 1993 they used revelations about illegal funding of the party (the Filesa scandal) in an attempt to force resignations among their rivals. However, Guerra's supporters used their majority on the party executive to ensure that the question of responsibility for party corruption would be left until after the election.

The dimensions of conflict

It is possible that the type of governmental structure adopted by the socialists encouraged conflict between different sectors of the party once it had gained office. The existence of a powerful *vicepresidente* and of another 'super-ministry', with the finance minister deciding all appointments pertaining to the economy, meant that there were two extremely coveted positions which party groups sought to conquer. The governmental structure may have made the executive itself more of an arena of conflict than in other countries.

However, open power struggles within the socialist government occurred only in 1985 and 1990. To account for their absence at other times one should mention that, with the exception of González and Guerra, members of the party executive have not tended to double as government ministers: a fact that helped reinforce the tremendous dominance of the two Sevillians until 1991.[35] Only González and Guerra were present in both the government and party executive throughout the period 1982–91. It should also be noted that liberals and *guerristas* have not been the only groups present in the government, where social democrats and other moderates have always played a minor role. Moreover, as prime minister, González for a long time was able to play an effective mediating role between the liberals and *guerristas*. From March 1991 he frequently used Narcís Serra (Guerra's replacement as *vicepresidente*) as a peace-maker during internal party disputes.[36] The situation changed in the early 1990s when mediation became less effective as liberal–*guerrista* conflict brought about a rapidly deteriorating relationship between the government and the party executive.

A more distinctive dimension of conflict in the PSOE is the regional one. Although in other countries there may be sub-national exceptions to a national pattern of intra-party conflict, sub-national variation is much more complex and persistent in the Spanish case. National leaders of the PSOE have had considerable success in subordinating local party groups but at the expense of enhancing the power of intermediate authorities, above all at the regional level. Regional power has grown both because of devolution and through the encouragement by national party leaders of regional delegations. Provincial party federations now usually agree to form part of a regional delegation to the party congress, rather than send their own.

Hence the regional level has become a very significant 'site' or 'arena' of conflict in the PSOE. Regional and regionally specific issues at times give rise to conflict, although equally, as noted, the centre–periphery cleavage cuts across other cleavages and thus serves to prevent ideological polarisation in the party.

The stance of regional barons varies from case to case. Increased regional autonomy has been defended by leaders and activists in Catalonia and Andalusia. However, party federations in some of the least developed parts of Spain, such as Extremadura, have supported strong centralism as the best means of securing a national redistribution of wealth.

Pro-regionalism is not always manifest within the PSOE where there is a similar trend in society. If the Catalan socialists do to some degree reflect the sentiments of Catalan nationalism, the Basque socialists have shown far less sympathy for Basque nationalism. The latter has a much more pronounced separatist orientation than does Catalan nationalism, and historically the Basque Nationalist Party emerged as a reaction against the industrial revolution. Basque socialism, on the other hand, was based originally on workers who migrated to the region in response to new industrial employment.[37] The much stronger historical ties between party and proletariat in the Basque Country (and Asturias) are reflected today in the existence of stronger 'workerist' factions in northern Spain compared with the PSOE elsewhere.

Throughout the country, however, there is very limited factional *organisation*. This reflects both a traditional reliance on strong personal leadership in the PSOE and the statutory intolerance of well-organised factions. With the exception of IS, internal party groups in the 1980s tended either to be 'clans' of like-minded elite figures, or an individual to whom followers were linked at least as much by patronage as by ideas. Unable to survive or succeed simply through collective action within the party, such groups have relied on occupying positions within the party or the state structure and then using these to build further support by clienteles. Even when in firm control of the party apparatus during the 1980s, the *guerristas* often acted with the sectarian exclusiveness of an organised faction. However, they have never accepted that a *guerrista* faction exists: until Guerra's departure from the government, their claim was that the whole party was devoted to Alfonso.[38]

Given this low ideological threshold, conflict within the party has had the character of power battles between elite groups and a challenge to the leadership by activists 'from below' has seemed unlikely. However, in recent years CEPES has been trying to mount an ideological challenge within the party. By 1991, the PSOE's disaffected activists were substantial enough in number to contemplate their own coordination and to develop a left-wing alternative both to the government's economic policies and to the party's internal authoritarianism. A CEPES conference held in November brought together former socialist ministers and officials (including former foreign minister Fernando Morán), IS activists, UGT leaders and former communists. Among the main criticisms voiced of the government and its liberal wing were that they assimilated 'modernisation' to merely economic growth. The conference attracted an impressive list of participants.[39]

This did not necessarily herald the rise of right–left conflict in the PSOE, and if such a conflict were to develop the regional factor could well continue to overshadow it. The rise of a party left wing would be resisted by the regional barons, whose own influence would be diluted if left–right factionalism were to find greater expression at regional party level. Moreover, the development of CEPES will be handicapped by its lack of activist support in the party and the group's internal diversity (including the social distance between the academic-led IS and mainly blue-collar UGT). Even less likely is collaboration between CEPES and the *guerristas*. Not only did Guerra's followers mobilise energetically against the UGT/CCOO general strike in 1988: they also put pressure on the German Social Democratic Party

in an effort to prevent its deputy, Friedhelm-Julius Bencher, from participating in the CEPES conference.[40] Yet the very existence of CEPES shows
that authoritarian party comportment is being challenged: just a few years
ago, dissidents would not have dared to meet openly.

The management of conflict

It is ironic that González and Guerra opted for a tight managerial regime, for
during the final years of Francoism they had been leading figures in the battle
for renewal of the old exile-dominated PSOE and had accused its leader,
Rodolfo Llopis, of himself confusing political discipline with military discipline.[41] Yet right up until this pair's public divergence in 1991, their
internally authoritarian organization reflected a preference for imposed unity
over negotiated consensus.

Their standard means of securing party unity was to offer activists the
alternative of rewards for loyalty or harsh penalties for dissidence. In a
relatively small party seeking to fill an expanding number of public
positions, which formed the basis of political, administrative and managerial
careers, activists who took the official line were rewarded with posts very
quickly (even former communists). Those who dissented had only a small,
hostile audience within the party, and to seek external support constituted
grounds for exclusion. Suspension or expulsion from the party, often with
little regard for the notional rights of the victim, often had career implications and almost invariably ended in political frustration. For those deeply
committed to political activism, ideological self-policing has been very
common in the PSOE because of a belief that there is 'no world elsewhere'.
Although there is a small socialist party within the IU, it has failed to develop
during the last decade and remains a clearly junior partner to the communists.

In addition to the traditional stick, there is the carrot of cooption.
Although denied freedom of debate, party intellectuals have been provided
with opportunities for conferences (often at attractive coastal locations) and
for publication. Moreover, cooption was attempted in a bid to neutralise
debate following the launch of CEPES. An effort was made through the
party's Pablo Iglesias Foundation to integrate this left-wing initiative into an
officially sponsored exercise in pluralist debate which would focus on specific
policy questions.[42]

At government level, González relied until 1991 on maintaining a delicate
balance between the liberals, generally holding the economic portfolios, and
the *guerristas*, who besides being present in the cabinet delivered party loyalty
and organised the electoral victories. The liberal–*guerrista* partnership was
always an uneasy one, but at least there was no fundamental divergence over
basic questions of economic, foreign or defence policy. For several years,
González served as arbiter between these two main contenders for power, his

own authority based upon his high popularity and the inclusion always of a handful of relatively independent ministers who were personally loyal to him. Government reshuffles were in part an attempt to 'fine-tune' the balance within the government.[43]

However, González's balancing act eventually proved unsustainable. Internal tensions in the aftermath of the general strike and then the Juan Guerra scandal affected the efficiency of his government to such a degree that in 1990 parliament only approved one complete piece of legislation, apart from the budget.[44] A desire to make the Spanish economy internationally competitive and to improve his government's public image eventually persuaded González to give the liberals their head in the government. By this time González had also become annoyed at the way in which spokesmen in the *guerrista* party apparatus contradicted ministerial statements and at the refusal of Guerra to weaken *guerrista* dominance on the party executive at the 1990 Party Congress (despite González's own entreaties).

There is a sense in which Guerra fell victim to public opinion. By October 1990 polls showed that more Spaniards favoured his departure from the government than his continuation.[45] González finally tried to break the impasse, not by fighting an open battle within the party, but by using his freedom of manoeuvre as prime minister to reshuffle his government. He was not able to avoid a battle, however. Despite the subordination of party to government during the 1980s, the party has not been reduced to a mere cipher of the government. Indeed, in the months leading up to the election in 1993, the *guerrista*-controlled party asserted itself by pushing ahead with strike legislation that had been negotiated with the UGT, and which was being questioned by most members of the government. Only the announcement of an early election frustrated the bill.

It is not easy to differentiate between the managerial techniques used in party and government, since González is leader of both. As general secretary of the PSOE and as prime minister (in a strongly 'presidentialist' executive) he has repeatedly used the threat of resignation when faced with opposition.[46] He did this most recently in April 1993, threatening to resign if party leaders did not take responsibility for the Filesa scandal. Although he compromised on this occasion due to the nearness of a general election, this type of threat has been a credible one since 1979. In that year González did resign as party leader and in doing so exposed the inability of his rivals to produce a more credible alternative. He was back within months, with increased authority. Since then, he has repeatedly threatened Spaniards with his resignation. In 1986 he implied that he would resign if the NATO referendum went against him, and in 1990, during the early months following the Juan Guerra revelations, he declared that he would resign if critics forced Guerra to go. At other times he has tried to overcome difficulties in the PSOE by having his confidants circulate rumours that 'Felipe is tired of government', that he is 'contemplating resignation', or that his ambitions extend to the presidency of international organisations.

González has exploited the fact that he has remained at the head of the popularity polls for more than a decade; he knows too that the media is broadly sympathetic, ready to rally to him when his permanence in office seems uncertain. Unchallenged in the PSOE leadership since 1979, his departure could bring great disunity to the PSOE for there is no clear, undisputed successor to him, nor is there much experience of pluralism in the party executive.

The impact of internal party conflict

On balance one must conclude that recent internal conflict has had more negative than positive results for the PSOE. In 1990 party factionalism affected the Spanish policy-making process negatively, greatly reducing the legislative productivity of the Socialist government. The problem of immobilism seemed to have been resolved by Guerra's removal from the government, but in the longer term it threatened to recur, this time due to government–party conflict rather than splits within the cabinet (although within the government there were pale reflections of this conflict, especially over plans to introduce greater 'flexibility' into the labour market).

In 1993 tension between the *guerrista*-controlled party apparatus and government ministers forced González to call an early general election on 6 June, for fear that the divisions would deepen with disastrous electoral consequences for the party. The PSOE's lead in the opinion polls had disappeared a few weeks earlier as a result of the depressed state of the economy and the emergence of corruption as a political issue. Yet polls conducted prior to this did not show any clear correlation between public support for the PSOE and the resurgence of factionalism in the party.[47] This may be because the public focused chiefly upon the government, which gained in coherence following Guerra's departure and did not immediately encounter opposition to its policies from within the party apparatus. Moreover, there were occasional well-publicised displays of government–party harmony designed to show voters that the socialists were at least as united as their rivals. Only on the eve of the 1993 election did the discord within the PSOE reach such levels that it undermined public confidence in the socialists' suitability for office.

On the other hand, there are ways in which the recent increase in pluralism within the PSOE could become beneficial to the policy-making process in the longer term: clearly not if it is simply a matter of deeply antagonistic factions echoing the personal attacks made by Guerra upon Solchaga and by Solchaga upon Guerra, but certainly if a climate conducive to a critical discussion of policy matters were to emerge. The rubber-stamping role of the Socialist Parliamentary Group and party congresses during the 1980s fuelled public scepticism about the quality of socialist party democracy, and helps explain why the PSOE appeared to have run out of legislative steam by the end of the decade. It remains to be seen, however, whether the authoritarian management of the PSOE has eliminated its capacity for fruitful political debate.

Whether the party can arrive at a satisfactory compromise between unity and diversity, conflict and cohesion, could well be influenced by new developments in Spanish politics following the 1993 general election. If inter-party pacts are necessary for the socialists to remain in office, the choice of partner or partners could provide a new source of division within the PSOE. While one sector of the party would prefer to collaborate with the centre-right Basque and Catalan nationalist parties, another would prefer to come to terms with the IU. Electoral defeat, on the other hand, would provoke recriminations between *guerristas* and *renovadores*.

Yet even a PSOE that was spared such tensions and continued to enjoy electoral success would probably find the quasi-monolithic model of the 1980s both inappropriate and impossible to maintain in the future. The party itself has developed and at least its leaders, at all levels, seem keen to exert a degree of influence. Perhaps then we have seen the last of those party congresses that were as 'bland, uneventful, colourless and smooth as a play being performed on the stage for the third year running'.[48]

Notes

1. Sartori, G., *Parties and Party Systems* (Cambridge: Cambridge University Press, 1976), p. 85.
2. Share, D., *Dilemmas of Social Democracy: The Spanish Socialist Workers' Party in the 1980s* (Westport, CT: Greenwood, 1989), chs 4–5.
3. Gillespie, R., *The Spanish Socialist Party: A History of Factionalism* (Oxford: Clarendon, 1989).
4. Preston, P., *The Coming of the Spanish Civil War* (London: Macmillan, 1978); Graham, H., *Socialism and War: The Spanish Socialist Party in Power and Crisis, 1936–1939* (Cambridge: Cambridge University Press, 1991).
5. Juliá, S., 'Pasiones Socialistas', *El País*, 6 October 1991. (All references to *El País* are to the daily edition, except where specified.)
6. Hine, D., 'Leaders and Followers: Democracy and Manageability in the Social Democratic Parties of Western Europe', in W.E. Paterson and A.H. Thomas (eds), *The Future of Social Democracy: Problems and Prospects of Social Democratic Parties in Western Europe* (Oxford: Clarendon Press, 1986); Gillespie, R. and Gallagher, T., 'Democracy and Authority in the Socialist Parties of Southern Europe', in T. Gallagher and A.M. Williams (eds), *Southern European Socialism* (Manchester: Manchester University Press, 1989).
7. *El País*, international edn, 6 January 1992; *Oxford Analytical Daily Brief*, 20 July 1992.
8. *El País*, international edn, 4 November 1991.
9. Personal interview, Madrid, 27 November 1991.
10. *Cambio 16* (Madrid), 950 (5 February 1990).
11. *El País*, 3 August 1985.

12. *El Socialista*, 513 (15 November 1990).
13. Sotelo, Ignacio, 'Paradojas y aporías de los socialistas en el poder', *Leviatán*, 13 (1983).
14. Gillespie, R., 'The Break-up of the "Socialist Family": Party–Union Relations in Spain, 1982–89', *West European Politics*, Vol. 13, No. 1 (1990); Juliá, S., *La desavenencia: Partido, sindicatos y huelga general* (Madrid: El País/Aguilar, 1988).
15. Hine, D., 'Factionalism in West European Parties: A Framework for Analysis', *West European Politics*, Vol. 5, No. 1 (1982).
16. Share, op. cit.
17. Gillespie, 'The Break-up'.
18. *Cambio 16*, 950 (5 February 1990) and 970 (25 June 1990).
19. Gillespie, R., '*Programa 2000*: The Appearance and Reality of Socialist Renewal in Spain', *West European Politics*, Vol. 16, No. 1 (1993).
20. *El Mundo*, 6 November 1991.
21. For summaries of the differences between the liberals and *guerristas*, see *Mercado*, 510 (11 November 1991) and *Cambio 16*, 974 (23 July 1990).
22. *El País*, 25 January 1988.
23. *El País*, 31 December 1987, 21 April 1989, 11 January 1990.
24. *El País*, 30 November 1987.
25. On Democracia Socialista, see *El País*, 18 November 1989, 1 March 1990; *El País*, international edn, 7 May 1990, 5 November 1990; and *El Socialista*, 15 March 1990. The new party won a mere 5,000 votes (0.49 per cent) in the Basque regional elections of October 1990).
26. By 1990 the average age of party members was 45, having been 47 in 1980. Party membership had reached 260,000, from 107,000 in 1981. See PSOE, 32 Congreso (1990), *Memoria de gestión de la C.E.F.-C.F. y C.F.C. (1988–1990)*, pp. 9, 27; Gillespie, R., 'Spanish Socialism in the 1980s', in Gallagher and Williams, op. cit.
27. *El País*, 14 October 1991.
28. On the relationship between the PSC and the PSOE, see G. Colomé, 'The "Partit dels Socialistes de Catalunya"', in J.M. Maravall *et al.*, *Socialist Parties in Europe* (Barcelona: ICPS, 1991), pp. 45–8.
29. *Cambio 16*, 1043 (18 November 1991). Guerra hardly endeared himself to regional party leaders by calling them *califas* (caliphs).
30. *El País*, 13 November 1991: at this time central government accounted for 60 per cent of state expenditure, autonomous communities 24 per cent and municipal government 16 per cent. The distribution advocated by Guerra was 50:25:25.
31. *Cambio 16*, 1042 (11 November 1991).
32. *El País*, international edn, 25 June 1990.
33. *Cambio 16*, 1023 (1 July 1991); *El Independiente*, 19 October 1991.
34. *Cambio 16*, 983 (24 September 1990).
35. Heywood, Paul, 'Governing a New Democracy: The Power of the Prime Minister in Spain', *West European Politics*, Vol. 14, No. 2 (1991), p. 102.
36. *El Siglo* (Madrid), 18 November 1991.
37. Fusi, J.P., *Política obrera en el País Vasco 1880–1923* (Madrid: Turner, 1975).
38. *El País*, 22 April 1990.
39. *El País*, 16–19 November 1991.
40. *El País*, 16 November 1991.
41. *Le Socialiste* (Paris/Toulouse), 2 November 1972.
42. *El País*, 28 November 1991.
43. *Tiempo* (Madrid), 18 July 1988; *El Globo* (Madrid), 11 July 1988.

44. *El País*, international edn, 17 December 1990, 7 January 1991.
45. *El País*, international edn, 1 October 1990.
46. Heywood, op. cit., p. 111.
47. *El País*, international edn, 6 January 1992.
48. Shapiro, L., 'Keynote-Compromise', *Problems of Communism* (Washington), Vol. 20, No. 4 (1971), p. 2. Shapiro was describing the 24th Congress of the Communist Party of the Soviet Union.

4 'The war of the roses': conflict and cohesion in the Swedish Social Democratic Party

David Arter

In a multi-party marketplace, underpinned by a PR list voting system, the parliamentary supremacy of the Swedish Social Democratic Party, Sveriges Socialdemokratiska Arbetareparti (SAP), has had few equals in the western world. Indeed, when viewed in a comparative light, its achievements appear unique on three counts.[1] First, there is the size of its popular support. In the general elections between 1944 and 1985, SAP polled an average 45.7 per cent of the active electorate and in five of the contests held between 1938 and 1968 it managed over half the votes cast. Second, SAP has boasted considerable longevity of governmental tenure. At the time of the general election in September 1991, SAP had governed for 56 of the 70 years since the first Riksdag (parliamentary) election conducted on the basis of universal suffrage in 1921. Finally, there is SAP's exclusive hold of the reins of power. For over four decades, the party has governed Sweden singly-handedly. In combination, these three strands make out a powerful case for SAP enjoying what Sartori calls 'predominance' in the Swedish party system. Moreover, two of its long-serving prime ministers, Tage Erlander (1946–69) and Olof Palme (1969–76, 1982–86) acquired international reputations, while the party's contribution to the Swedish model of welfare capitalism has been widely admired across Europe.

Challenges to the cohesion of social democracy

The heyday of social democratic domination may, however, be over. True, in 1993, SAP could boast being the third largest party in the Nordic region, surpassed only by the 41.3 per cent gained by the Icelandic Independence Party in 1991 and the 39.7 per cent of the Danish Social Democrats the previous year. SAP's 37.6 per cent in 1991 nevertheless represented its poorest performance since 1928 and paralleled similarly disappointing showings by the Norwegian Labour Party (DNA, 34.3 per cent in 1989) and Finnish Social Democrats (24 per cent in 1991). SAP, moreover, is no longer so clearly the natural party of government in Sweden. Certainly, since the shift to a unicameral legislature in 1970,[2] it has not monopolised power to the same extent as earlier. Thus SAP languished out of office for two consecutive parliamentary terms between 1976 and 1982, and after 1991 was once again the leading opposition party. In office, moreover, it has no longer commanded majority support in the Riksdag. Hence SAP governed from 1970 to 1976 and 1982 to 1991 as a minority cabinet, relying on legislative coalitions with one or more of the opposition parties to realise its policy goals. Indeed, as a minority governing party between 1982 and 1991, the SAP entered legislative coalitions with all the main bourgeois parties – the Moderates (conservatives), Liberals and Centre (formerly Agrarians) – as well as the radical leftist Left-Communists – Vänsterpartiet Komunisterna (VpK) – since 1990 called simply the Leftist Party.

From its earliest days, SAP aspired to be a catch-all party and espoused an ideology with a broad-based appeal. At the 1911 Party Conference it formally defined the concept of social democracy as 'a united force of all "small folk", whether workers, handicraft-workers or small farmers', while as early as 1895 Hjalmar Branting's reference to the 'people's party model' and Per Albin Hansson's celebrated notion of the 'people's home' in the 1930s were both imbued with the spirit of national consensus. It is quite conceivable that without this 'coalition mentality' at the societal (electoral) as well as governmental level, a welfare state might never have become as highly developed.

A broad-based party, of course, will almost certainly constitute an internal coalition – that is, an accommodation of various elements, views and interests – and this structural heterogeneity is likely to create intermittent managerial problems. An interesting 'outsider's view' of SAP as a complex, at times viscous internal coalition, binding the hands of its leadership, can be gained from an exchange in September 1989 between Ingvar Carlsson, the SAP chair and prime minister, and one of the leading opposition figures, the Liberal chair, Bengt Westerberg. In an interview in the independent daily newspaper *Dagens Nyheter*, Carlsson admitted that he had often considered the merits of coalition government and went on to state that he had nothing in principle against such an arrangement. In response, Westerberg, while acknowledging potential advantages and disadvantages in formal cooperation (of whatever sort) with SAP, stressed how the latter was itself a coalition and that when an internal (compromise) agreement had been reached, this left the leadership little room for manoeuvre in negotiating with other parties.[3]

As a 'people's party', the traditional strength of Swedish social democracy has pivoted on four party-voter axes. First, there has been a high level of cohesion on the part of the blue-collar working class. In the 1960s, 78 per cent of industrial workers supported SAP, a higher proportion than in any other Nordic social democratic-labour party. Second, the party has recorded significant (and increasing) support from those in lower middle-class clerical positions. In 1964, 46 per cent of these white-collar workers supported the SAP. Third, the alliance of 'small folk' was completed by dint of the fact that SAP gained the backing of a majority (53 per cent in 1964) of the rural 'proletariat' of farm workers and smallholders. This markedly coalitional character of SAP's support stood in sharp contrast to the historically class-based nature of the vote for the main bourgeois parties. The principal electoral 'blind spots' of the SAP have been the farmers and 'old middle-class' professions.[4] Moreover, in addition to these three main party support networks, there developed strong bonds of solidarity between SAP and the blue-collar trade union confederation, Landsorganisationen (LO), based on a system of collective affiliation.

SAP–LO cooperation, to be sure, has on occasions been severely tested. For example, in 1948 the government insisted on moderate wage claims to combat inflation and Erlander informed LO that, since the economy simply could not withstand disruptive action, if LO and the central employers' organisation Sveriges Arbetsgivareföreningen (SAF) failed to make a responsible incomes agreement, the trade union movement could 'shop around for another government'. Generally though, LO (backed by SAP) and SAF worked hand in glove to make harmonious labour relations a key component of the so-called 'Swedish model'. Through its leading economists, Gosta Rehn and Rudolf Meidner, moreover, LO was able to exert significant influence over the economic policy of the SAP governments in the 1950s. SAP and LO also worked closely at this time on the controversial scheme for mandatory supplementary (incomes-related) pensions – the Allmän Tillaggspension (ATP) proposal.[5] While it may be argued that after the ATP controversy, SAP lacked a major issue with which to mobilize voters, relations with LO remained good throughout the 1960s.

Since the 'golden era' of a booming economy and amicable labour relations in the 1960s, macro-changes in the socio-economic climate of Swedish politics have conspired to challenge the cohesion of social democracy and strain SAP's internal coalition. Four hypotheses will form the basis of our subsequent examination. The first derives from the impact of the social structural transformation which began in the first postwar decade. In recent years, it is suggested, the reorientation of policy needed to maintain SAP's appeal to the growing body of salaried employees has undermined the strength of allegiance of the party's working-class constituency and injected heightened volatility into its overall support base.

As early as the 1950s, the shift from the land, followed shortly by the first signs of de-industrialisation, led to a sharp decline in the economically active population engaged in farming, a relative drop in the number employed in blue-collar industrial labour and to a concomitant growth in the tertiary sector. Those parties anchored in the farming constituency (Agrarians) and working class (Social Democrats) were challenged to respond to the gradual blurring of the class contours of politics. The case for postwar adaptation was implicit in the observation of Birgersson *et al.* on the 1950s: 'The shift to salaried employment and the growth of service industries, when coupled with the marked rise in living standards, would explain much of the declining vote share of both the Social Democrats and the Agrarians' [who governed in a coalition between 1951 and 1957].[6] The Agrarians, indeed, changed their name to Centre Party in the last-mentioned year. From the SAP viewpoint, two central questions follow. One, what is the current voter profile of SAP and how far has it traded its cloth cap to become essentially a 'new middle-class' party? Two, to what extent has any alteration in the internal balance between SAP's main support groups served to weaken the partisan identification of its followers and created a propensity for working-class and/or middle-class voters to defect (at least in the short term)?

The second hypothesis focuses on the manifold problems for a small exporting nation like Sweden attendant on the steady erosion of its industrial base from about the early 1970s onwards. The 'structural deficit' between the goods-producing and the service-producing sectors of the economy has caused, *inter alia*, balance-of-payments problems, a shortfall on national account and, by extension, increasing difficulties in sustaining existing levels of welfare provision. For the SAP cabinets between 1982 and 1991, more-over, faced by the need to implement an austerity programme (to hold down wages, dampen consumer spending and control inflation, which was in excess of Sweden's main competitors), applying the economic brakes, it is contended, inevitably generated tension and conflicts of interest between members of SAP's internal coalition – especially between the cabinet and LO – over the politics of distribution. Perhaps the central question in this context concerned the likely effects of retrenchment on the Swedish model of industrial relations and in particular the special relationship between SAP and LO.[7]

The third hypothesis highlights the remarkable impact of 'green' issues in Swedish politics since the late 1960s. Indicative of the growing salience of ecological concerns, especially among young voters, was the Centre Party's strong performance at the 1968 election. On a very high turnout of 89.3 per cent – more than half of all voters backed SAP – the Centre Party, which had projected a high environmental profile, emerged as the largest non-socialist party, a position it consolidated in the early 1970s. Like Austria, Sweden in 1970 staged a referendum on the future of nuclear power – the outcome was interpreted by the Riksdag as a decision in favour of phasing out nuclear power (by the year 2010) – while on the eve of the 1988 election (at which the Greens surmounted the 4 per cent barrier to enter parliament), an astonishing three out of four voters stated that the environment was the most important campaign issue.[8] Against this backdrop, it is suggested that a corollary of the accentuated progress of post-materialist ideas in Sweden was the inevitable generation of cross-pressures within SAP over environmental questions, since by their nature 'green issues' do not conform to the traditional left–right dimension in politics. Where, then, has SAP stood on questions juxtaposing the interest of the economy and the need to protect the environment, and has there been a tendency to resort to uneasy compromise solutions – half red, half green?

A final hypothesis is prompted by the radical restructuring of the geo-political landscape of Europe following the autumn revolutions of 1989. The disintegration of the Soviet empire in eastern Europe, the collapse of the Soviet Union itself and the overarching membership of the Conference on Security and Cooperation in Europe (CSCE) – which proclaimed a charter for the 'New Europe' in November 1990 – marked the final end of the cold war and meant that in a real sense Sweden's widely respected policy of neutrality had been overtaken by events. The dramatic course of events also facilitated Swedish involvement in a seemingly exponential process of European integration with the European Community (EC) in the van. At the time of the first British and Danish overtures to join the Common Market in 1961, the Swedish premier, Erlander, ruled out a Swedish application despite a vigorous pro-membership lobby from the Moderates and industry. He insisted that it would necessitate adopting a new foreign policy and risk creating the impression both at home and abroad that Sweden was straying from its traditional policy of neutrality.[9] In the totally transformed conditions of 1990, however, Sweden applied for full member-ship of the EC. Yet against this background of accelerating integration, it is hypothesised that in the manner of its Danish and Norwegian fraternal parties, the question of EC membership would divide SAP into opposing camps – the 'pro-marketeers' willing to ratify the Maastricht Treaty unconditionally or when made contingent on certain opt-out clauses, and the 'anti-marketeers' refusing to abandon a long-serving policy of non-alignment in favour of involvement in a future political and defence union. It should be recalled that defence issues have divided SAP in the past. In the late 1950s there was the real danger of an internal split over the proposed development of Swedish atomic weapons. The central question, then, might well be: could the SAP unite behind a treaty which contained a long-term commitment to a common defence?

The following section of this chapter analyses the main lines of conflict in SAP, distinguishing between the structural strains and issue cleavages reducing partisan cohesion. Two primary structural strains are identified: the tension in the electoral arena between working-class and middle-class social democrats; and the internal friction, particularly between SAP and LO, over the implications of restraint in the management of the economy. In the context of structural strains, it is pertinent to recall former SAP finance minister Kjell-Olof Feldt's depiction of the SAP as a forum for the resolution of competing interests. Alluding to the second half of the 1980s, Feldt observed that interests increasingly came into conflict as common ideas lost both their gloss and glue. Two issue cleavages (among several in recent years) are given prominence – the split between the 'concrete socialists' and 'eco-socialists' over the question of the future of nuclear energy; and the division between 'pro-marketeers' and 'anti-marketeers' over the question of Sweden's application for full EC membership. The basic argument, however, is that although SAP, the predominant governing party in Sweden, has been a 'broad church' and displayed intermittently high levels of (largely) issue-based division, there has been little in the way of factionalisation (that is, the formation of interest groups with a clearly defined personnel and outlook), and, indeed, a relatively low incidence of fragmentation (that is, splits leading to the creation of electorally significant breakaway parties). This is especially so when compared to the experience of its fraternal parties in Finland in the 1950s, Denmark in the 1970s and Britain in the 1980s.

The main conflict lines in SAP

THE TENSION BETWEEN THE INTERESTS OF MIDDLE-CLASS AND WORKING-CLASS SOCIALISTS IN THE ELECTORAL ARENA

Starting in the mid-1950s, SAP's leadership worked to broaden the party's catchment of 'small folk' so as to include more of the growing body of persons employed in what could be described as 'middle-class' positions – especially those in the expanding service industries. Accordingly, SAP began to project an image of itself as a party of all wage-earners and the mutual interests linking manual with white-collar workers were stressed. Above all, the basic principle of the welfare state was adjusted to make a stronger appeal to the middle class which in turn undoubtedly benefited from the introduction of, among other things, income-related health insurance and supplementary pensions schemes. Benefits, in short, were related to incomes.[10] Elements of the middle class were also attracted by SAP's pervasive reputation as the party most competent to govern and the party of national leadership. Accordingly, middle-class socialism gained ground. By 1956, 24 per cent of the middle class voted SAP, but by 1988 this had risen to 35 per cent.[11]

While the electoral alliance of middle class and working class in support of social democracy largely held firm during the long years of economic prosperity, the advent of retrenchment and, ultimately, the lurch towards recession in the early 1990s tested SAP's ability to reconcile the interests of its two constituencies. By the 1980s there was evidence both of a weakening in allegiance and, more strikingly, increased volatility among SAP voters. True, the strength of partisan identification with SAP remained relatively high when compared with other main parties, especially among an older cohort of voters born in or before 1930. Nevertheless, it declined in the 1980s. Whereas in 1976, 50 per cent of SAP voters identified themselves as loyal supporters of the party – ironically the 42.7 per cent SAP polled in the general election that year was its worst performance since the 1920s — this had fallen to 41 per cent in 1988.[12]

Significantly, too, there was a growing proportion of SAP voters splitting their vote, that is to say, backing another party in at least one of the three simultaneous elections held on general election day — the Riksdag, county council and municipal ballots. In 1982 only 5 per cent of the social democrats who supported SAP at the Riksdag election voted for another party at the municipal level; six years later, this had risen to 12 per cent.[13] The greater instability of the SAP vote was, to be sure, part of a wider phenomenon, accompanied by the heightened importance of issues, the campaigns and, above all, the media. By 1988, in fact, the media had taken virtual control of the campaign agenda from the political parties.

Crucially for the SAP's future as an electoral party, however, there has been a slow decline in the political cohesion of the working class. In 1956, 72 per cent of working-class voters supported SAP; by 1988 this had fallen to 65 per cent; and by 1991 it had plummeted to barely 50 per cent. Consistently throughout the second half of the 1980s, survey data showed that SAP was experiencing greatest difficulty in holding on to its traditional support. It was by no means coincidental that in June 1985 the quarterly barometer of the polling agency Svenska Institutet för Opinionsundersökningar (SIFO) pointed to a loss of SAP support among young people, the low-paid and trade unionists and that in January 1990, at the time of the radical tax reform agreement with the Liberals, opinion polls again indicated that SAP was losing the loyalties of the low-income groups, LO members and voters in the larger towns.

Doubtless circumstantial factors played a part in accounting for the heightened volatility of traditional working-class voters — not least the unpopular economic policies of their 'own government'. The February 1990 government crisis, when the Carlsson cabinet resigned following the Riksdag's rejection of its proposed wage freeze and strike ban, is a notable case in point. The planned embargo on strikes catalysed grassroots protest in the labour movement and prompted wholesale defections from the ruling party. Although the reconstituted Carlsson government quickly dropped the strike ban, the electoral damage was probably already done. More generally, there appears throughout the 1980s to have been a mismatch between the policy directions of the SAP cabinet and the policy anticipations of ordinary SAP voters. A detailed study of the 1988 general election indicated that as many as a quarter of SAP voters placed themselves to the left of the party. A still larger group in 1990 held that the SAP cabinet had gone too far to the right in its public sector cuts and in promoting a tax reform package that did nothing to reduce disparities in wealth.

It would seem reasonable to conclude, therefore, that in addition to a gradual, long-term decline in the political cohesion of the working class, the unprecedented volatility of the SAP's blue-collar vote in 1991 was tied to a number of short-term factors and, in particular, dissatisfaction with the economic deals between the minority SAP government and the 'middle parties', the Centre and Liberals. It may not be inappropriate to note, moreover, in the context of the Riksdag breakthrough of a populist movement called New Democracy, which played on racial prejudices, that a significant number of working-class voters were also opposed to the type of liberal immigration policy backed by SAP. Support for the view that the exodus of traditional SAP voters in 1991 was a temporary aberration – and that there exists something of a 'homing tendency' among disgruntled workers – can perhaps be found in the evidence of a rapid revival of SAP's fortunes when it was displaced from government. Only a month after the September 1991 election, SAP witnessed a 1.1 per cent improvement in its standing and by December 1991 its support stood at 40.9 per cent, a level comparable with May–June 1989 when the decline began and vastly better than April 1991 when SAP slipped to a nadir of 28.7 per cent in the opinion polls. At the beginning of 1993 SAP registered a remarkable 48.4 per cent in the SIFO poll, albeit 5 per cent less in the rival TEMO ratings.[14]

When looking ahead to the medium term, a vital challenge to SAP can be found in the evidence of a steady erosion of the class allegiance of the younger generation. This is clearly reflected in the increasing age and declining number of SAP members – down from 1.2 million (out of an electorate of about 6 million) to barely a million over the course of the 1980s. The problem should not be exaggerated. At the end of the 1988 general election, a larger proportion of young voters (45.6 per cent) voted SAP than among the electorate as a whole. But over a quarter of all 18–20-year-olds did not vote, more than double the rate of abstentionism among first voters in the two previous general elections. The propensity for abstention ('sofa voting') appears greatest among young working-class men in the larger towns.[15]

The further challenge facing SAP in continuing to attract the white-collar vote warrants a brief mention too, especially in view of the perceived impossibility of maintaining the welfare state at existing levels of provision. Feldt's radical tax reforms in 1990, which were designed to enhance productivity – by abolishing national income tax for 85 per cent of wage-earners and shifting the weight of taxation to goods, capital and services – greatly benefited the middle class. Raising and widening the base of VAT hit the poor hardest. But against the backdrop of broad cross-party agreement that Sweden was living beyond its means and must trim the sails of state, the nascent debate within SAP (discussed more fully later) about reverting to flat-rate rather than incomes-related benefits sorely tested the allegiance of the middle class. Precisely what happened to the SAP vote in September 1991 is not yet clear, although exit polls indicated losses to the Centre, Liberals and especially Christian Democrats, as well as a trickle to the Moderates. Much as elsewhere in the Nordic region, the two largest Swedish parties, the SAP and Moderates, increasingly compete for the floating middle-class vote in the urban centres.

'WELFARE SPENDERS' VERSUS ADVOCATES OF PUBLIC SECTOR RESTRAINT

When in power as a minority government between 1982 and 1991, a source of deep friction within the social democratic movement was the need to curtail public spending in favour of a programme of restraint. Austerity measures were almost bound to depress the sciatic nerve of a party celebrated for building a system of 'womb-to-tomb' protection. Indeed, they proved the source of a left–right split that divided SAP from the levels of the cabinet and parliamentary group down to the grassroots, as well as alienating the trade union wing of the labour movement and its leading organ, LO. The resignation of Kjell-Olof Feldt as minister of finance in February 1990 was a logical, albeit dramatic, manifestation of this conflict.

The case for restraint was overwhelming. A significant increase in the tax burden during the SAP government from 1970 to 1976 and the expansion of public spending during the bourgeois cabinets of 1976 to 1982, meant that the Swedish economy was ill equipped for the downturn it experienced at the time SAP returned to office in 1982. There was, for example, a massive budget deficit of Kr.90 billion, while unemployment was rising. An unprecedented 16% devaluation, followed by a rigorous diet of measures, was initially successful – both wage-earners and pensioners refrained (as instructed by the government) from demanding compensation for the inflationary effects of devaluation – and, briefly, the Swedish economic situation improved appreciably. Throughout, however, inflation remained higher than in Sweden's main competitors and export firms lost vital market shares. Indeed, Feldt has claimed that from the middle of 1984 the government lost control of the economic reins at the very time the international economy moved into an upturn. The austerity that he canvassed also left the finance minister at loggerheads with the labour movement, members of SAP's Riksdag group, cabinet colleagues and even the prime minister, Olof Palme, himself.

From a social democratic viewpoint, there were two obvious problems associated with pursuing a tight line on public spending. First and foremost, it appeared to challenge the welfare culture deeply ingrained in the ranks of the party and traditional perceptions of SAP as the beneficent provider. For the 'welfare spenders' it was a matter of principle to challenge the undogmatic, if not exactly unscrupulous, stance of the finance minister on the mixed economy and the welfare state. In cabinet, both the industry minister, Thage Peterson, and the minister of social affairs, Sten Andersson, displayed a lack of sympathy with Feldt's concern for restraint, while Andersson's pledge, during the 1985 election campaign, to reimburse pensioners for the inflationary effects of devaluation was, it seems, made without the finance minister's knowledge and not communicated to him until it was too late.[16] Moreover, in his volume *Samtal med Feldt (A Conversation with Feldt)*, published in 1984, the finance minister proceeded to slaughter a number of SAP's 'sacred cows' – *inter alia* canvassing the case for introducing an element of private competition into the provision of welfare services (common ground with the Moderates!) – and this caused a rift with Palme that was never really mended.

Second, it was not easy to reconcile austerity with the types of election promise routinely demanded by SAP's party conference and LO's counterpart – promises that, of course, would unquestionably enhance SAP's retaining power. Ironically, in his account *Alla Dessa Dagar (All Those Days)*, Feldt cites his own campaign speeches in 1988 to illustrate the way SAP 'pumped up' its performance in government – practically 'abolishing the economic crisis' – so as to accommodate its two main electoral titbits, increased parental insurance and longer annual holidays.[17] The cabinet succumbed to pressure from LO for six weeks' annual holiday, while extended parental insurance was adopted ostensibly because it had been prioritised by the party conference. At the 1987 Party Conference, Palme's successor as prime minister, Ingvar Carlsson, stated that parents must have more time with their children, and that accordingly parental insurance would be doubled to eighteen months.[18] Subsequently admitting his error of judgement, Feldt signalled in cabinet that these commitments could be funded out of economic growth, rather than increased taxes. He later admitted that he had been gripped by election fever to the extent that he had completely forsaken the thesis that he had striven to convert colleagues to before the 1982 election: namely, that the important thing for a party is not so much to win an election, but *how* it wins it. Irresponsible promises, it was inferred, should be avoided at all costs – particularly when the need for austerity is paramount.[19]

Third, a policy of restraint was almost certain to antagonise the trade union movement by tying the hands of LO in the collective bargaining process. Indeed, LO's refusal to cooperate with its 'own government' prompted Feldt in 1990 to insist that its continuing intransigence presaged the imminent collapse of the renowned 'Swedish model' of amicable industrial relations. From the middle of 1984, LO, under its chair, Stig Malm, apparently ceased in practice to support austerity measures and became the government's foremost critic. On the very evening of his election, Malm evidently declared that the finance minister had forfeited his stock of trust in the labour movement. These latent strains between the government and LO on economic policy flared into the open in the so-called 'war of the roses' on 1 May 1989. Malm inveighed against the cabinet for its proposal temporarily to raise VAT by 2 percentage points so as to dampen down overheating in the economy. Carlsson retaliated by indicting LO and its leadership with an irresponsible attitude to the economy.[20] Not surprisingly, perhaps, plans from the Ministry of Finance in January 1990 for reduced public spending met with opposition from LO, which countered by threatening to destroy Feldt's radical tax reform blueprint. When the government almost caved in to LO, Feldt spoke of a 'last chance for the Swedish model'.

In seeking to lead SAP along the road of restraint, Feldt's personality and outspoken style did not perhaps facilitate his task. He was always a rather controversial figure in his own party. As early as 1981 he antagonised left-wing sections of SAP by stating that it would be necessary to abolish the controversial employee investment funds if the corporate sector continued its stubborn opposition to them, and hardly endeared himself to the 'welfare spenders' when later he insisted that during a period of austerity there must be cuts even in the childcare sector.[21] When Feldt left politics on 16 February 1990, the day after the Carlsson government had resigned following the Riksdag's rejection of its proposed wage freeze and strike ban legislation, he admitted that constant opposition from the labour movement had been the principal reason for his decision. Significantly, his successor, Allan Larsson, reaffirmed the Feldt line, although when a Kr.10 billion austerity package, which the reconstituted SAP government agreed with the Liberals in April 1990, involved compromising the SAP's much publicised election commitment to extend summer holidays and parental leave, dissatisfaction permeated through the party. The austerity measures were approved in the parliamentary group only after a fractious debate and the chair of the Riksdag Finance Committee, Anna-Greta Leijon, resigned her post and, indeed, her parliamentary seat over the party's broken election promises.

'CONCRETE SOCIALISTS' VERSUS 'ECO-SOCIALISTS'

Green issues have played a remarkably prominent role in Swedish politics since the late 1960s when the Centre Party, ironically appropriating many of the ideas of the so-called New Left, began to project a strong environmental profile. By 1973 the Centre had dashed the cross-party consensus on energy policy and announced its opposition to any further expansion of the nuclear power programme, while during the 1976 general election campaign, its leader, Thorbjörn Fälldin, pledged that if he became prime minister no new atomic reactors would be loaded with fuel and all nuclear power installations would be dismantled by 1985.

For much of the 1970s SAP formed part of the pro-nuclear mainstream, but the Three Mile Island reactor accident near Harrisburg, Pennsylvania, in March 1979 prompted the party to re-examine the premises of its nuclear energy policy. It discontinued its cooperation with Ola Ullsten's Liberal minority government (the Centre had abandoned a three-party non-socialist coalition in October 1978 over the loading of two more reactors) and, shortly afterwards, SAP canvassed a referendum on the future of nuclear power, which it proposed to hold in spring 1980 – that is, after the general election of September 1979. SAP also stated that it preferred not to adopt a final stance on nuclear power until after the publication of the findings of an investigation into the Harrisburg incident.

The nuclear power referendum on 23 March 1980 aligned the Moderates, Liberals and SAP against the Centre, the VpK and the Christian Democrats (Kristen demokratiska Samling, KdS). There were three options, and 'line 2' backed by SAP, LO and the Liberals, which (like the Moderates' 'line 1') advocated a long phase-out, received 39.3 per cent of the vote. 'Line 3', the anti-nuclear option, polled 38.6 per cent and 'line 1', which did not set out a specific policy for run-down and, therefore, appealed to the pro-nuclear lobby, managed 18.7 per cent. The turnout was 75.7 per cent. Importantly, both the Liberals and SAP contained influential groups favouring the expeditious closure of all existing nuclear plant. On the eve of the referendum, only 67 per cent of Social Democrats – admittedly a marked improvement on the 50 per cent of two months earlier – identified with 'line 2' and it is notable that women were particularly active in Socialdemokratiska arbetsgruppen för en alternativ energipolitik (SAFE), the Social Democratic Working Group for Alternative Energy Policy, which campaigned for 'line 3'.[22] In any event, by mid-June 1980, the Riksdag approved government legislation reaffirming the phasing out of nuclear power in Sweden by the year 2010 – a year initially suggested in a SAP proposal.

Energy questions were not especially high on the Swedish political agenda in the early 1980s, but following the Chernobyl disaster in Ukraine, a special Ministry of the Environment and Energy was created in October 1986 by Carlsson, the SAP prime minister, as part of a cabinet reshuffle. The new department was headed by Birgitta Dahl, formerly energy minister. At this juncture, the two 'green' parties in the Riksdag, the VpK and Centre, came up with independent plans for the rapid run-down of nuclear energy. The VpK envisaged the completion of the phase-out by 1996 at the latest; the Centre fixed its deadline for the closure of all nuclear power plants at 1999.

The nuclear power issue grouped the parties in a manner that cut across the traditional left–right ordering in the Riksdag. Thus, whilst the Centre and VpK urged a punctual start to the phase-out schedule, Westerberg, the Liberal leader, insisted that this type of dogmatic rather than pragmatic approach to the nuclear question would place an incalculable burden on the economy, employment capacity and, indeed, energy provision. He predicted the introduction of electricity rationing and substantially increased energy prices. The Moderates, for their part, did not even bind themselves to the 2010 deadline for completing the run-down. Carlsson, the prime minister, stated that although he could not accept the timetable of the two 'green' parties, 2010 would none the less be an absolute condition of subsequent government legislation on the matter. In the event, the extent of inter-party division had not narrowed after the failure on 12 February 1987 of a third round in the leadership talks on the energy question.[23]

There existed deep division within SAP on the nuclear issue. The Women's Organisation (Kvinnoförbundet), Youth Organisation (Sveriges Socialdemokratiska Ungdomsorganisationen, SSU) and Brotherhood Movement (Bröderskapsrörelsen) demanded an early closure of two reactors (at

Barsebäck), while the youth leader, Anna Lindh, even contemplated a deal with the Centre on the question. In contrast, before the Chernobyl disaster at least, individual Social Democrats had tabled 'motions' in the Riksdag envisaging the use of nuclear power *after* the 2010 deadline. At the time of Palme's assassination in February 1986, there was a clear division in the SAP Riksdag group over the timing of the run-down.[24] The most vehement opposition to the proposed run-down came from LO and, in particular, the largest member, the Metal, Manufacturing, Paper and Mineworkers' Union. Yet on 15 May 1987, Dahl put before the Riksdag a bill laying down a schedule for the transition from nuclear power in which the first reactors would be taken off stream during 1993 to 1995.[25] The following year parliament sanctioned the closure of two reactors — in 1995 and 1996 respectively — subject to the competitiveness of the core electricity-intensive industries being maintained, carbon dioxide emission levels remaining at least constant and none of the untrammelled rivers in the province of Norrland being sacrificed for hydro-electric development. Significantly, at a public hearing of the Riksdag's Economic Committee on 7 April 1988, there was criticism of the programme of closures and experts from LO, the white-collar Tjänstemännens Centralorganisation (TCO) and industry brought out the risk of spiralling electricity prices and their corollary, rising unemployment.[26]

Division in the governing party intensified in August 1989 when, in an interim statement, the so-called 'programme of the '90s' committee, led by Anna-Greta Leijon, contested the mutual compatibility of the stated goals of the Riksdag's energy legislation.[27] LO, moreover, now pressed for the development of the four untouched Norrland rivers so as to provide some compensation for the predicted energy shortfall resultant on the abolition of nuclear power. LO's second chair, Rune Molin, along with the SAP district organisation and LO's regional organ in Norrbotten, were reported to favour such a step as a means of preserving jobs and preventing emigration from the region.[28] Indeed, over the summer of 1989 the leaders of the four biggest trade unions publicly canvassed a postponement of the run-down schedule. However, the environment and energy minister, Birgitta Dahl, repeated her commitment to adhere to the Riksdag's decision to begin the phase-out in 1995.[29]

At this departure, the prime minister acted in two ways to achieve a measure of party cohesion on the nuclear power question. First, there was the appointment in a reshuffled cabinet of LO vice-chair Molin as industry minister, with responsibility also for energy questions — which were thus removed from the controversial Dahl. She continued as minister of the environment.[30] Second, a special committee of inquiry, comprising the LO leader, Stig Malm, Dahl, Molin and Ingvar Carlsson, was set up and this reported that it would be possible to abolish nuclear power subject to certain conditions being met.[31] Later, however, Malm publicly criticised the government's decision (reiterated by Dahl) to adhere to the 1995–96 start of the phase-out — as its point of departure in forthcoming talks with the

Liberals and Centre – pointing to LO studies demonstrating the extent of the expected electricity deficiency.

However, at the 1990 SAP Conference the government was given a free hand to negotiate with the so-called 'middle parties', the Centre and the Liberals, on the run-down of nuclear power without any obligation to start in 1995–96. Conference nevertheless insisted that the last reactor be taken off stream by 2010, although a condition of granting the cabinet flexibility in its bargaining stance was that the wind-down would not endanger overall energy provision.[32]

Against all the odds, on 15 January 1991 the prime minister, Carlsson, successfully reached agreement with the opposition-based Liberals and Centre on a five-year energy programme, which, in concentrating on renewable domestic energy sources and increased saving, was designed to facilitate the abolition of nuclear power while also determining when the run-down of reactors could start.[33] The deal represented a considerable sleight of hand since no reference was made to a specific timetable for the phase-out, and yet neither was the principle of the ultimate abandonment of nuclear power explicitly challenged. Tensions remained below the surface. SAP and the Centre presumed that the 2010 deadline for all closures still obtained; Westerberg, for the Liberals, however, insisted that sufficient alternative energy supplies would have to be forthcoming and electricity prices remain competitive.

There is a postscript to the nuclear power question. During the summer of 1992, one of the Barsebäck reactors developed a fault and five aggregators had to be shut down. This meant the closure of about half the plant's productive capacity. Public opinion did not, however, express itself in favour of a total close-down, nor did the government act to take Barseback off stream. Indeed, opinion polls early in 1993 indicated that over 80 per cent of people did not believe nuclear power would be abolished by 2010. In any event, there remained no realistic alternative to nuclear energy – which presently supplies about 54 per cent of Swedish electricity – and, ironically, no realistic alternative is likely to be developed as long as nuclear power remains in production. It may well take another nuclear disaster in the USA or Europe to concentrate the minds of Sweden's political leaders on implementing the phase-out, although there continues to be vigorous opposition within SAP to the continuing use of nuclear energy.

In addition to the nuclear power question, SAP has been split in recent years on a number of regional environmental questions. The plan for a combined road and rail link over the Sound between Kastrup in Denmark and Limhamn in southern Sweden is a notable case in point. At the 1987 SAP Conference, there was strong opposition to this proposal, particularly from the party's Skåne district (in which Malmö is situated), which favoured a railway tunnel under the southern Sound, primarily because of the increase in cars and increased pollution that would be generated by a road bridge. This was also the view of the Young Socialists, whose chair, Anna Lindh, characterised the bridge project as typically '*passé* – a '60s project'.[34] Significantly arrayed against a road-rail link was the old anti-nuclear alliance from 1980 of the Centre, VpK and Christians, plus the 'Environmental Party – the Greens', which had been formed by 'line 3' activists.

When SAP divisions on the question intensified,[35] an internal debate was instigated and, on 20 April 1990, the prime minister, Carlsson, was able to report an 'overwhelming majority' of the *partistyrelse* (party executive) in favour of a road-rail bridge on both economic and environmental grounds.[36] Proponents increasingly presented it as a 'bridge to Europe' – a bridge of opportunity – linking Sweden with the EC's thriving internal market, which, through the European Economic Area (EEA) blueprint, Sweden had applied to join. After a three-hour debate an overwhelming majority of SAP's Riksdag group came out in favour of the Öresund bridge, with the result that opponents like Birger Rosqvist, chair of the Traffic Committee, and Kent Carlsson of the SSU were obliged to accept the decision and, in Rosqvist's case, steer the measure through parliamentary committee.[37] Finally, after a 13-hour debate in Spring 1991, a Riksdag majority of 229–85, with five abstentions, approved the construction of a combined road-rail bridge over the Sound. During occasionally acrimonious exchanges, the communications minister, Georg Andersson, attempted to appease the protesters by promising an international panel of experts to monitor the environmental aspects of the construction and undertaking to raise the matter with the Danish government. Opponents of the bridge were implacable and dubbed Andersson a 'concrete socialist'. A hard core of 'eco-socialists', moreover, held out: among the SAP parliamentarians voting at the final division on the bridge, 133 voted 'yes' and nine 'no'.[38]

'PRO-MEMBERSHIP' VERSUS 'ANTI-EC' SOCIAL DEMOCRATS

Carlsson's minority SAP cabinet was instrumental in instigating the moves that in summer 1991 led to a Swedish application for EC membership. The fundamentally altered geo-political conditions in the wake of the autumn 1989 revolutions facilitated matters. At the SAP conference in December 1990, Carlsson observed that in a Europe in which the old east–west antagonisms had largely forfeited their significance, the traditional obstacle to Sweden joining the EC, a historic policy of armed neutrality, had lost much of its moral force. He did not then spell out that economic imperatives and, in particular, the need to sharpen the competitive edge of Sweden's export industries, stabilize the exchange rate and attract foreign investment, had in practice dictated the approach to Brussels. Among leading industrialists, the Volvo head, Per Gyllenhammer, strenuously canvassed full membership and, in time, LO became convinced that Sweden's celebrated welfare model would be jeopardised if export industry, deprived of adequate outlets within the EC, did not generate the wealth to sustain it. Cross-party support for application was achieved remarkably quickly. In November 1990, Riksdag agreement was reached between the SAP government and all the opposition parties, except VpK and the Greens, and on 12 December 1990, with dissent only from the aforementioned parties, parliament voted overwhelmingly in favour of seeking EC membership, albeit with the important caveat of preserving Swedish neutrality. On 1 July 1991 Sweden formally applied to join.

In so proceeding, the national political elite had apparently paid little heed to the state of public opinion. Certainly, when SAP's relegation to opposition after the September 1991 general election reduced to a degree the premium on a unitary posture, the party modified its stance to reflect growing reservations in the ranks about full EC membership. The announcement by the new Moderate-led coalition under Carl Bildt of a referendum on EC membership to coincide with the September 1994 election doubtless prompted recollections in SAP of the difficulties experienced at the 1980 nuclear power referendum when the party had its own line. In any event, since opinion polls indicated 47 per cent of SAP supporters were opposed and only 33 per cent in favour of the EC, the party leadership declared that it would not canvass an unqualified 'yes' but illuminate both sides of the argument in what it described as an 'educational campaign'. True, this was not presented as a change of stance. The new party secretary, Mona Sahlin, insisted: 'We will work for a "yes" vote while providing citizens with as much information as we can on one of the most difficult decisions of my generation.'[39] But, significantly, Inga Thorsson, the party's disarmament expert – who in the 1950s had been a prominent opponent of Sweden's acquisition of 'tactical' atomic weapons – announced she would vote against membership on defence and security grounds, and there was a groundswell of opposition in the Women's Organisation, the Brotherhood Movement and the SSU. The Stockholm youth branch, for example, endeavoured (unavailingly) to enforce a party 'primary' on EC membership by collecting the necessary number of signatories.

On the eve of the formal commencement of negotiations on Swedish accession in February 1993, there was a widespread discrepancy between the attitude of voters and leaders on the question of EC membership. This was the case in all the political parties except the Leftist Party, the Moderates and to some extent the Liberals. According to survey data from the Central Statistical Bureau, only 8 per cent of SAP voters said they would definitely vote 'yes' at the forthcoming referendum, whereas 37 per cent would definitely oppose membership;[40] in New Democracy, 'anti-marketeers' were twice as numerous as definite 'pro-marketeers'; and while half the Christian Democrat supporters were against, only one-fifth favoured membership and the remainder were undecided.[41] The Centre Party, representing the traditional farming constituency, was as badly divided as SAP. Against this backdrop of a deeply divided public, two pressure groups, formed in 1992, competed for influence. The one, 'No to Europe', acquired increased momentum after the Danish rejection of the Maastricht Treaty in a referendum on 2 June that year; the other, 'Yes to Europe', was backed by SAF and, indeed, industry as a whole.

In addition, a third (cross-party) organisation, the Europaforum, emerged at the beginning of 1993. Like 'line 2' in the 1980 nuclear power referendum, it positioned itself between the two existing groups, lending critical support to Swedish membership and undertaking to view the course of negotiations from a wage-earner's, women's and environmental perspective. The initiators sought to create 'a left and bourgeois alternative to Europe' – their credentials and reputation vested Europaforum with a strong anti-establishment profile – and to mobilise those disaffected with the irrational outpourings of the 'no' lobby, but disinclined to fall in with the 'yes' group promoted by the corporate sector. Notable among the eight-strong executive were two Social Democrats, Margot Wallström and the Christian pacifist Greger Hatt from the party's Brotherhood Movement.[42]

For SAP's leadership, the key management question at this stage was the most appropriate way of handling the question within the party. Pressure was building up to hold a membership ballot. Sten Johansson, editor of the agenda-setting party journal *Tiden*, a former advisor to Olof Palme and an opponent of Swedish accession, argued that polling members was the best way of legitimising the ultimate stance taken by SAP at the forthcoming referendum.[43] Equally, there was criticism in the party ranks of Carlsson's apparent equivocation on the issue while emphasis was also given to the need to seize the initiative from the party's 'no' lobby.[44] In an interview in *Dagens Nyheter*, Carlsson responded to his critics by expressing his continuous and unambiguous support for full membership and held out the prospect of cross-national solutions to the growing unemployment problem. He nevertheless disassociated himself from the work of an expert group within the Liberal Party which apparently envisaged future Swedish membership of an EC-based defence union. 'There is nothing in the EC that allows it to assume military responsibility for Sweden and Finland', he asserted.[45] Elsewhere, Carlsson publicised his close contacts with Delors, González, Rocard and other leading European socialists, and brought out his commitment to the politics of European integration – the potential afforded by cross-national policy coordination – before the economics of it.

Yet it is symptomatic of the split in SAP on the EC issue that at a joint meeting of the party executive and parliamentary group on 19 January 1993, held to determine the appropriate conditions of entry and the party's overall EC strategy, a decision was simply deferred until 1994. It was agreed to call an extraordinary party conference in summer 1994 at which either a 'yes' or 'no' vote would be recommended to party supporters. However, it was stressed that the referendum result alone would determine the allegiance of the SAP's Riksdag group which would adhere to the popular verdict, irrespective of personal convictions. The party, in short, was openly divided and would not become involved in the referendum campaign in its own name. At the same 19 January meeting, SAP's party executive formulated a set of conditions that were intended to constitute an agenda for the detailed negotiations on Swedish entry. Two stipulations were given particular importance. First, there was the demand that the traditional Swedish policy of military non-alignment (the term 'neutrality' was avoided) should be maintained and the Swedish government was urged to issue a statement making clear that membership of the Western European Union was not a current issue, that is in need of resolution in the short term. Second, it was urged that any decision on a common currency and central bank (European Monetary Union) be postponed until the next major EC 'review summit' in 1996. Bildt, the prime minister (who hinted obliquely at the possibility of holding a Danish-style referendum on EMU) supported SAP's terms of entry, despite having earlier appeared to accept the Maastricht Treaty unconditionally.[46] Several commentators, however, pointed to the hazards of seeking a deferral of or even an opt-out from EMU which, they noted, formed a core element of Maastricht.[47]

Bildt also concurred with the remaining SAP objectives for EC entry. These included acceptance of the 'openness' (public scrutiny) principle regarding legislation; provision for the Riksdag to monitor and influence the course of the EC negotiations; and the insistence that if Sweden did join, a purpose-specific EC parliamentary committee would be created as a scrutinising body. Swedish was also to become an official EC language. Furthermore, Sweden's free-trade agreement with the southern Baltic republics was to be protected — it was hoped that similar arrangements would be forged between the Baltics and the EC — while sanctions against a third party were to be preceded either by a resolution of the UN Security Council or, in exceptional circumstances, the Riksdag's consent. Importantly, in domestic affairs, SAP insisted that collective agreements should apply to all work carried out, even by foreign contractors, and also that Sweden should be able to maintain existing regional policy support forms.[48] Ironically, while SAP was deeply split on the EC question, the government and leading opposition party executive were broadly in agreement on the central prerequisites of Swedish admission.

Having examined the structural strains and a number of the issue cleavages confronting the SAP in recent years, it might reasonably be concluded that SAP has none the less proved a remarkably cohesive force on the political left. This is specially so in view of the catch-all nature of its electoral support, its several constituent organisations and, not least, the numerical size of its Riksdag group, which has been easily the largest of the parliamentary parties. SAP has also been called upon to withstand the pressure of managing an economy heading towards recession, accommodate sensitive environmental issues — like nuclear power — which have cut across the traditional left–right continuum, and negotiate the strongly polarising issue of EC membership, which has divided all the other Nordic social democratic–labour parties. True, the point about relative cohesion should not be exaggerated. There has been evidence of reduced grassroots solidarity and diminished support for SAP among its traditional electoral constituency. There has also been intermittent conflict over economic management between the party and LO. As we have seen, several issues bisected the electoral, organisational and parliamentary arenas in the party. Nor can it be said that there exists an internal consensus about the future policy direction of social democracy (discussed later) as Sweden approaches the twenty-first century. Equally, there has been no significant fragmentation in its ranks, that is to say, the formation of separate and significant dissident parties, in the manner in which there was a Social Democratic Opposition (TPSL) in the Finnish Eduskunta in the late 1950s, the Centre Democrats left the Danish Social Democrats in 1972 over issues that included EC membership, and the 'Gang of Four' broke with the British Labour Party in 1981.

Two minuscule maverick groups do warrant a brief note, however, not because they have posed or are likely to constitute a serious challenge to SAP, but because their critique has highlighted the dilemma facing a broad-based party like SAP in reconciling the disparate interests housed under its roof. The first splinter group, the Arbetarlistan (Workers' List), was officially launched as a political party in May 1990 by a 20-strong body of union activists within SAP.[49] Its programme of demands were 'redder' and 'greener' than those of the 'mother party', and in aspiring to achieve a radical synthesis of red-green policies it was critical of SAP leaders, dismissing them as career politicians lacking an understanding of the problems of ordinary people. Founded in the wake of the two 'lib-lab' pacts – Social Democrat-Liberal legislative coalitions – on tax reform (January 1990) and austerity (April 1990), the Arbetarlistan castigated the 'inverted Robin Hood politics' of robbing the poor to feed the rich, namely SAP's policy on income distribution, as well as advocating new tax reform, the protection of the welfare state and the introduction of genuine measures of economic democracy. Clearly the new party wanted above all to compete with SAP for traditional working-class votes, especially those of the low-paid trade unionists. At the same time, by opposing nuclear power and EC membership, it perhaps hoped to attract an 'eco-socialist' element. At the polls in September 1991, the Arbetarlistan platform was indistinguishable in its essentials from those of the Leftist Party and the Greens, while the undoubted electoral protest concentrated not on the ground to the left of SAP, but on the political right, with the emergence of two new parliamentary parties, the Christian Democrats and New Democracy. The Leftist Party, in short, sank almost without trace.

The second dissident group, the Kvinnoparti (Women's Party), founded in June 1992, originated in unrest in SAP's Women's Organisation about the way, largely under trade union influence, the party appeared to have ridden roughshod over its agenda of reforms.[50] Elements in the women's movement argued, for instance, that in LO's hands, their demand for a reduction in working hours had been converted into a call for six weeks' annual holiday (adopted by SAP, of course, during the 1988 general election campaign), while there was also discontent with the way the Women's Organisation's opposition to the Öresund bridge and nuclear energy, and its campaign for further measures on health care, had proved largely unavailing. In response to the rebels' threats to form a separate women's party, the chair of the Women's Organisation, Margareta Winberg, suggested the formation for the 1994 general election of female lists of candidates within SAP. In the event, this initiative proved insufficient to contain the disgruntled, although it is important to note that the Women's Party (Kvinnoparti) did not comprise exclusively former Social Democrats. Proposing to run candidates in 1994, the principal demands of the new party include legislation on a six-hour working day, protecting the welfare state and, of course, greater equality between the sexes, particularly in respect of education, incomes and appointments to posts in senior management.[51]

Sources of cohesion in SAP

If, as Edmund Burke once suggested, 'party is organised opinion', then an explanation of the basic cohesion of the SAP could lie in the adhesive properties of an all-embracing ideology. Indeed, at the macro-analytical level, it might be contended that underpinning both the strength of the party's support and its predominant unity of purpose has been a fundamental congruence between the values of social democracy and those of the wider Swedish political culture. SAP has been both the embodiment and *embouchure* of a fundamental socio-political consensus predicated on the notions of equality, solidarity and social justice, and informed by a pragmatic approach to the resolution of conflict. This was essentially the thrust of Henry Milner's study, *Sweden: Social Democracy in Practice*.[52] By extrapolation, partisan cohesion would be viewed as the corollary of broad-gauge 'ideological integration' and a series of traditional policy goals which, deriving from SAP's basic value system, have emphasised expanding the welfare state, promoting a thriving private sector so as to finance it and, by baking a large enough cake of economic growth, to redistribute wealth to the poorer sections of society. The smaller the cake, of course, the fewer the crumbs to go round – something which proved a conundrum for the SAP governments of 1988–91.

If, however, in line with Feldt's thesis outlined earlier, social democracy as a common ideology is perceived to have lost much of its force as a partisan coagulant, a more instrumental line of reasoning might point to the way, in a competitive multi-party marketplace, the introduction in 1971 of triennial elections – giving the Riksdag the shortest parliamentary term in Europe – has placed a premium on (at least) the appearance of sustained unity for parties wishing to hold power. Plainly, too, the minority status of SAP governments in recent years has elevated the importance of 'backbench' loyalty (Riksdag seating is in fact by region and not the more usual party grouping) at crucial parliamentary votes. Over the last two decades, to be sure, SAP's Riksdag group has displayed growing independence of the political executive – a product, in no small measure, of the greater licence it enjoyed during the 1976–82 opposition years. But the erosion of the numerical base of SAP governments in the assembly in the 1980s – together with the growing unreliability of the VpK as a legislative ally – meant that pressure on SAP backbenchers to toe the party line increased.

Another factor when analysing the sources of cohesion within SAP has been the leadership style of Ingvar Carlsson, who was unanimously appointed to the highest office – having been deputy chair – on 1 March 1986, 24 hours after Palme's assassination. In contrast to the somewhat domineering manner of his predecessor, Carlsson brought to the premiership the reputation of a conciliator, and developed this role as mediator-in-chief to hold together the coalition of competing interests making up the party. Feldt, the long-serving finance minister, has even suggested that, in view of the 'end of ideology' in the party, the ability to work towards compromise solutions has become a *sine qua non* of successful SAP leadership.

Carlsson's contribution to party cohesion has, perhaps, been more apparent in the sphere of close liaison with the leading organs of the party machine than in the area of cabinet management. In the latter context, Olof Ruin has brought out the way SAP prime ministers have not generally had to reconcile the differing party factions in their distribution of ministerial portfolios simply because factions as such have not really existed. LO members have been routinely included in government – about two-fifths of SAP's Riksdag group in recent years has comprised LO members – but, otherwise, the prime minister's hands have not been tied.[53] Where Carlsson has excelled, however, has been in his sensitivity to the need to seek to harness grassroots opinion in the party. A former SSU chair, he has grasped the importance of avoiding a rift between the government/shadow cabinet and the party in the country. The risk of this has increased as party conference, now held every three years, has exhibited a growing concern to twist the arms of ministers by moving detailed directives and resolutions. Accordingly, Carlsson has endeavoured to involve the party board and executive committee – the two highest-ranking bodies between conference – in the preparation of issues for governmental decision to a greater extent than before. Carlsson, in short, has tried to enlist the backing of the representative organs of the party before coming to a final decision.

The social democratic movement's cohesion was potentially enhanced, its organisational structure modified and LO's political influence almost certainly reduced as a result of the abolition in 1991 of the collective affiliation of union members to the party. The formal move to end collective affiliation stemmed from the trade union confederation rather than SAP: at the 1986 LO conference, the chair, Stig Malm, even described the system of collective affiliation as a 'millstone round the neck of the labour movement' (though not all delegates agreed). The question, however, had been the subject of intermittent debate within the party for over two decades. That SAP's 1987 Conference voted overwhelmingly to support an executive committee proposal to end nearly a century of collective affiliation was integrally bound up with the mathematics of the partisan balance in the Riksdag. In particular, the VpK let it be known that after years of abstaining on the question, they would back one of the (regular) bourgeois motions seeking to proscribe collective affiliation to political parties unless the SAP (minority) government got in first with a similar proposal of its own.[54]

Since the ending of collective affiliation in 1991, SAP's membership has declined. At the beginning of 1993 it stood at 260,000 – compared with about one million in 1987 – of which 15–25 per cent were members of social democratic workplace organisations. The new form of collaboration between the party and labour movement has taken the form of *organisationsanslutning* ('organisational affiliation'), which permits union clubs or sections to affiliate to a local *arbetarkommun* (SAP branch). But union members wishing to join the party must themselves take the initiative to do so.

The increased 'structural distance' between the party and trade union confederation rid SAP of the formal association with what in recent years has been one of its most hawkish elements. LO was consistently critical of the legislative deals that SAP entered into with the main bourgeois parties, both as a minority party in government and, after September 1991, as the leading opposition party. For example, on 7 June 1989, a legislative coalition was formed between SAP and the Centre in the Riksdag's Finance Committee which facilitated the introduction of a so-called 'obligatory saving' – to run from September 1989 to the end of 1990 – of 3 per cent on all wage-earners' taxes as a means of dampening down consumer demand.[55] This was necessary when it became obvious that the cabinet could not muster a parliamentary majority for a general increase in VAT. The compulsory savings initiative was strenuously opposed by the Liberals and Moderates; proved extremely unpopular within SAP; prompted vocal protest from the pensioners' organisations; and created extensive dissent in LO.[56] LO also sniped at the January 1990 'lib-lab' deal on tax reform;[57] opposed a similar pact on a package of austerity measures three months later; remained disenchanted with the historic 'national handshake' between the Moderate-led coalition and SAP on three crisis agreements between 20 and 30 September 1992 – agreements that almost certainly avoided the need to devalue the Swedish crown (significantly, there was no complementary crisis between LO and the employers organisation SAF);[58] and criticised the government–SAP deal on 16 December 1992, raising taxes and requiring more savings, as the Swedish economy teetered on the brink of depression.[59] Yet under the leadership of Stig Malm – who was re-elected unopposed for a further five-year term in June 1991 – LO's political influence may well have declined, at least within SAP. Furthermore, while SAP's cohesion potential has risen accordingly, Malm's leadership has been the subject of criticism from member unions who have sought greater devolution and power within the confederation.

W(h)ither Swedish social democracy?

At a European socialist leaders' meeting in Brussels in January 1993, there was much optimism about the future of socialism on a continent in which communist parties had virtually disappeared and the New Rightist professions of the 1980s had heralded the economic crisis of the 1990s.[60] In the Nordic region, however, political debate has been punctuated by intermittent talk of 'social democracy in crisis', and 'obituary notices' have even appeared in several leading newspapers. For example, Arve Solstad, in the Norwegian daily *Dagbladet*, described social democracy as a 'period piece'. The era of social democratic dominance was over, he insisted, because the parties had achieved most of their historic objectives.[61] Although the former Finnish Social Democrats' leader, Ulf Sundqvist, was quick to repudiate such a view,[62] Nordic social democracy will nevertheless need to adapt, redefine its goals and modernise its programme if it is, indeed, to avoid an identity crisis. This is equally true for SAP, despite the fact that in opposition from 1991, its lost support has largely returned. What, then, are the principal planks of SAP's policy agenda – the challenges – for the 1990s?

First and foremost, there is the question of how SAP intends to approach the reconstruction of the welfare state, given that Sweden can no longer afford to maintain existing levels of provision. As the party secretary, Mona Sahlin, noted recently, the state cannot continue to provide citizens with benefits that are generous enough to preserve their living standards.[63] One approach, and the one possibly favoured by an internal programme committee (which was to report to the September 1993 Party Conference) is to raise taxation.[64] Another, mooted by the former finance minister, Feldt, is to jettison the principle of incomes-related benefits based on means-testing. Since a commitment to income security for all cannot be maintained, the way forward, according to Feldt, would be to provide basic protection for all, namely a fixed benefit unrelated to income.[65] To the objection that a system of universal basic security would, in practice, be *selective* in its operation – because only the most disadvantaged would profit – Feldt countered (controversially) that this was probably the only way of preserving the universalist character of welfare provision and, in any event, it gave the better-off an excellent opportunity of demonstrating solidarity towards the less privileged sections of society.

A second crucial challenge for SAP in the 1990s will be to generate a credible economic strategy – that is, one providing at once the prospect of much needed jobs for men and women and consolidated living standards for the majority of citizens. Delivering the economic goods to the middle classes will be particularly problematic in the context of a budget deficit which in

February 1993 stood at over Kr.200 billion. Even on the optimistic assumption of a 3 per cent growth scenario, public spending cuts are inevitable, unemployment will come down only slowly and the pressure to increase taxes will mount.

In such circumstances, it seems imperative for SAP to champion a radical cause which will serve as a standard-bearer for the future and avert a possible crisis of identity within the social democratic movement as a whole. In the postwar period, the ATP supplementary pensions scheme of the late 1950s and the employee investment funds of the 1970s have proved such causes. True, it might be argued that SAP's commitment to introducing the LO-inspired employee funds scheme, which was implemented in 1983 in the teeth of vehement opposition from the bourgeois bloc and business community,[66] was largely a quid pro quo for trade union support on economic policy and, in particular, initial backing for Feldt's tough anti-inflationary programme which followed the 1982 devaluation. There is no evidence, moreover, that the funds issue was a vote-winner. But with future membership of the European Union likely to increase further the 'democratic distance' between the people and the political elites in Stockholm and Brussels, and with a clearly widespread sense of low subjective competence (powerlessness) among citizens, a 'bottom-up' participatory approach to economic management appears essential to rekindle enthusiasm for social democracy as a genuine popular movement. In short, emphasising the 'by' element – the *democracy* – in social democracy appears the best way to mobilise support on a broad front and counter charges that, unlike the 'green' parties, SAP lacks a radical agenda.

Notes

1. Åke Mauritzen, 'Socialdemokratins samhälle', *Nordisk Kontakt*, 8/1989, pp. 69–71.
2. Björn von Sydow, *Vägan till enkammarriksdagen. Demokratisk författningspolitik i Sverige 1944–1968* (Stockholm: Tiden), 1989.
3. 'Statsministerin kan tänka sig en koalitionsregering', *Nordisk Kontakt*, 12/1989, pp. 74–75.
4. Sten Berglund and Ulf Lindström, *The Scandinavian Party System(s)* (Lund: Studentlitteratur) 1978, p. 108.
5. Leif Lewin, 'The Supplementary Pension System', in L. Lewin *Ideology and Strategy. A Century of Swedish Politics* (Cambridge: Cambridge University Press) 1988, pp. 204–38.
6. Bengt Owe Birgersson, Stig Hadenius, Björn Molin and Hans Wieslander, *Sverige efter 1900* (Stockholm: Bonnier Fakta), 1981.
7. The advent of a three-party bourgeois coalition in 1991 coincided with Sweden's plunge into its worst economic crisis since 1945. Plainly, as the 1993 Finance Bill noted, high unemployment, falling output, serious imbalances in the financial sector, a large deficit in public sector finances and the depreciation of the Swedish krona will

bring acute pressures for many people. *Economic Policy Statement by the Swedish Government*, January 1993, p. 2.

8. David Arter, 'A Tale of Two Carlssons: The Swedish General Election of 1988', *Parliamentary Affairs*, Vol. 42, No. 1, January 1989, p. 88.

9. Stig Hadenius, *Swedish Politics During the 20th Century* (Borås: The Swedish Institute), 1988, p. 115.

10. Hans Bergström, 'Sweden's Politics and Party System at the Crossroads', in Jan-Erik Lane (ed.), *Understanding the Swedish Model* (London: Frank Cass), 1991, pp. 18–19.

11. Diane Sainsbury, 'Swedish Social Democracy in Transition: The Party's Record in the 1980s and the Challenge of the 1990s' in Lane (1991), op. cit., p. 47.

12 Ibid., p. 41.

13. Bergström, op. cit., p. 13.

14. 'Ny demokrati framåt efter krispaketen', *Nordisk Kontakt*, 12/1992, p. 92.

15. 'Unga valjäre röstkolkade mest', *Nordisk Kontakt*, 6/1989, p. 71.

16. Kjell-Olof Feldt, *Samtal med Feldt*.

17. Kjell-Olof Feldt, *Alla dessa dagar*.

18. 'Familjepolitik och skattepolitik huvudfrågor i nästan års val', *Nordisk Kontakt*, 13/1987, pp. 63–64.

19. Hans Norrbom, 'Kjell-Olof Feldts bekännelser', *Nordisk Kontakt*, 4/1991, pp. 111–13.

20. '"Rosornas krig" på första maj', *Nordisk Kontakt*, 6/1989, pp. 65–66.

21. Hans Norrbom, 'En omstridd politiker', *Nordisk Kontakt*, 4/1990, pp. 105–6.

22. Robert C. Sahr, *The Politics of Energy Policy Change in Sweden* (Ann Arbor: University of Michigan), 1985, pp. 103, 120.

23. 'Ingen femparti uppgörelse om kärnkraftens avveckling', *Nordisk Kontakt*, 4/1987, pp. 71–72.

24. 'Avvecklingen av kärnkraft påbörjar redan år 1995', *Nordisk Kontakt*, 9–10/1988, p. 79.

25. 'Första reaktorn ur drift 1993-95', *Nordisk Kontakt*, 8/1987, pp. 64–65.

26. 'Förtida kärnkraftsavveckling möter kritik', *Nordisk Kontakt*, 5/1988, pp. 60–61.

27. 'Målkonflikter i energipolitiken enligt socialdemokratisk 90-talsgrupp', *Nordisk Kontakt*, 10–11/1989, p. 72.

28. 'LO föreslår utbyggnad av skyddade älvar', *Nordisk Kontakt*, 5/1989, p. 71.

29. 'Energibeslut kan rivas upp', *Nordisk Kontakt*, 14/1989, p. 74.

30. 'Ingvar Carlsson ombildar sin regering', *Nordisk Kontakt*, 2/1990, pp. 72–74.

31. 'Kärnkraften splittrar s', *Nordisk Kontakt*, 10–11/1990, p. 74.

32. 'Kärnkraftsavvecklingen skjuts upp?', *Nordisk Kontakt*, 13/1990, pp. 69–70.

33. 'Energiuppgörelse i hamn utan årtal för avvecklingen', *Nordisk Kontakt*, 1/1991, pp. 90–91.

34. 'Starkt motstånd mot Öresundsbro', *Nordisk Kontakt*, 13/1987, pp. 68–69.

35. 'Fortsatt socialdemokratisk oenighet om brobeslutet' *Nordisk Kontakt*, 4/1990, p. 89.

36. 'Första etappen klar för Öresundsbro', *Nordisk Kontakt*, 6/1990, pp. 68–69.

37. 'S-ja till Öresundsbro', *Nordisk Kontakt*, 7/1990, p. 73.

38. 'Klar majoritet för brobeslutet', *Nordisk Kontakt*, 6/1991, pp. 100–1.

39. 'Risk för partisplittring efter växande EG-motstånd', *Nordisk Kontakt*, 3/1992, pp. 82–83.

40. Sten Johansson, 'Oppen strid inom S oundviklig', *Dagens Nyheter*, 7 January 1993, p. 4.

41. 'Vain 20% Kds:n kannattajista Ruotsin EY-jäsenyyden kannalla', *Kristityn Vastuu*, 14 January 1993, p. 1.
42. 'Samarbete över partigränser för EG', *Dagens Nyheter*, 17 January 1993, p. 7.
43. Sten Johansson, 'S måste medlemsomrösta', *Dagens Nyheter*, 9 January 1993, p. 4.
44. Birgitta von Otter, 'Sluta tiga, Carlsson!', *Dagens Nyheter*, 13 January 1993, p. 4.
45. 'Ja till EG räddar jobben', *Dagens Nyheter*, 14 January 1993.
46. 'Ett bra dokument', *Dagens Nyheter*, 20 January 1993, p. 6.
47. 'Socialdemokratins EG-vånda', *Dagens Nyheter*, 20 January 1993, p. 2.
48. 'S vill vänta med EMU-beslut', *Dagens Nyheter*, 20 January 1993, p. 6.
49. 'Nytt parti bildar i konkurrens med socialdemokraterna', *Nordisk Kontakt*, 2/1990, p. 77.
50. 'S-kvinnor vill bilda eget parti', *Nordisk Kontakt*, 2/1992, p. 115.
51. 'Kvinnoparti i nästa val', *Nordisk Kontakt*, 6/1992, p. 79.
52. Henry Milner, *Sweden: Social Democracy in Practice* (Oxford: Oxford University Press), 1989.
53. Olof Ruin, 'Three Swedish Prime Ministers: Tage Erlander, Olof Palme and Ingvar Carlsson', in Lane (1991), op. cit., p. 64.
54. 'Kollektivanslutningen till SAP avskaffas', *Nordisk Kontakt*, 13/1987, p. 69.
55. 'Mildare åtstramning efter uppgörelse', *Nordisk Kontakt*, 8/1989, pp. 54–55.
56. 'M och fp vill riva upp beslutet om tvångssparandet', *Nordisk Kontakt*, 12/1989, p. 79.
57. 'Statsskatten slopar för nio av tio inkomsttagare'.
58. 'Historiskt handslag över blockgränsen lugnade marknaden', *Nordisk Kontakt*, 9/1992, pp. 84–85.
59. 'Svensk ekonomi befarar gå mot en depression', *Nordisk Kontakt*, 12/1992, pp. 86 *et seq.*
60. 'Europas plågoris samlar s', *Dagene Nyheter*, 16 January 1993, p. 13.
61. Arve Solstad, 'Socialdemokrati i krise, har gjort sin gjerning', *Nordisk Kontakt*, 9/1991, pp. 14–15.
62. Ulf Sundqvist, 'Socialdemokratin – dödförklarad i förtid', *Nordisk Kontakt*, 11/1991, pp. 26–28.
63. 'Lovande s-debatt om välfärden', *Dagens Nyheter*, 17 January 1993, p. 2.
64. 'Försiktig kliv åt vänster', *Dagens Nyheter*, 16 January 1993, p. 13.
65. Feldt insisted that although the Moderate-led coalition was committed to the principle of universal welfare benefits, its cuts in sickness benefits from 90 per cent to 70 per cent had hit the poor the hardest. See Kjell-Olof Feldt, 'Byt princip för välfärdsstaten', *Dagens Nyheter*, 20 January 1993, p. 2.
66. Thus on 4 October 1983 about 75,000 people demonstrated against the funds in Stockholm. However, according to Riksdag legislation in December 1983, five regional employee funds were established and instructed to buy shares on market terms. Each fund was directed to show a profit, although none would be permitted to own more than 8 per cent of any company. Funds were to be financed by a new profit-sharing tax and by an increase in the existing employee fees for supplementary pensions.

5 Towards party irrelevance? the decline of both conflict and cohesion in the Norwegian Labour Party

Knut Heidar

A party without conflict is a dead party. Such parties are monolithic and usually unable to gain support or raise expectations. But a party of total internal conflict will also soon expire – at least in electoral terms. This is the dilemma for all parties, social democratic ones included. It is, however, possible to argue that social democratic parties have had the lion's share of internal strife. Most of them were seriously affected by schism within the international labour movement in the wake of Lenin's coup in Russia in 1917. Furthermore, socialist ideology allowed ample room for debates about the correct, even 'scientific' interpretation of the Revolution. Social democrats became – after the Second World War – parties of government and they were soon sought out by scores of single-issue organisations. In short, there was a rich potential for a 'conflict of interests'.

Cohesion does not presuppose lack of conflict. In fact, the test of cohesion comes with conflict and the 'healthy' state of a party would probably include a bit of both. Cohesion is, however, the rationale behind party formation in the first place: staying together, even if disagreeing on some secondary issues, gives strength. In politics it is rational to accept minor policies contrary to one's own beliefs or interests in order to fight together for the important issues. Indeed, this is precisely the kind of calculation every voter must undertake before making a choice at the ballot box. Conflict, on the other hand, is integral to politics. To fight for interests and debate the goals of political change without the use of force is in fact the democratic alternative to totalitarian command. In party politics staying together does not exclude fierce debate and that is why we can find conflictual parties with a high level of cohesion. Just as we find parties with minimal conflict and poor cohesion, the two do not necessarily go together as outlined in Table 5.1.

Table 5.1   Party types according to levels of cohesion and conflict

PARTY CONFLICT

		Low	High
PARTY	Low	Party irrelevance	Party of factions
COHESION	High	Honeymoon party	Party of democratic centralism

A party scoring low on both conflict and cohesion is a party where members, activists and leaders do not care much about each other. In policy terms the party organisation is largely irrelevant, and the 'party' as such is basically only an organisational framework for nominating candidates for elections and a useful label to evoke old electoral identities. The 'party of factions' has intense conflict between different internal tendencies, but there is very little attempt to curb organised factionalism. The 'honeymoon party' has a high degree of internal cohesion, and at the same time has few policy differences — at least openly expressed. Lastly, the party of 'democratic centralism' is a closed community engaged in intense struggle, and is the type of party where members are tied together as in a *beltespenning* (the legendary way of duelling with knives in pre-industrial Norway when two men were strapped together to fight it out).

My argument in this chapter is that the Norwegian Labour Party (Det Norske Arbeiderparti, DNA) is moving towards party irrelevance. During the 1980s the party moved both towards lower levels of conflict as well as poor party cohesion. This explains why DNA, in the new debate about membership of the European Community, managed to avoid the internal turmoil created by the same issue 20 years before. To present the argument in a provocative and admittedly exaggerated way: the party's organisation is on the decline as a meaningful political entity.

The argument will be developed, first, in a short presentation of three periods in DNA's history, each illustrating one of the party types sketched above. Second, I shall (in some more detail) present material to corroborate the 'decline of conflict' argument in the two decades following the first debate on EC (which took place in 1970–73). Third, I will deal with evidence on the 'decline of cohesion', again starting with the 1972 débâcle when the old values of organisational solidarity came under heavy pressure. Finally, I shall briefly discuss some of the causes for this development and focus in particular on the changes in party generations during the 1970s.

Background

DNA was founded in 1887 and its electoral breakthrough came after the turn of the century. The party was radicalised during the Second World War; at the Party Conference in 1918 the revolutionary opposition won control from the old moderate social democrat leadership and in 1919 DNA became a member of Comintern. During the following eight years the party experienced two party splits and one merger. The old-guard social democrats split to found their own party (the Social Democratic Party) in 1921 and the communist left marched out of the DNA at the 1923 Party Congress. In 1927 the trade union movement guided DNA and the Social Democratic Party towards a merger. Both the party takeover by the left in 1918 and the split with Comintern in 1923 created intense in-fighting at all levels of the party. At no other time in the history of the labour movement, however, did the culture of organisational solidarity dominate party rhetoric to such an extent. The different tendencies in the class struggle were supposed to fight it out inside their class organisation. But not through organised factions of course, and when a decision was reached, the minority were 'obliged' to stay loyal in the external struggle. Anything else would be to weaken the organised force of the labour movement – splinters would be traitors to their class. In the early 1920s the DNA leadership accepted this version of democratic centralism – at least in theory, but DNA was a mass party with a practice that differed sharply from the Leninist model. In this period the party was like a pressure cooker – which exploded twice.

DNA formed a minority government in 1936 and was returned to the Storting with a solid majority after the Second World War. In the 1940s and 1950s DNA stood for industrial growth and the welfare state, enlisting the help of Keynesian macro-economic planning to modernise Norwegian society. The organised labour movement was to be a key factor in building a more equal society, old programmatic 'dogmatism' was brushed aside, and traditional demands to 'socialise' industry were taken out of the party agenda. Membership and party activity were still at a high level at the same time as both the old solidarity culture and fighting the communists gave unity and purpose to the DNA.

The 1960s saw an end to the old solidarity and the rise of internally and externally propulsed factionalism in the DNA. During the 1960s the party found itself faced by a 'third alternative', a non-communist competitor to the left: the Socialist People's Party (Sosialistisk Folkeparti, SF). An internal opposition also emerged in the 1960s – primarily within the youth organisation – as a result of the international reaction to the Vietnam war. The climax came with the debate on Norwegian entry into the EC, of which the leadership in the party, the trade union movement and most DNA parliamentarians were in favour. However, in an unprecedented step, an internal party opposition group organised an 'Information Committee Against Membership' in December 1971. The political thrust of this organisation was a disagreement with the leadership over the possibility of creating a more equal, more 'socialist' Norway within the EC. A referendum was held in Norway in 1972 and EC membership was narrowly rejected (by 53 per cent to 47 per cent). The internal struggle created lasting bitterness and was a tacit dimension in the turbulent internal factionalism of the party from 1972 to 1981.

The decline of conflict 1972–92?

The DNA Congress in the autumn of 1992 decided to support a second Norwegian application for membership of the EC. The debate was heated both at the branch level in the run-up to the congress and at the party congress itself. Still, according to commentators, the debate bore no comparison to the one 20 years earlier. The problem, however, in discussing intensity of conflicts and in comparing the different conflict situations, is both to define a 'scale of conflict intensity' and to find appropriate indicators. Clearly, the most we can hope for is an assessment based on the description of the major party clashes as portrayed in the literature on the party.

MEMBERSHIP OF THE EUROPEAN COMMUNITY?

The first struggle over the issue of membership 1971–72 has been described as intense and bitter: old friendships fell apart, quite new and surprising alliances emerged. The left wing within the trade unions and DNA fought shoulder to shoulder against the 'reactionary' farmers' union and faced, among the most ardent proponents of membership, old comrades from within 'the movement'. After the defeat of the referendum of September 1972 the DNA government stepped down. But inside the DNA the feud continued over the nominations for the 1973 Storting election. In March the next year a majority of the leaders in the Information Committee decided to leave the DNA to join the new electoral front – Socialist Election Alliance (Socialistisk Valgforbund, SV) – created by the SF, the Communist Party and 'independent socialists'. Prominent members of the Committee had already had their party membership suspended, but the main reason for the split was that they were not satisfied that enough anti-market representatives had been placed in 'safe' constituencies before the Storting election. Nevertheless, the majority of anti-membership activists, and quite a few prominent leaders, decided to stay in DNA.

In spite of the 1973 election defeat a DNA minority government – supported by the SV – returned to power. Most of the old party leadership had kept their positions, but the left of the party (which by and large had been on the anti-membership side in the EC debate) was not satisfied with its share of the spoils. The conflict which emerged over the election of a new party leader at the 1975 Congress was not directly related to the EC issue. Although both contenders for the leadership had been in favour of membership, neither was closely tied to the old pro-EC camp. They reflected in a moderate way the traditional left–right axis within the party. Most anti-market activists sided with the left-wing candidate, the deputy chairman, Reiulf Steen, who was elected, but the compromise was that the other candidate, Oddvar Nordli, would take over as prime minister if the possibility arose. This 'balanced' arrangement came about after an intervention of the retired party leader (and prime minister for most of the postwar period), Einar Gerhardsen. He feared another destructive conflict within the party which might – again – end in a split. The intense debate over the new leader completely dominated party activities before the 1975 Congress.[1]

DIVIDED LEADERSHIP 1975–81

The separation of the leadership positions – chairman and prime minister – institutionalised the left–right conflict within the party. This gave the government a difficult time as it could not take the support of the party organisation for granted. Among the substantive issues fuelling internal party friction were the emerging environmental questions. These split the old left of traditional 'electrification socialism' and the young generation advocating more 'green' policies. Even more critical, though, was the debate on national and international security triggered by the NATO 'twin-track decision' of 1979: to negotiate with the Soviet Union first and if not successful to deploy so-called 'Euro-missiles' later. Party opinion was quite unprepared for the potential new arms spiral implicit in this decision and it also opened up an old, hidden dimension in party debates based on scepticism about the role of the USA in international affairs: the anti-NATO sentiments were coupled with those of the anti-Vietnam-war dissidents of the late 1960s. The leadership – including the party chairman – had to take to tactical steps like parallel diplomatic missions to Moscow and Washington, to convince the DNA parliamentarians. The controversy, however, continued both inside and outside the party. In Norwegian politics the twin-track decision became a rallying point for left forces in general and the Left Socialist Party (Sosialistisk Venstreparti, SV) (which was the 'electoral alliance' from 1973, minus the communists, which had become a party) in particular. The peace movement collected half a million signatures on a petition against missile deployment and quite a few communes and counties declared themselves 'nuclear free zones' with the support of DNA representatives. The peace movement was provided with another rallying point with the proposal (which reached parliament early in 1981) to store equipment for US military forces in Norway. This was (according to the US Department of Defense) necessary to counter the military build-up by the Soviet Union on the Kola peninsula. The peace movement argued that storing this equipment would contribute to increased international tension and also being close to breaching the policy – established in the late 1950s – not to have foreign bases on Norwegian soil. Both debates were used by conservative politicians to indicate the inherent untrustworthiness of DNA in matters of national security; of course, this accusation was furiously rejected by DNA, which pointed to the fact that it was the DNA government which had had to take responsibility for both the NATO twin-track decision (which it had actively participated in making) and for the final decision to build a military depot in central Norway.[2] Not until 1984 did DNA reach a compromise in the Euro-missile debate that all factions could accept – and even then it was half-hearted.

In the meantime DNA had gone through another leadership debate. This time the wider party was not involved to the same extent as in 1975, but the top-level struggle also mobilised some rank-and-file members. In January 1981 the prime minister announced his resignation for health reasons. In a rare political thriller the secretary of the environment, Gro Harlem Brundtland, was elected as the new prime minister through a series of informal and later formal party meetings. A 'write-in campaign' for Mrs Brundtland from the party 'grassroots' was alleged to have contributed to her selection and at the party congress a few months later the incumbent party chairman, Reiulf Steen, was forced to step down in favour of Mrs Brundtland. She was a popular choice, giving DNA a boost in its rather miserable poll rating, but her selection could not keep the centre-right parties from winning a majority at the Storting election in the autumn of 1981, and DNA went in opposition for the next four and a half years.

CONSOLIDATION 1981–86

From 1981 to 1986 Mrs Brundtland consolidated the party, and it was Mrs Brundtland who managed to work out a compromise in the missile debate and to lead the party through a fairly good election in 1985. After the conservative 'bourgeois' government was defeated in parliament in April 1986 – when the right-wing populist Progress Party sided with the left to oppose a rise in the petrol tax – she again became prime minister. The political problems of her second government (1986–89), came not so much from internal conflict as from dissatisfied voters and the resentment of sections of the trade union movement. The economy was under pressure and a devaluation just after she took office was followed by policies to regulate wages. In addition, high interest rates and – from 1988 – a dramatic increase in unemployment, made trade union support less than half-hearted. The party left expressed dissatisfaction with the government's lack of effective economic policies; a dose of old-style Keynesian medicine was required, they argued. The government, however, held the view that under the new, liberalised, international economy the old medicine would not work.

PROGRAMME REVISIONISM: THE 'FREEDOM DEBATE'

The political climate changed as Norway entered the 1980s. The 'bourgeois' coalition headed by a conservative prime minister, Kåre Willoch, had followed the international trends with its programme to 'roll back the frontiers of the state'. Reaganism and Thatcherism were forceful inputs into the general debate and the government played the 'dynamic tax-policy' card, arguing that lower taxes would fuel the economy and in the end give increased public revenues. Private local radio stations were allowed and the government launched a programme to slim down public bureaucracy and make it more responsive. Deregulation of the credit market was initiated and private interests were invited to enter education, the health sector, nurseries, and so on. Although this privatisation was initially conceived on a small scale, the direction was clear.

At its 1981 Congress DNA had adopted a new programme of party principles which did not arouse much controversy within the party, but were more than just a rewrite. They were cast in an analytical sociological language in which the party faced 'new challenges' which demanded 'new answers', and socialism was 'not a condition, but a process'. The 1969 programme of principles had stated rather bluntly that the goal of the party was 'a socialist society'. Now this socialist 'process' was directed at three particular goals: freedom, democracy and equality ('equal worth'). Later in the programme 'solidarity' – central to 'democratic socialism' – was added to the list. The important new twist to the 1981 programme was the strong emphasis on the labour movement as a 'freedom movement'. Freedom was linked to solidarity and equality as the main values guiding the social democratic project. Possible trade-offs between freedom and equality were brushed aside.[3] The official party history describes the 1981 programme as 'a lot more pragmatic' as the new programme also left out the old demand to establish public control over banks and credit institutions.[4]

Shortly after the 1985 election the DNA leadership announced plans for a broad internal party debate to be called the 'freedom debate'. Politically, this was a reaction to the policies of the 'bourgeois' government since 1981, in particular to the increased salience of 'private solutions'. The main purpose of the campaign was therefore to 'recapture' the concept of 'freedom' for the labour movement, and organisationally the debate was planned to culminate in the formulation of the 1989 election manifesto. The 'freedom debate' raised – from different angles – the question of the proper balance between state and markets, between the public and the private. The aim was to promote discussions on what was a proper social democratic answer – relevant for the 1980s. To achieve this the party leadership set out to challenge two DNA traditions: the rooted belief in the value and extension of the public sector; and close ties with the trade unions. During the 1970s and early 1980s an expanding public sector with detailed regulations and a growing bureaucracy had (as the electorate's belief in state intervention dwindled) become increasingly troublesome parts of the social democratic project. The anti-state rhetoric of the 'bourgeois' parties no doubt found fertile ground in strategically important sections of the electorate, and DNA leaders considered this a threat both to the party and to the welfare state. They prepared for a counter-offensive by presenting two general points on party policies to the DNA's membership. First, the choice of policies should be made on the basis of what benefited the consumer, not the producers in the trade unions. Second, DNA had to come to terms with more variation in policy approach. Centralised policies treating everyone alike would not necessarily produce the best solutions.

In the aftermath of the 'freedom debate' and the centrist leaning 1986–89 government, there was some public debate about the general direction of DNA policies. This was also fuelled by a steep rise in the unemployment figures but at the party congress in the spring of 1989 there was only meek, almost symbolic opposition. Economic setbacks made prospects dim for expensive reforms, and the leadership had its way with a moderate election manifesto for the 1989–93 term which put more jobs, greater solidarity and improving the environment high on the agenda. A rebellion did come, however, over the election of a new deputy leader. The candidate favoured by the top leadership had to share the job with a former trade union leader, Torbjørn Berntsen, who campaigned as a representative of the 'old groups' within the labour movement. The leadership also met defeat on a proposal to end the collective trade union affiliations to the party. These were minor obstacles, however. After the congress parliamentary politics prevailed as usual, the important task being to keep the conservatives out of power.

A MEEK OPPOSITION

Opposition to the new ideological signals of the 'freedom debate' was scattered. Even though Gallup poll figures in 1989 showed that 25 per cent of DNA voters thought DNA had moved too much to the right 'these last years',[5] there was not much internal opposition. The deputy party leader (1981–89), Einar Førde, later summed up his experience: 'DNA is one of the least idea-oriented social democratic parties I know'.[6] Possibly the critics held back in order not to harm the minority DNA government in 1986–89, but this had not silenced the left wing in the past (it probably had more to do with the general decline in party activism). The grassroots did not turn out in great numbers to participate in the 'freedom debate' (they rather enjoy their individual freedom in front of the TV), nor did the youth movement, tradi-tionally the guardians of ideological causes, fly the red flag. In contrast to the late 1970s – when the DNA government made compromises to the left and experienced a viable left-wing opposition – the DNA left had by the late 1980s faded under the impact of a new international climate and the domestic electorate 'right-wing wave'.

A few critical voices still addressed publicly what they judged to be a scrapping of traditional values within the party. Just after the 1985 election Torbjørn Berntsen had complained that he, with his trade union and industrial background, was not given a sufficiently influential position within the parliamentary party group. This outburst triggered the 'identity debate'. In policy terms, the leader of the Municipal Workers' Union, Liv Nilsson, was predictably outspoken in her criticism of the signals in the 'freedom debate' opting for 'private solutions'. Nilsson was a member of the DNA Central Committee and had already offended party culture by arguing that she was the *representative* of her union within that committee.[7] The public quarrel came over how to create new nurseries. The DNA manifesto for the 1987 council elections emphasised the need for more places for pre-school children, and the question was if this should be the exclusive task of the councils or whether one should encourage the creation of private and 'cooperative' nurseries. Mrs Nilsson held the traditional social democrat view that a public sector solution had a value in itself which could not be reduced to a question of cost and expedience, and at the 1987 Congress she argued strongly that a 'deideologisation of the means can well lead to the goals not being achieved'.[8]

Although publicly a muted opposition, the internal concern was widespread. The old party leader, Reiulf Steen, often considered a protector of the left, had – in a private telephone conversation – given the following description of the kind of society sought by the 'modern' right wing within the party: 'A welfare society for the affluent middle class . . . It will be a kind of mini-America. Where the conservatives and DNA compete for power, without anybody being able to see much difference between them'.[9] Steen had lost the leadership contest in 1981, but the new leadership of Mrs Brundtland along with electoral trends and a new international climate had quietened the old party left.

Opposition to the new party line had, however, some backing from the old academic left. In 1988 a former Left Socialist Party MP, Professor Ottar Brox, published a book defending 'traditional social democracy'.[10] But Brox had the rhetorical problem that he was on record as being fairly critical of 'traditional social democracy' during its alleged golden age. From within the party, Professor W.M. Lafferty argued that the new party discussion on 'freedom' was 'bourgeois territory',[11] and he agreed with critics on the right that there was a conflict between freedom and increased pluralism on the one hand and solidarity/equality on the other. Professor Lafferty feared that the DNA leadership, by 'stumbling into the desert of instrumental materialism', ran the danger of replacing the ethical basis of social democracy with a 'technique'.[12] In Lafferty's view the 1975–81 period – with a minority DNA government supported by the SV – had seen the culmination of the 'social democratic state'.[13] This was the period when DNA, in practical politics, came closest to the 'social democratic idea' which was about uniting classical socialism – meaning equality in property and status – with democratic decision-making in all spheres of society.

In a response, Einar Førde argued that Lafferty was right in seeing the 1980s as a time for change of course for DNA –but it was a change of means, not of basic values.[14] The change, according to Førde, was in line with international trends within social democracy: upgrading markets, downgrading state solutions. And in fact the 1980s had been an important ideological phase in the history of DNA – being closer to 'real ideological debate than at almost any time in our history'.[15]

THE EUROPEAN ISSUE AGAIN

The 1989 election brought the centre-right coalition back to power – but only for a short period. The conservative-led government of Jan P. Syse fell after one year because the three parties were unable to agree in the negotiations on the European Economic Area to be established between EFTA and the EC. In November 1990, when Mrs Brundtland formed her third government (a minority one), the European issue had again become central, despite having been 'exiled' for nearly 20 years from Norwegian politics. Still, the 'ghosts' from 1972 reappeared to DNA in the shape of a fear of another split in the party – this time possibly bringing its vote below 30 per cent. The SV and the agrarians were ready and eager to pick up the deserters if the Labour leadership moved too quickly on its pro-EC policies.

In organisational terms, the party elite played its cards carefully. The party secretary – who had opposed EC membership in 1972 – was critical of the way the organisational weapon had been used to further the pro-membership cause during the previous European debate. The new debate was conducted in a much more open atmosphere and the party members were encouraged to express their opinions freely. The 1990 Congress discussed the procedure for the emerging debate and decided to create study groups in order to sound out membership opinion before the final decision was to be taken in November 1992. During this internal debate the leadership did not express a definitive view on EC membership, so that even the prime minister, who could not avoid expressing views on European developments in general, did not draw any conclusion until a meeting of the county party in Hordaland in April 1992 (although no one ever doubted her firm commitment to membership). At the congress in November 1992 the party decided to support an application for membership, but at the same time it decided to reconsider the question when the negotiators had worked out the conditions for Norwegian membership. Meanwhile the Norwegian Storting had decided in October 1992 to ratify the EFTA–EC agreement on an EEA treaty.

This more open party process paid off in terms of internal conflict level. Obviously there had been debate, and anti-membership views had been presented by prominent DNA members in government as well as in parliament, but basically the 'waiting game' of the pro-leadership paid off. In addition, the EEA agreement caused strategic difficulties for the 'anti-European movement' by splitting its forces. By 1993 no institutionalised expression of opposition (like the Information Committee of 1971) had emerged within DNA. There was, of course, resistance to membership both from key individuals (some seen by the press as making a bid for the leadership),[16] and from important sections of the party, namely the northern counties. Still, the level of conflict had not matched the 1970s.

The decline of cohesion 1972–92?

Cohesion is about sticking together, either because of agreement or because the party members for some reason think they should bury disagreements. The reasons for burying disagreement may be the use of brute force, cultural constraints, rational calculation, and so on, but the ultimate value should be that the representatives of the party ought to act in a concerted manner.

ORGANISATIONAL TRENDS

Our first question is whether there is any change in the organisational framework of DNA within which cohesion can find a fertile ground. The 1972 Information Committee had as its rationale the fact that the leadership used the organisation in an undemocratic manner to favour the pro-European point of view. In 1972 as well as in 1992 the party laws had a paragraph setting out the conditions for suspending or excluding a member, and, although the article was slightly changed, to 'breach party laws, programmes or guidelines' was still grounds for exclusion.[17] Active party members had their membership suspended in 1972, but not in 1992, and the organisational structure of the 1990s was basically the same: the local branch was the primary membership unit, the commune, the county and the national party were the levels above and the biennial congress was the highest authority in the party. The congress elects the leadership and makes the final decisions on the party programme. In spite of DNA's stability of organisational structure, the way the party organisation works at the time of writing (1993) is quite different, however. First, the party culture has changed substantially. In the 1970s the old guard still set the tone – with their perception of the need to stand united against the 'bourgeois forces' in society and retain a unity tempered in the bitter struggles against the communists just after the war. Unity and subordination were cultural realities within the party and some no doubt saw as illegitimate the continued fight against European membership after the congress had decided the party view.[18] At the special party EC congress in 1972, there was laughter around the hall when the entire delegation from the northern county of Nordland voted 'yes' to membership. Everyone knew there was massive opposition to the EC in that county among DNA members and voters as well as the society at large.[19] By contrast, in the party debate before the 1992 Congress all the northern county parties came out against membership.[20] The change presumably resulted not solely from higher democratic motivation, but also from the diminished effectiveness of potential organisational manipulation that had come about in between times.

After 1967 DNA congresses were opened to the media. This 'openness', however, did not in itself mean much as the important committees still met behind closed doors. The memoirs of key DNA figures in the 1950s and 1960s give the impression of highly centralised decision-making: 'Some of us had been talking together' is an expression often used by the old party leader Einar Gerhardsen in his memoirs. In his era the 'some of us' were the most trusted cabinet ministers, the party secretary, the leader of the trade union movement and the editor of the central DNA newspaper. But this tight control was lost in the 1970s. Old organisational values had evaporated during the unruly EC debate, and the wartime generation had departed. The changing media also played a part. More important, probably, were the general social changes. These were reflected in the composition of the 1985 Congress: 57 per cent of the delegates were then public employees; only 12 per cent came from industry; 46 per cent had a university-level education.[21] The party secretary in 1985 explained the need for a more open policy process in the party by pointing to a new kind of member who demanded respect for his or her points of view.[22]

Another change affecting the inner life of the party has been the increase in party bureaucrats at the central party office and the decline in membership. The public finance of parties, which was introduced in 1970, increased steadily over the years making better professional staffing possible.[23] In terms of nominal members DNA has had mixed fortunes during the 1980s – rising from 153,000 in 1980 to 176,000 in 1985 and then declining again to 121,000 in 1990. (In the 1970s the figures were around 150,000.) A decline in membership, it seems, took place only in the latter part of the 1980s, but figures stabilised again in the early 1990s. The party entered government in 1986 just as organisational renewal was put on the agenda with the 'freedom debate'. In 1989 the party secretary acknowledged, however, that DNA had not been able to combine government power with a 'lively and critical debate within the party'.[24]

The labour movement as a whole – trade unions, the cooperatives, and so on – also faced problems. The decline (if not the death) of the traditional working class during the 1970s removed the social glue necessary to hold 'the movement' together. (Indicative of the decline of solidarity were the quarrels with the public employee unions mentioned earlier.) The increased independence of the press owned by the labour movement also caused problems for the party; the party has about 20 per cent of the national daily circulation and important regional strongholds. During the last two decades the labour press has increasingly operated on a professional basis and felt free to criticise and 'unmask' DNA politics and politicians almost as much as other media.[25]

The use of professional surveys became more common in the 1970s. Party headquarters increasingly used them to test public opinion, bypassing both the media and their own organisation. Labour and Conservative were the only parties to subscribe to the *Norwegian Monitor*, a systematic (and expensive) effort to discover the political and economic attitudes of changing socio-cultural groups within Norwegian society.[26] DNA became a more 'open party' during the 1980s – to paraphrase its 1987–88 organisational campaign, however, openness was not only a necessary adjustment to a new political context, but also an organisational benefit to be enjoyed by fewer and less involved party members.

PARTY ELITES AND PARTY VOTERS

The two main party elites – in the organisation and in the Storting – overlap to a high degree: by and large the top organisational leaders also have a seat in parliament. The tendencies to left–right struggles in the 1970s did not stem from a split between party and parliament, the split ran through both. Nor is there a tendency to increased dissention within the DNA parliamentary group. In the important EEA decision in the Storting in October 1992 only three DNA MPs voted against the treaty. This, of course, could reflect relatively little disagreement over this treaty inside the parliamentary party, but it could also reflect the strong norms which still prevail in terms of majority decisions within the group.

The arena for increasing dissent is, however, the media. There has clearly been a development of more external party debates over the last 20 years. The 'some of us have been talking together' process of closed party decision-making has been changed into 'some of us have been on television'. Systematic research is not available so an illustrative example will have to do: in September 1992 DNA presented the programme for the 1993 election to be debated at the November Congress. But the hope that this would boost party support by capturing the attention of the media was disappointed. The DNA leader of the city council of Oslo, Rune Gerhardsen (the son of the old leader) had gone on television the previous night with the leader of the SV, Erik Solheim, to plead for closer cooperation between the Norwegian left-wing parties. Together they had worked out a private programme for *rapprochement* which they launched on television as the party programme was presented. Immediately the staging was denounced as 'disloyal' by the party leader, but she added: 'if Rune Gerhardsen knows what he is doing'.[27]

Few doubted that he did. The party secretary complained that this was not cleared with the party headquarters, and Gerhardsen was generally condemned by the leaders of the county parties for his private initiative. According to authoritative party opinion Gerhardsen had crossed the border of legitimate activities for such a major party figure. But the same deputy leader who strongly criticised Gerhardsen, Torbjørn Berntsen, had himself been very active in the media when launching his candidature before the 1989 Congress – taking media attention away from the issues. He did not, of course, enlist help from a competing party, so his campaign is not strictly comparable to Gerhardsen's. My point here, however, is that control over the organisational arena does not have the same value to the leadership as it did 20 years ago and that party discipline at the elite level is much weaker.

This weakening of willingness to stay firmly with one's party also holds for the voters. In Norway, as in most of western Europe, there is an increasing volatility in the electorate.[28] The change is not dramatic, but compared to the stable 1960s it is clearly visible: voters, including Labour voters, have started to choose. This again is an important fact when considering the trend towards less cohesion within the party organisation: staying together may still be important in order to reach a decision in parliament, but the cost is also higher in the sense that party voters who are of a different opinion might choose to vote for another party at the next election. One of the first to see that was the elder Gerhardsen, when he argued at party's EC congress in 1972 – as a pro-European – that

if the party did not have any well-known members and spokesmen who were against membership, they ought to get hold of some – in order to make it clear for everyone that one can belong to the Labour Party even if voting [no] in the referendum.[29]

Generational shifts in party politics

When the DNA leader and prime minister, Gro Harlem Brundtland, confirmed in September 1992 that she considered the actions of Rune Gerhardsen to be 'disloyal', she also made it clear that to herself and quite a few of DNA's leaders and members the organisation still matters. The incident made it clear that DNA is not without cohesion, but nor is it without conflict. Even if the tendency is for there to be less conflict, and that it takes a more personalised direction than it used to, the party is no mere label for whoever collects your membership fee – it does put constraints on your politics as well as upon your actions. The DNA, therefore, is not 'irrelevant' in the sense discussed at the beginning of this chapter, but there is still little doubt about the direction of development.

Why has the party moved towards both less conflict and less cohesion? Any answer would have to be tentative, but it is a safe bet that we have to search for it both inside and outside the party organisation. A pressure-cooker can take a higher pressure in the same way as a party with a strong cohesion can take a higher level of conflict. The first EC debate in the 1970s is crucial in this respect: to the new generation entering the party ranks at that period, the use of the party whip was illegitimate. What happened during the 1970s was a clash between two generations – the old one with solidarity and loyalty engraved on all their political behaviour, and the young generation who had been through a quite different school. The newcomers were better educated, they were more mobile, socially as well as geographically, and they were more used to the open politics of a society where the media played an active part. What was normal party discipline for the old generation was unacceptable oligarchy for the young. During the 1980s a new party leadership actively engaged itself in 'modernising' the party organisation, trying to make it more open to new groups and to face a more uncertain environment.

Outside the party organisation there is the well-known change in the media which makes the slow organisational procedures of a traditional political party difficult to follow at the same time as it invites a more personalised politics. Besides the changes in social structure creating a more urbanised middle class, there are also the higher educational levels which contribute to the breakdown of 'the party' as an important and stable point of reference in the lives of voters, members and leaders. In short, today there are alternatives to the DNA in leisure, social milieu and career opportunities which did not present themselves to the older generation.

Notes

1. Nyhamar, C.J., *Nye utfordringer 1955–1990* (Oslo: Tiden), 1990, p. 307.
2. See ibid., pp. 465–97.
3. The importance of 'freedom' was certainly not new in party programmes. The programme of 1949 makes this very clear, but it dealt more with freedom *from* than freedom *to*. See Lorenz, E. (ed.), *Norsk sosialisme i dokumenter* (Oslo: Pax), 1970.
4. Nyhamar, op. cit., 1990, p. 355.
5. *Arbeiderbladet*, 27 February 1989.
6. Førde, E., 'Ideologi i Gros tid', in R. Hirsti, *Gro – midt i livet* (Oslo: Tiden), 1989, p. 44.
7. See, for example, the discussion at her controversial re-election in 1987: DNA, *Landsmøteprotokollen 1987* (Oslo: DNA), 1988, pp. 191–93.
8. *Landsmøteprotokollen 1987*, p. 115.
9. The statement came in a secretly taped, private and very frank telephone conversation in 1981, see Johansen, V. and Jørgensen, P.T., *Edderkoppen* (Oslo: Aventura), 1989, p. 90.
10. Brox, O., *Ta vare på Norge!*, (Oslo: Gyldendal), 1988.
11. Lafferty's views are expressed in Lafferty, W.M., 'Den sosialdemokratiske stat', *Nytt Norsk Tidsskrift*, Vol. 3, No. 1 (1986); and Lafferty, W.M., 'DNAs nye retning', *Nytt Norsk Tidsskrift*, Vol. 4 (1987).
12. Lafferty, 'Den sosialdemokratiske stat', 1986, p. 36.

13. Lafferty, 'Den sosialdemokratiske stat'.
14. Førde, op. cit., 1988, pp. 41–57.
15. Ibid., p. 47.
16. The key being the leader of the city council in Oslo, Rune Gerhardsen, the son of the national 'father figure' leader of successive DNA governments in 1945–65, Einar Gerhardsen. In the autumn of 1993 the *Social Democrats against EC* (Sosialdemokrater mot EF, SME) was founded. The leader was Mr. Halvard Babbe, an MP and previous Secretary of Trade and Commerce.
17. See 'Laws for the Norwegian Labour Party', section 12.1.
18. See, for example, the bitter attack by the party secretary at the time on Einar Gerhardsen's acceptance of the 'anti-membership group' within the party, Bye, R., *Sersjanten* (Oslo: Gyldendal), 1987.
19. Gleditsch, N.P. and Hellevik, O., *Kampen om EF* (Oslo: Pax), 1977, p. 81.
20. *Arbeiderbladet*, 27 April 1992.
21. Heidar, K., Partidemokrati pa prove (Oslo: Universitetsforlaget), 1988, pp. 45–63.
22. I. Leveraas at the 1985 Congress.
23. Svåsand, L. and Strøm, K., 'Organizational Developments in Political Parties', in Svåsand and Strøm (eds), *Challenges to Political Parties*, forthcoming.
24. *Dagbladet*, 25 October 1989.
25. Østbye, H., 'Media in Politics', in Strøm and Svåsand, *Challenges to Political Parties*, forthcoming.
26. DNA, however, has now dropped this.
27. *Arbeiderbladet*, 2 September 1992.
28. Aardal, B. and Valen, H., *Velgere, partier og politisk avstand* (Oslo, Statistisk Sentralbyrå), 1989, Valen, H., Aardal, B. and Vogt, G., *Endring og kontinuitet* (Oslo: Statistik Sentralbyrå), 1990.
29. DNA, *Landsmøteprotokoll* (Oslo: DNA), 1972, p. 90.

6 The French Socialist Party: presidentialised factionalism

David S. Bell and Byron Criddle

Before the 1970s the French Socialist Party was one of the least effective of European socialist parties. From its creation in 1905 it was an intrinsically factionalised party comprising clearly delineated groups which had indeed been distinct parties before 1905, representing reformist and maximalist traditions. After 1920 when it lost much of its manpower and resources to a new communist party, it suffered a competitive environment which precluded easy access to government. After 1945, when communist rivalry racheted upwards to communist dominance of the left, the party entered a period of decline and marginalisation which lasted until the 1960s.[1] Yet from such a condition it was to emerge by its adaptation under François Mitterrand's leadership in the 1970s to a political environment and system of electoral competition offering great opportunities to a skilfully led and government-oriented social democratic party.[2] This chapter focuses on the contemporary party during the particularly propitious decades of the 1970s and 1980s and the rather less certain period that opened up in the 1990s.

In the context of the post-1958 presidentialised political system, which came to bipolarise electoral competition into right and left in the 1960s, the party rose to dominate the opposition to a right-wing coalition continuously in office between 1958 and 1981.[3] With a leader, Mitterrand, skilled in the arts of party management, the party – or rather more accurately Mitterrand – mobilised a broad range of dissenting opinion against a recession-damaged conservative government, and captured in 1981 the commanding height of the French political system, the directly-elected presidency. Socialist governments – the first ever to rest on a parliamentary majority composed of a single party – were installed from 1981 to 1986, and others, albeit relying on only a relative parliamentary majority, between 1988 and 1993; between 1986 and 1988 and after 1993, conservative governments 'cohabited' with the continuing presidential incumbency of Mitterrand.

Mitterrand had taken control of the party in 1971 and led it to office ten years later. In the 1980s it scaled 30 per cent of the vote in three successive elections, and in 1988 Mitterrand was re-elected to the presidency by a wide (54 to 46 per cent) margin. Thereafter, however, support fell dramatically away as it came, in its turn, to pay the price for economic recession and for staleness born of a long period in office. In the 1993 general election the previously dominant party of the 1980s was reduced to 20 per cent of the vote and 67 seats in a 577-seat National Assembly, and for the second time in Mitterrand's presidential incumbency power had to be ceded to a right-wing government – and this time much less ambiguously, on account of its massive parliamentary majority.

The party of the 1970s and 1980s was the party of the man who had fashioned it into an instrument for launching himself into the French presidency.[4] Yet the party Mitterrand had taken over in 1971, the Parti Socialiste (PS), had itself been refashioned two years before from a confluence of the old Section Française de l'Internationale Ouvrière (SFIO, the party founded in 1905) and other groupings of the non-communist left, including Mitterrand's own organisation, the Convention des Institutions Républicaines (CIR, a grouping of vaguely left-wing 'clubs'). The SFIO itself had originally been forged out of pre-existing parties representing distinct traditions – social democratic reformist and maximalist marxist – and in which in time intermittent participationist practice came to be resisted by radical rhetoric. Factional conflict in the interwar era revolved around disputes over participation in 'bourgeois' governments, an issue over which the Radical and thus participation-inclined 'Neo-Socialists' left the party in 1933, or around the matter of the scale and pace of the Socialist-led Popular Front government's reforms; and in 1940 the party's former secretary-general, Paul Faure, led a significant defeatist pacifist minority into support for the Vichy regime. After the Second World War participation became rather more routine, but factional disputes arose over policy matters such as decolonisation (Algeria) or over the exercise of power in the party.

The experience of the party in the Mitterrand years, however, was to see it controlled by a heterogeneous alliance around a pragmatic figure with 'republican' rather than socialist roots, who, responding to the transformed institutional culture of the Fifth Republic, converted it into a force in which factionalism became wholly subordinated to the needs of winning and then retaining the French presidency. Like Jaurès in the SFIO after 1905, Mitterrand possessed a talent for bringing together diverse groups in a common cause. Having in 1965 assembled a broad alliance – including the communists – for his first presidential bid, he took over the PS in 1971 with the votes of its right and left wings – with the municipal socialists with their large memberships in the Nord (led by Pierre Mauroy) and Bouches-du-Rhône (Gaston Defferre) and with the party's avowedly 'Marxist' faction, the Centre d'Etudes, de Recherches et d'Education Socialistes (CERES), led by Jean-Pierre Chevènement. This alliance cemented *la ligne d'Epinay*, the strategic orientation set by Mitterrand in

1971 and involving an alliance with the Communist Party (PCF) around a joint platform.[6] This was to be the political instrument for the party's renewal, for the negotiation of a joint programme with the communists, and for Mitterrand's subsequent strong showing in his second presidential campaign in 1974. The *mélange* of traditions involved in Mitterrand's alliance of factions in 1971 confirmed its essentially electoralist impulsion; namely a strategy to mobilise the large communist electorate in the cause of electing a socialist government. This strategy, however, by giving the PS the electoral boost it needed in the 1974 presidential election and in subsequent by-elections and opinion polls, destabilised the alliance with the PCF which, in order to reassert its physical dominance retreated into a series of polemics against Mitterrand and the PS. Such assaults inevitably undermined the factional alliance behind Mitterrand, with CERES echoing much of the PCF critique of the Socialist Party.[7] In consequence, in 1975 Mitterrand's disparate coalition was replaced by one more impervious to PCF attacks and more conducive to reassuring voters to the party's right: out went CERES and in came Michel Rocard's almost avowedly social democratic group, perceived, in a party where social democratic references were virtually unheard of, as to the right of all other factions.[8]

This second coalition was itself destabilized by the PCF sabotage of the joint programme of the left in 1977 (*la rupture*) and by wrecking tactics designed, successfully, to thwart a left victory at the 1978 general election. Rocard's faction, judging the alliance of the left a hopeless cause, used the occasion to press the claims of a Rocard presidential candidacy for 1981. Rocard made a number of speeches and attacks which confirmed him as a public favourite but which disrupted the party, threw Mitterrand on to the defensive, and ensured for Rocard an enduring dislike among many party activists, as reflected at the rancorous Metz Congress in 1979.

While this congress did not see the break up of Mitterrand's re-formed party, and thus confirmed the extent to which the process of reuniting the left could be judged a success and the PCF campaign to destabilize and break the PS a failure, the congress was exceptionally bitter, and rivalries and animosities then stirred, lingered on into the early 1990s. The Mitterrand faction bestriding the centre of the party, despite its vigorous defence of the leader, did not achieve an overall majority and had to retain its grip on the party through a realliance with the CERES faction which had been reviled since 1975, while Rocard and Mauroy were pushed off the ruling Secretariat.[9]

With Mitterrand's domination of the party thus secured, the presidential challenge from Rocard duly collapsed in the autumn of 1980 with Mitterrand's declared decision to run posing a dilemma for Rocard who had to work conspicuously for victory even though his prospects depended on the failure of Mitterrand's strategy and the weakening of his grip on the party. Rocard had, however, positioned himself in the vital 'social democratic' ground over which future party battles would be fought and which would be relevant to the success of the PS as a governing party after 1981. His 'moderate' posture was also to pay dividends when French politics changed in the mid-1980s following the steep decline of the PCF.[10]

With Mitterrand's outflanking of Rocard in early 1981, the basic strength of the new party began to reassert itself and Mitterrand emerged in the opinion polls as the front-runner and despite its 'War of the Roses' the party reunited behind Mitterrand's third presidential bid. The party demonstrated an unexpected unity with Rocard and Mauroy playing full parts in the campaign. Such unity − a major factor in the 1981 presidentials − significantly contrasted with the disunity of the incumbent right.

With Mitterrand in the Elysée, all party faction leaders, Rocard, Chevènement and Defferre were given senior (minister of state) status in government, while Mauroy was made prime minister. Rocard, however, was punished for having challenged Mitterrand by being sent to the marginalised planning ministry, where he languished until March 1983 when a government U-turn from reflation to retrenchment put his strategy unavoidably on the agenda once again. The post-victory Valence Congress of 1981 also saw all factions − now decapitated by ministerial office − relegated to minorities, and the promotion of Mitterrand loyalists to all important posts in the party, as in the government.[11]

Mitterrand's strategy appeared to have been vindicated by the 1981 victory, and his subtle form of anti-communism was about to eliminate the PCF by bringing it into government and so deprive it of its protest articulation, or 'tribune', function. However, the rhetorical 'rupture' with capitalism, trailed in PS pronouncements before 1981, soon ran into economic problems. Mitterrand was pushing rapid reforms against other members of the party including the prime minister. The finance minister, Jacques Delors, made himself the spokesman for a more restrained approach to the economics of growth, contesting the policy of reflation from below (by popular consumption), and calling for restraint on public spending and a 'pause' in the reform programme (a less than innocent remark since it recalled Léon Blum's vocabulary at the time of his Popular Front government's U-turn in 1937). Rocard was unable to speak out, but Delors did; the result was that Delors' popularity rose to make him one of the stars of the government. Delors had made his career under Mitterrand's patronage but, less even than Rocard, had been unable to establish a base in the party and was therefore unable to capitalize on a popularity which made him a potential future presidential contender.

When the policy U-turn eventually came in 1983, and the economic expansion was slowed down, the CERES left's Chevènement quit the government and in 1984 a church schools' nationalisation bill, dear to party activists, was withdrawn. The role of these two humiliations for the Mitterrand visionaries was to throw into doubt the entire project. The result was a predictable U-turn in the party, which began to describe itself as 'social democratic', to take up the catch-all themes of 'modernity' and to abandon Marxist vocabulary. The scene was set for the deradicalisation of the party's discourse by the educative impact of government office after 1981.[12]

In government, after 1981 it was considered disastrous to allow factional war to erupt into congress battles, and a series of single resolutions (or resolutions and amendments ending in composites) were imposed at each congress until that at Rennes in 1990. At the Valence Congress of 1981 a single motion was presented. At the Bourg-en-Bresse Conference in 1983, Chevènement, having left the government in protest over economic policy, was proposing a siege economy and his CERES amendment took 18.1 per cent of the votes, but was readily composited with the other main resolutions. At the Toulouse Congress in 1985, in the run-up to the 1986 parliamentary elections, it was Rocard who was booed as he tabled a dissenting resolution. He too had quit the government (in opposition, ostensibly, to the introduction of proportional representation for the 1986 election), and garnered a healthy 28.6 per cent of the vote; but again a unanimous composite was agreed by the end of the congress.

The Lille Congress of 1987 was held during the 'cohabitation' of President Mitterrand with the right-wing government led by the neo-gaullist prime minister, Jacques Chirac. In such a particularly fraught battle between the president and the right, the party was in no mood to cause problems and accordingly, the congress was almost drained of interest, with the leadership organizing a vast rally on the last day for want of anything to occupy the agenda. But during this time the party underwent a little noticed change: it discarded revolutionary rhetoric to become a genuine party of government (although its statutes were not altered until 1990).[13]

The 1990 Rennes Congress saw emerging conflict over the post-Mitterrand succession with the implosion of his faction and rivalry between its leading contender, Laurent Fabius, and Lionel Jospin, and between them and the perennial presidential aspirant, Rocard. In January 1992 a *modus vivendi* was reached between Rocard and Fabius in the run-up to important elections, with Fabius taking the leadership while virtually conceding Rocard's claims to the 1995 presidential nomination.

But March 1993 saw the party going down to a crushing defeat that implied the loss of all the electoral ground gained in the twenty years of Mitterrand's hegemony. In anticipation of such a defeat Rocard, in February 1993, had launched a proposal for a 'big bang' to create a reformed Socialist Party encompassing 'centrist' voters from the right, the growing ranks of youthful idealists in the green parties, and those communists disaffected by the PCF's sclerotic stalinism. Immediately after the election, Rocard staged a takeover of the leadership at a meeting of its directing committee, ousting Fabius, a move prompting Chevènement to declare his own exit from the party. Thus 1993 saw the party in a state of severe demoralisation and confusion.

Measuring the factions

In French left-wing parlance 'faction' is a term used to describe a group within a party or a union, directed from outside. Militant in the British Labour Party, or *Unité et Action* in the FEN (Fédération de l'Education Nationale — French teachers' union) are 'factions', but there are none such in the PS. The pejorative meaning given to the term is one reason why it is not considered respectable, but the existence of *currents* of opinion and highly structured groups competing within the organisation has been a feature of French socialism from its origins. We shall call these 'factions', contrary to French political usage.

French socialism, while an early growth in Europe, was very badly divided between rival groups formed around individual leaders. These groups were united in 1905 into the SFIO, but the price of this fragile unity was the recognition of the existing 'factions' — the former political parties which had coalesced to form the SFIO. This continued throughout the lifetime of the SFIO (1905–69) with groups being organised, and with the competition between them being one of the principal features of the life of the party. One of the factions, the 'Neo-Socialists' was expelled in August 1933 and took with it several federations and leaders (into the Parti Socialiste Ouvrière et Paysan). The party was also divided by the defence question into the 'Paulfauristes' (later to become Vichyite) and Blumists before the War.

After the War, Guy Mollet (leader from 1946 to 1969) proposed the elimination of factions and abolished them on the party's Directing Committee by having it elected on a single winner-takes-all slate. Nevertheless, although Mollet retained the leadership of the SFIO for the rest of its history, it was plagued by intense battles over issues such as Europe and the Algerian war. The rivalry between Mollet (ostensibly of the left) and Defferre enlivened the last two decades of the SFIO.

The new Parti Socialiste, formed in 1969, was intended to repeat the process of amalgamation of the left as conducted by Jaurès in 1905. Nevertheless, the founders were mindful of the lessons of the factional fighting of the old SFIO. The result was an ambiguous compromise which outlawed organised *tendances* (a rule of which CERES was later to fall foul), but re-established the system of electing the leadership by proportional representation on the basis of signed resolutions voted on at party congresses. These resolutions became the basis for the estimation of the strength of factions, if not of their coherence, given that people sign for very different reasons, and although there were powerful sub-factions not officially so counted.

Resolutions are published in the party's *Le Poing et la rose* with a list of signatures appended. These are then sent down to activists for debate, amendment and voting.[14] The leadership of the party at local level is decided by votes on these resolutions. Resolutions have to poll over 5 per cent of the activists in order for their backers to be represented on the

131-strong Directing Committee, which then elects the first secretary, the Executive Bureau (27) and the National Secretariat (the latter of variable size, though 13-strong in 1992). The Secretariat is the key to the struggle and its places are occupied by the majority in the party (that is, the supporters of the majority resolution, if there is one): the distribution of Secretariat posts thus becomes a major factor in the process of compositing rival resolutions. Within the Secretariat, the control of the party organization is a key post, with its holder regarded as the party's second in command. For most of the 1980s it was held by Jean Poperen, but on falling out with Jospin (leader from 1981 to 1988), he was replaced at the 1990 Rennes Congress by Marcel Debarge. With Fabius' takeover as leader in January 1992, it went to a Rocardian. Other Secretariat posts of importance are those of finance, the federations, elections, information, and party education. There are no fixed hierarchies and some posts can become significant objects of struggle, such as (in the 1970s) workplace sections, and then disappear. Local (*département*-level) federations are run along similar lines with posts divided according to faction strength.

The party congress, held over a weekend every two years, is formally the focus for decisions on strategy and leadership. In fact the compositing of resolutions – the important wrangling – goes on behind closed doors without the ordinary delegates having a much better idea of what is happening than the attentive reader of the press. The committee for compositing the resolutions (on which the factions are represented proportionally) meets on the last night of the congress, and sometimes can sit for days, as at Rennes (1990), where, because of quarrels over the attribution of delegates, bargaining in the committee did not start until the last hour of the congress and went on to the following week.

The factional line-up

Just as the party, in response to the institutional demands of the Fifth Republic, was presidentialised by Mitterrand, so its factional conflicts came to be characterised by rivalry between those seeking, like Rocard, and Fabius, or more questionably Chevènement, to inherit the presidential mantle, or whose ambitions lay more realistically in running the party (such as Mauroy and Jospin).[15] Factions more ideologically defined – such as CERES and the Poperenists – adapted to presidentialism less easily, and were accordingly marginalised.

The most important faction until the early 1990s was the Mitterrand faction which, although never surmounting 50 per cent, managed, through alliances, to dominate the party in one form or another for twenty years following Mitterrand's coup in 1971. This group was itself composed of diverse currents and after 1986 suffered from quarrels between rival presidential hopefuls. The term 'Mitterrandist' denotes nothing specific other than a devotion to the 'works and acts' of François Mitterrand. The perception – correct as it turned out – was that Mitterrand was the only possible leader of the left in the 1970s as its only credible presidential figure, and that the alliance with the PCF – his strategic choice – was the only possible route to power. Part of Mitterrand's political force was an astonishing ability to speak with many voices (now through Fabius, now through Joxe) to the bafflement of opponents and to the gratification of the variety of interests and sub-currents brought together in a personal coalition around the leader.

Mitterrand's 'left' strategy was in fact a strategy to stifle the PCF in a close embrace, and to replace communist with socialist electoral hegemony. It paid off in 1981 despite there being no perceptible Mitterrandist ideology, agenda or programme. The Common Programme of the left (1972–77) was, for example, never *Mitterrand*'s programme, and was ignored by him in his 1974 presidential campaign. In a long career he had moved seemingly from right to left across the ideological spectrum, leaving few footprints; it was impossible to say who the real Mitterrand was. There was a vague appeal to social justice and a preference for strong state intervention in Mitterrand's later (presidential) pronouncements, but not enough to be incompatible with the centrist (usually Catholic) social reformists wooed after 1986 for electoral reasons.[16]

In Mitterrand's faction the first important sub-group was the former Convention des Institutions Républicaines set up in the early 1960s outside Mollet's SFIO. This 'first generation' of Mitterrandists prospered mightily in the distribution of government posts under Mitterrand's presidency. It included Edith Cresson, Pierre Joxe, Roland Dumas, and Louis Mermaz. Mitterrand's friend, the late Georges Dayan, played a key role in promoting a second generation (non-CIR Mitterrandists who entered the PS without preliminaries) as a sort of talent-spotter. This second group, sometimes called '*sabras*', entered the party under Mitterrand's aegis as it rose electorally in the 1970s, and acquired a reservoir of individuals to staff the apparatus and to negotiate with the PCF. These '*sabras*' included Paul Quilès, Lionel Jospin (who replaced Mitterrand as party first secretary in 1981) and Laurent Fabius.

Other 'personalities' with some independent standing rallied to the Mitterrand banner during the 1970s, notably Jacques Delors. To these may be added the many sub-currents which while retaining an identity around a leader of their own, were in almost permanent alliance with the Mitterrandists: notably, the 'left-wing' Poperen, and, more important because of their 'block votes', the moderate leaders of the Nord and Bouches-du-Rhône, Mauroy and (until his death in 1986) Defferre.

Mitterrand's faction – as the party's legitimist core – survived the policy U-turn of 1983 and the replacement of the Mauroy government (1981–84) by one led by Fabius (1984–86), but the simultaneous movement of the PCF into rancorous opposition in 1984 meant the end of Mitterrand's 'left union' strategy — and a turn to the centre. This duly paid off in the presidential election of 1988 where Mitterrand secured re-election by 54 to 46 per cent. What shattered the faction, however, was the quarrel between Fabius and Jospin and the centrifugal forces unleashed by the race for the post-Mitterrand presidential nomination. Pierre Mauroy (backed by Jospin) defeated Fabius (Mitterrand's candidate) to become first secretary in 1988.[17] In January 1992 Mauroy gave up the leadership of a diversifying, failing and increasingly unpopular party, which no longer seemed to be an essential part of the presidential weaponry. By 1992 Mitterrand had no further use for his faction nor it for him.

The Mitterrand faction was not inheritable by the most presidentially ambitious of its leaders, Fabius, despite his attempt to present himself as the heir-apparent. Born in 1946, the son of a rich Parisian antique dealer, he had an impressive start at the elite 'Sciences-Po' University and Ecole Nationale d'Administration (ENA) before entering the Conseil d'Etat. He joined the PS, aged 27, in 1973, and in 1975 became Mitterrand's economics adviser, heading the party's economics group, and by 1977 was both an elected local official (mayor), and on the party's Directing Committee. In 1978 he was elected to the National Assembly for Seine-Maritime and rose rapidly in Mitterrand's entourage. He made a famous contribution (attacking Rocard) at the Metz Congress, at which Mitterrand is supposed to have said that Fabius was the person 'who best expressed my thoughts'. After the election of 1981 he was made minister of the budget (1981–83), industry minister (1983–84) and then prime minister (1984–86). He held the powerful and sensitive post of president of the (hung) National Assembly from 1988 to 1992 before becoming the party's first secretary. In order to build support for the Rennes Congress of 1990 he worked the party's 'rubber chicken circuit', outdoing even Rocard in his wooing of the activists. He also had enemies, and there were doubts over his abilities (in particular, his steadiness under fire), his immense smoothness, rich bourgeois origins, and (if unspoken) his Jewish background. He had, from being an 'archaic' revolutionary, become the leading 'moderniser'. His self-presentation as prime minister was as a deutero-Rocard, emphasising the dynamics of the market, restructuring, competition and technology. The problems of inequalities and the rise of the National Front were later adopted as issues. For Fabius the party also required modernisation — his bull point at Rennes in 1990. He, like Rocard in the latter's 1993 initiative, envisaged the creation of a bigger party, enlarged to include 'sympathisers', reducing membership fees, increasing workplace sections, increasing the number of women, and encompassing former communists. He had the support of many former Mitterrandists, and was seen as the 'presidential' hopeful by the faction; in 1992 a deal with Rocard allowed him to control the party. Fabius was not able to capitalise on this alliance to secure control of the apparatus because he was closely watched by Rocard's supporters and because of the debilitating, wracking and continuing threat of prosecution over the use by the French health service of Aids-contaminated blood while he was prime minister. Strong in Seine-Maritime, his fief, Fabius also made breakthroughs in the big Bouches-du-Rhône and the Pas-de-Calais federations. The struggle with Jospin (education minister after 1988) pushed Fabius into the teachers' unions and earned him the support of the FEN leaders, André Henry and Jacques Pommantau, and many teachers who resented Jospin's weak reaction (as minister) to Islamic fundamentalism (the issue of veils in schools), the communist-led Syndicat National de l'Enseignement Secondaire (SNES) teachers' union and the Church. He was ousted by Rocard after the 1993 elections but remained strongly supported in the parliamentary party.

Fabius' rival, Lionel Jospin, another Mitterrandist 'sabra', came from an SFIO family, via Sciences-Po and ENA, originally intending a diplomatic career. He joined the new Socialist Party in 1971 (as a result of a friendship with Pierre Joxe), entered the Secretariat in 1973, took charge of the monitoring of PS–PCF relations, and became spokesman on Third World affairs in 1975. The hammer of CERES in the Paris federation, he was elected a Paris councillor in 1977, and a Paris deputy in 1978. In 1979 he became the party's international secretary and was seen as a possible 'dauphin' from that time by wide sections of the party, a feeling confirmed when he was made first secretary as Mitterrand withdrew to fight for the presidency in the 1981 elections. In 1986 he became deputy for Haute-Garonne and from 1988 to 1992 was education minister. He had opportunities – both as first secretary (1981–88) and as education minister, but made little of them. His position by 1990 was that of a blocking – 'not-Fabius' – force, with little expectation of his own advancement, and by 1993, losing his Assembly seat, he had virtually backed out of party politics.[18]

Among Mitterrandist fellow-travellers was Jean Poperen. Poperen was in the Communist Resistance with his brother (Claude, once a PCF politburo member) but was excluded from the PCF in 1958 and became one of the founders of the Parti Socialiste Unifié (PSU) (from which he was in turn excluded in 1967 by Michel Rocard). He created his own small left grouping, the Union des Groupes et Clubs Socialistes (UGCS), and joined the new Socialist Party in 1969. He first associated with CERES but joined the Mitterrand majority in 1975 and remained in it thereafter while retaining his factional identity. He became the party's 'number two' in 1981 but enjoyed poor relations with Jospin, who deprived him of his Secretariat post in 1987. Elected deputy for the Rhône in 1973, in 1988 he became minister for relations with parliament ('chief whip'). At the 1990 Rennes Congress his small group polled a mere 7 per cent, drawing ironically, given his repeated strictures against the old SFIO, from the old socialist areas in the Loire and the Midi as well as from areas of Rocardism, from secularists (Poperen being vigorously secularist on the issue of private schools and Islamic fundamentalism), and from left-wingers objecting to the party's centrist drift.

Pierre Mauroy (president of the Socialist International after 1992) rose as head the federation of the Nord, less a faction than a continuation of the old socialist municipal tradition of the SFIO activist base which the Nord retained in the lean years. It was Mauroy who brought Mitterrand to the leadership of the PS in 1971 and remained a faithful supporter thereafter – even during 1979–81 when he was with Rocard in 'opposition'. He was the party's 'number two' from 1971 to 1979 and prime minister from 1981 to 1984 but, despite support for a reconstructed alliance of the left, he was no radical in government and called for restraint well before 1983. He ran the party as first secretary from 1988 to 1991, but was hamstrung by the factional rivalries and relinquished the position to Fabius.

The most innovative of the factions, though not the most politically astute, has been that of Michel Rocard.[19] The core is the group – mostly Catholic and former Confédération Française Démocratique du Travail (CFDT) – which followed Rocard through the PSU, was seen as the most credible instrument for the renewal of the non-communist left, and then into the new Parti Socialiste after the presidential election of 1974. The group was formed around the most eminent of the post-Mitterrand presidential possibles – but had neither been well structured, nor made the impact that might have been expected given the 'failure' of Mitterrand's leftist strategy. Challenging Mitterrand in 1980 was, in retrospect, a mistake. Michel Rocard, born in 1930, had a remarkable early career – in common with most leading socialist figures of the 1980s – at Sciences-Po and ENA, becoming an *inspecteur des finances* and an SFIO member. Leaving the SFIO in 1958 over its Algerian policy, he continued an active political career while a civil servant and was close to Mendès France. He became secretary general of the PSU in 1967 and entered a 'radical' phase. As PSU presidential candidate in 1969, he polled 3.6 per cent and then defeated the former Gaullist premier, Couve de Murville, in the Yvelines by-election in the same year. In 1973 he lost the seat, but took a big part in Mitterrand's presidential campaign in 1974 and joined the Parti Socialiste at the 'Assises', organised by Mauroy the same year. He entered the party's Secretariat in 1975 and in 1977 became mayor of Conflans St. Honorine (in his former Yvelines seat). During the Nantes Congress of 1977, ostensibly criticising CERES, Rocard began to make a more distinctive mark as a 'social democrat' (if not himself exactly using the term), and in 1978 regained his parliamentary seat.

The devastation of the left by the PCF's sabotage of the 1978 election caused Rocard to move out of cover and contest Mitterrand's strategy of alliance with the communists as well as the PS's 'archaic' stances, and launch a bid for the 1981 presidential nomination; hence the clash at the Metz Congress in 1979. When Rocard's presidential bid failed in the face of Mitterrand's decision to run, Rocard had to keep his head down as his faction became the object of attack. He was 'rewarded' with the planning ministry in 1981, and the difficult agriculture ministry in 1983, but resigned in 1985. The resignation enabled Rocard to regroup his support in the country, and strengthen his faction to the extent of polling almost one in three of the votes at the Toulouse Congress in 1986. Subsequently no majority in the party was available without the Rocardists. The policy U-turn and the collapse of the alliance with the communists seemed to have brought the Rocardist hour, but the suspicion of Rocard in the party was intense, and a 'Foot/Healey' problem remained: Rocard (like Healey) was unpopular with activists but a winner with public opinion. It was a mark of the desperation of Mitterrand that Rocard was made prime minister in 1988, acknowledging that he was indisputably the person best placed to open out political appeal to the centre and to manage the post-1988 hung parliament.[20] Rocard's tenure at the Matignon (1988–91) was prolonged by the Gulf crisis (1990–91) but, if the relationship with the president was glacial from the outset, Rocard did succeed in leaving a mark on government and left office still a very popular politician.

The Rocard faction has operated under different organizations and mastheads. It was organised by the 1990s, around the publication of *Lettre d'information*, and the *Convaincre* society. An important and innovative aspect of Rocardism – in fact its main strength – was the faction's ability to play simultaneously on two registers: public opinion and party opinion. The use of public opinion against the party activists meant that Rocard's network of sympathising 'fellow-travellers', journals and free-floating intellectuals was of prime importance. Notwithstanding Rocard's own Protestant background, a Catholic bias was reflected in the social composition of the faction, with strength in the areas into which the socialists moved after 1971 (the west, the Paris region, Savoy, Gers and Vaucluse). Unable to make much headway in the old SFIO areas, and failing to take over the Bouches-du-Rhône after Defferre's death, the Rocardists compensated by concentrating on public opinion and at the 1990 Rennes Congress prudently eschewed mounting an attack on other factions.[21]

Rocard's originality lay in style, method, outlook and ideology. He abandoned the impenetrable leftist 1960s jargon of the PSU to come up with a form of 'straight talking' (*parler vrai*) which invariably involved telling unpleasant social democratic truths to socialist activists with a provocative lucidity. The pragmatic and didactic method, direct from Mendès France, allied to a social democratic/'Mendèsiste' search for consensus, was illustrated by the settlement he negotiated in New Caledonia in June 1988, and in his general management of the hung parliament after 1988, which involved the placating of centrist opinion.

He was the first to point out the inadequacy of the old-fashioned nationalization and state-centred socialism as well as to deliver lessons on the necessity of the market and on its superiority to state planning. Thus was reformism defended with vigour and against the supposedly 'revolutionary' currents of the Parti Socialiste. Rocard's concept of 'self-management' – later replaced by 'autonomy' – meant in reality a limited role for the state: a recognition that society should drive the state and not vice versa. In

economics he demanded a regulating state and a maximum of decentraliza-
tion. (He had spoken at the Nantes Congress in 1977 of a left divided into
'statist' and 'pluralist' cultures.) This, however, did not make him an extreme
free-marketeer, rather the advocate of the need for the state to intervene to
protect the market from itself and to correct its short-termism – a mixed
economy in which the state reduces inequalities. In sum, socialism, for
Rocard, is not an ideology but a method (consensus), a value system and a
moral question. It is as near as any leading French socialist came to
delineating a social democratic theory.

In all this, Rocard managed to make himself disliked in the party. As
such, there had been no equivalent socialist leader since Guy Mollet. Many
members feared, quite rightly, that there was no place for them in the
Rocardist scheme of a vast rally to bring together unions, interest groups
and individuals to create a broad presidential coalition. Moreover, the
period which Rocard spent at the Matignon (1988–91) was not without its
critics; in particular, the 'social deficit' (the unattended-to poverty and
unemployment) was attributed to his inaction. The refusal to promise a
march to the sunlit uplands was also criticised: what is the left without a
vision?

Yet, leaving the Matignon in 1991, Rocard remained popular with public
opinion, and to that extent well on the road to a presidential campaign. He
was better-placed than any other possible socialist candidate with the
exception of Jacques Delors (whose poll rating was also good). He also
reflected a new form of socialism liberated from the PCF, and from the
state-centred solutions of the past. His stint as prime minister made him a
credible candidate with experience of major office, with apparent, if
unarticulated, Mitterrandist anointing. Rivalries inside the Mitterrandist
faction between Jospin and Fabius, aided his prospects, as did his seeming
'deal' with Fabius in 1992, until Rocard's administering of the *coup de grâce*
to Fabius in April 1993 when Fabius, an embattled leader who had led the
PS to humiliating defeat in the 1993 elections, was replaced by Rocard as
first secretary.

The faction attracting the most media and academic attention in the 1970s
was CERES, after 1986 renamed Socialisme et République (with a small
group remaining faithful to the old 'CERES' but which subsequently allied
to Poperen's group). The former CERES group remained, in the early 1990s,
led by the small circle around Jean-Pierre Chevènement – Pierre Guidoni,
Didier Motchane, Michel Charzat and Georges Sarre (the three musketeers
in the Dumas tradition expanded to five) and occasionally included others,
like Max Gallo. Publishing *République* and, in the past, many other journals,
it was notably prolific in writers.[22]

CERES, founded inside the old SFIO in 1966, had by 1969 made enough
progress to take over the party's Paris federation. In 1971 it contributed to
the coalition electing Mitterrand as leader. Its importance at that time was
that it was virtually the one structured faction in the party (indeed, 'a party

within the party') and played a decisive part in contributing to the party's renewal in respect of workplace sections, the youth movement and ideology. The faction was 'fellow-travelling' – not in a simple sense, but using communist pressure on the party to advance its own position. Hence it continually relayed PCF criticisms and accused the leadership of 'drifting rightward', breaking with Mitterrand in 1975 (when its congress vote stood at 25 per cent). The collapse of the PS–PCF alliance in 1977, on which it had grounded its identity and its power, was a blow from which it never recovered. Although the Metz Congress of 1979 brought it back into the leadership, it was at the price of the desertion of the bulk of its supporters and the terminal weakening of its intellectual support. Chevènement, a minister from 1981, left government in 1983, but returned as education minister from 1984 to 1986.[23] The possibility of CERES becoming a left-wing opposition was definitively past and the Marxist vision which it had vigorously promoted was dropped in 1986. The faction was fully reintegrated into the leadership and its acceptance of the government's policy in 1984 (more austere than in 1983) in its totality, had a devastating effect on CERES as a self-styled left-wing faction. At the Rennes Congress (1990) it fell to 8.5 per cent and was sidelined. An alliance with Poperen to constitute a new left, though an obvious option, was quickly dropped.

CERES was resented within the party for its echoing of communist criticisms as it took up an extreme *marxisant* stance in opposition to 'social democracy' – specifically to Rocard (dubbed 'the American left'), and also to a lesser extent, the later Fabius. It saw itself – as to some extent it was – the ideological pacemaker of the party, yet it was also a sort of intellectual inquisition on the lookout for 'social democratic' deviation. It also proclaimed itself to be the vanguard of the revolution and developed a theory of the revolution from below, guided by CERES and improbably including the PCF.

A distinct feature of CERES was its strong nationalism, expressed either in an extreme anti-Europeanism (or anti-Germanism) or anti-Americanism. CERES was the proponent of the 'Albanian' solution in 1983 – the protectionist answer to the balance-of-payments crisis of the time – and had an unmistakably Gaullist – ourselves alone – outlook on defence and foreign affairs. It was, in particular, one of the first groups in the party to rally to the French nuclear bomb. Chevènement, the group's presidential aspirant, had a brief period of glory as an orthodox minister of education (1984–86) but was a dissenting minister of defence before resigning (for the second time) in 1991 over the Gulf war and campaigned against the Maastricht Treaty on European Union in the 1992 referendum. By 1993 what remained of CERES was strong in the Belfort (Chevènement's seat, retained in the débâcle of 1993) and in Paris, but it had disappeared from about forty of the departments where the PS was globally strong. In April 1993, following Rocard's coup, Chevènement declared himself resigned from the party.

The Rennes Congress 1990

The apogee of the party's factional power struggle was reached at the Rennes Congress in 1990, two years into the Rocard government's term of office and with the party archons deciding that it had to display a full-throated consensus to the public to avoid the bruising struggles which had often damaged it in the past. This was in fact a necessity. French public opinion, already increasingly disenchanted by party strife, scandals and *la politique politicienne*, does not take kindly to arcane factional disputes and especially not in a governing party – as evidenced by the decline of the right in the 1970s.

But despite the imperative need to present a united face to the public, the Rennes Congress immediately descended into in-fighting, with the factional landscape revealed in full bloom. The difference from previous congresses where factional in-fighting had taken place, however, was that the competition was shorn of any ideological or issue-oriented content.[24] Because the party was in government without an overall majority, any policy issues presented too openly would have damaged the government. Moreover, centripetal forces were driving French politics to converge on the centre. Whilst Chevènement tried to sneak in an anti-European paragraph to the Congress's resolution, this was dismissed by Delors (who saw Chevènement as '*un cas désespéré*') and quickly removed so as not to impede the free flow of combinations.

The party struggle was about the post-Mitterrand era: over who would control the party and who would secure the 1995 presidential nomination when the president stepped down. Here the split in the Mitterrand faction became fully manifest, while plainly evident before the 1986 elections when Fabius and Jospin, the two major figures in the Mitterrand camp, had fallen out. The Rennes Congress found Fabius and Jospin at loggerheads, with Fabius making a failed run for the party leadership and encountering the same combination which had denied him – despite Mitterrand's blessing – the post in 1988. The congress confirmed that the Mitterrand faction was no longer directly amenable to presidential instruction (with instructions passed down to the faction leaders by the Elysée's envoy, Mme Cresson). Jospin, on the one hand – with a low popular rating – had no real possibility of taking the presidential nomination. Fabius, as a more credible presidential contender, could conceivably have expected a nomination from those in the party who did not want Rocard, but a degree of rather too obvious political manoeuvring, and an attempt to claim the position too brusquely, had again united a coalition against the former prime minister. Subtlety was not, however, to be expected from the man who as prime minister had managed in a TV 'face to face' to make even the neo-Gaullist leader Jacques Chirac appear sympathetic.

The line-up at Rennes delineated the putative post-Mitterrand factional configuration, with two groups emerging from the former Mitterrandist faction – those around Mauroy and Jospin, and those supporting Fabius:

Mauroy/Jospin	28.9%
Fabius	28.8%
Rocard	24.5%
Chevènement	8.5%
Poperen	7.2%
Others	2.0%

Mitterrandistes de foi dispersed themselves over the rival (ex-Mitterrandist) motions, with – for example – Mermaz aligning with Mauroy/Jospin, and Bérégovoy (finance minister 1984–86 and 1988–92, and to be prime minister in 1992–93) siding with Fabius. With Rocard's strong showing the party was effectively divided into three parts, and this, despite instructions from the Elysée enjoining unity, and similar, traditional cries from the conference delegates. The congress ended, for the first time in twenty years, without a deal being struck between the various factions. Mitterrand had sought traditionally either to impose unanimity or, failing that, to divide and rule. His concern in his second term was to prevent a clear successor emerging, no matter how desirable that was in the long-term interests of the party. Thus, the most obvious examples of presidential timber – Rocard and Delors – were kept without support, particularly the former, who was, as a popular, respected and beleaguered prime minister, always on the brink of taking the presidential nomination. Mitterrand's preoccupation had become increasingly with his place in history, to which end, in the short term, he sought to avoid becoming a lame duck president in the shadow of a designated successor. In this restricted sense the divisions of the Rennes Congress served him well.

Divergence between the interests of a declining president and those of the party were, however, increasingly hard to ignore. Various records were being broken; a record low socialist rating in the polls – a consequence in part of the ill-judged appointment of Edith Cresson as prime minister (1991–92); a record low Fifth Republic presidential rating for Mitterrand; and a financial scandal concerning the funding of Mitterrand's 1988 campaign and involving the president of the National Assembly (Henri Emmanuelli), to be followed in 1992 by the implication of Prime Minister Bérégovoy in a corruption case. The party had slumped since 1988 in all social categories: manual workers (−13 per cent), white-collar employees (−17 per cent), professionals (−14 per cent), secondary educated (−16 per cent) and under 35s (−15 per cent). Many supporters had deserted to the expanding Greens, and the party sought to woo them back by such means as including figures from the environmentalist movement – for example, Brice Lalonde – in the government. The impending loss of office with the end of the Mitterrand presidency was prefigured in an unconvincingly narrow acceptance of his

European policy in the September 1992 referendum on the Maastricht Treaty – and in the general election rout of March 1993.

Conclusion

The role played by François Mitterrand in the history of the contemporary French Socialist Party cannot be exaggerated. It was his leadership that transformed the party into a party of government – in the sense of being a party lacking any real autonomy of a socialist government – and thus exposed it to a process of 'maturation' it might otherwise have been denied. Both the party's general election successes – the landslide of 1981, and the near-victory of 1988 when it emerged a dozen seats short of a majority – were achieved in the wake of personal triumphs won by Mitterrand in presidential elections: his victory over President Giscard d'Estaing in 1981, and his convincing dispatch by an 8 per cent margin of Jacques Chirac in 1988. The implied electoral indispensability of Mitterrand was challenged only once – in 1978 by Michel Rocard – and did little to advance the challenger's prospects. Thus, in the twenty years of Mitterrand's hegemony, he – or his proxies within the leadership – encountered few of the difficulties associated with leadership-activist relations in European social democratic parties, and this notwithstanding the more avowedly 'Marxist' tradition reflected in French socialist rhetoric, a tradition sustained until the early 1980s by the postwar dominance of the landscape of the French left by the Communist Party.

In the 1970s, the 'one last heave' theory – applied in opposition parties slowly advancing on power election by election – was employed to justify 'free hands' for the leader, and rank-and-file submissiveness. The more idealistic activists were, in any case, reconciled to quiescence by the existence of an alliance with the Communist Party which prevailed, in one form or another, until the communists left government office in 1984. Thereafter, the Socialist Party entered openly into a more avowedly centrist phase. Shorn of the veto power of a (now declining) Communist Party, and – more important – denied an electoral majority by the demise of the communist *vote*, the Socialist Party was impelled to bid for votes in the centre. Such a strategy occurred *faute de mieux*, but it was equally implicit in the sort of Downsian electoral competition imposed by the presidential electoral system.

Once in office, after 1981, the alibis available to the party leadership (collectively no more or less than the expression of the will of the president of the republic), were legion. The first socialist government in a generation had to be given the benefit of the doubt, the financial orthodoxy imposed after 1983 being justified in terms of the government's need to survive the 1986 general election. Thereafter – with that election lost – the *cohabitation* of President Mitterrand with Chirac's right-wing government required the party's quiescence in order that Mitterrand might negotiate successfully the awkward passage to the 1988 presidential election at which socialist control over the government could be restored. That presidential election duly secured and parliament dissolved, the hung parliament then elected put a premium on supporting loyally Rocard's beleaguered minority government, constantly juggling with centrist deputies in order to preserve its parliamentary base.

Thus, one way or another, the Mitterrand years saw a party in which, whether in opposition or in office, discord was progressively submerged by electoral exigencies.[25] The supremacy of such electoralism was acknowledged at a special party conference in Paris in December 1991 where, in the run-up to regional (1992) and general (1993) elections, the party endorsed a policy statement embracing unequivocally the sort of social democratic reformism practised – if not preached – by each of the handful of socialist-led governments in France since Blum's Popular Front in 1936. The policy statement gained the endorsement of 81 per cent of the membership, with a mere 12 per cent opting for a 'socialist' alternative proposed by Chevènement, and 6 per cent for another minority position. The interpersonal in-fighting at the Rennes Congress was conspicuously avoided at the Paris meeting. Against a backdrop of the supposedly mobilizing catch-all themes of 'Europe' and hostility to the 'fascism' of the National Front, the factional leaders reallocated the contested roles between them: Fabius replacing Mauroy as leader, and Rocard being named as the 'virtual' presidential candidate. The blandness of the new programme served to highlight the essentially personal rivalries the party's factionalism had now come to express.

It was clear, however, that, post-Mitterrand, the party seemed set to face challenges quite unlike the games of musical chairs played out among its barons (or 'elephants' as they became known) during the years of office after 1981. The dislocation of the party into rival bands pursuing the post-Mitterrand presidential mantle, and the electoral collapse in 1993, appeared to threaten the analysis of the party as a consensus-based defactionalised party of government. The gap between the highly educated people in the party's elite and the rank and file, the alleged demoralisation of the latter over Mitterrand's centrist strategy in the elections of 1988, and the 'ideological draining' of the party, have all been alluded to elsewhere.[26] Much depended (in mid-1993) on the capacity of ambitious figures such as Rocard or Delors to mount a realistic challenge to the presidency on Mitterrand's departure, whether in 1995 or before. Rocard's initiative in February 1993 proposing a broadened coalition reflected the general problem facing social democratic parties everywhere, namely how to reconcile the decline of the blue-collar working class both with the 'post-materialist' interests of the younger voters and with the rising free-market demands of an individualist generation. It was not inconceivable that a viable alliance could be assembled around a figure such as Rocard and that such a candidacy would find endorsement within the party, where no ideological or programmatic differences existed between any of the serious contenders, whether Fabius, Delors or Rocard. The government-oriented culture of the party, established over 12 years after 1981, remained even in defeat in 1993, sustained by the continuing presidency of Mitterrand and the imminence of the election to determine his successor. Failure of the party to retain the presidency would, alternatively, take it into uncharted seas.

Scope for ideologically driven factionalism in the party – in all its guises since 1905 – had in any event been relatively constrained. After 1920 it was constrained by the restricted space the party occupied in a multi-party system, sandwiched between the Communist Party and the Radicals. While such constriction implied strategic choices over which factional conflict could and did emerge, the consignment to other parties of both 'hard' left and centrist opinion eased SFIO party management. Equally, after the War, political systemic constraints restricted the scope for factionalism, the Fourth Republic's survival requiring the SFIO's involvement in centrist coalitions whose *raison d'être* was the defence of constitutional government in the face of Communist and Gaullist opposition, and the maintenance of France's international alliances against the hostility of the same 'anti-system' parties. In effect, in coalition governments for all but five of the years between the Liberation in 1944 and the end of the Fourth Republic in 1958, the party became accustomed to the sort of governing responsibilities which served firmly to shape its culture in the Mitterrand years.

Culturally, the party was presidentialised after 1971. The key office in French politics being the presidency, intra-party factionalism revolves around winning the presidential nomination. Each faction, for credibility in this race, requires to be cosmopolitan, broad-ranging and ideologically diffuse, which is why CERES was never a serious runner in the presidential stakes. Survey evidence confirms that little differentiates the factions either in policy terms or in responses to such totemic invocations as 'Jaurès', 'Blum', 'Mendès France', or 'Marxism' – other than to identify the more clearly left-wing orientation of CERES.[27] What was uncertain before the end of Mitterrand's second term was how such a presidentialised culture might be eroded by the party's exclusion from the French presidency for seven years after 1995.

The system of presidentialism and the occupancy of the presidency by Mitterrand, converted the socialists into a catch-all party with much of the standard features of strong leadership, a subordinated rank and file, downgraded ideology, and non-exclusive linkages to particular clienteles. Of course, no party from the socialist tradition adapts effortlessly to such a model, and it required Mitterrand's capture of the presidency to complete the process. Power is a strong cohesive, and the suppression of the centrifugal forces inherent in factionalism followed from the centripetal effect of the leader elevated to head of state and of government. Equally, the electoral rout of 1993 marked the failure of a catch-all strategy and undermined the *raison d'être* of a *governing* party in which activists had been reduced to footsoldiers and factional leaders to courtiers. To some observers the 'governing' party had, in any event, been better regarded as of a more passive condition; that of – in the familiar expression – *un parti de godillots* (bootlickers). In this sense, the matter to be resolved after March 1993 was the identity of the boots to be licked as Mitterrand's presidency petered out.

In another sense, however, a 'leadership deficit' had affected the party after 1981, with Mitterrand's move from first secretary to Elysée and his replacement of himself with the loyal acolyte Jospin. This worsened after 1988 as the cohesive authority over the party of a president who would not run again, weakened. The successive first secretaries after 1988, Mauroy and Fabius, equally lacked authority, the first being elected (against Mitterrand's wishes) by those seeking to block the presidential ambitions of Fabius, who in turn, when he did finally manage to secure the leadership, was hamstrung both by resistance to his ambition and by the serious legal controversy over Aids-contaminated blood distributed during his prime ministership. Not until Rocard's ousting of Fabius in 1993 did the party again have at its head an incontestably credible presidential contender.

The larger question, not confined to France, of how to assemble in the wake of the Soviet collapse a social democratic response drawing upon the collectivist tradition, and in a national context to challenge the free-market liberal model, remained to be resolved. If the electoral collapse of 1993 marked the end in France of '*l'espérance collectiviste*', factional power play – opened at Rennes in 1990 – over the PS presidential nomination, would indeed carry no more significance than the reordering of deckchairs on the *Titanic*. But the nature of French electoral processes – frequent and multifarious (presidential, parliamentary, European, local) and conducive to both consensual Downsian strategies and the dislocating impact of proportional representation (in some elections) and of first ballot rivalries – could be expected to affect equally the resurgent right and the demoralised left. Shorn of the responsibilities of office and detached from a now bunkered, lame duck Mitterrand, the socialists, under a pragmatic, popular *présidentiable* such as Rocard, had much to play for if they could find the necessary unity.

Notes

1. On the SFIO at the liberation, see Graham, B.D., *The French Socialists and Tripartisme 1944–1947* (London: Weidenfeld), 1965; and, on the decline of the SFIO, see Roucaute, Y., *Histoires socialistes* (Paris: Ledrappier), 1987.
2. See Cole, A., 'Factionalism in the French Parti Socialiste, 1971–1981', Oxford unpublished D.Phil., Oxford; and the same author's 'Factionalism, the French Socialist Party and the Fifth Republic: An Exploration of Intra-party Divisions', *European Journal of Political Research*, Vol. 17 (1989), pp. 77–94.
3. Johnson, R.W., *The Long March of the French Left* (London: Macmillan), 1980.

4. Portelli, H., *Le Socialisme français tel qu'il est* (Paris: PUF), 1980; and Gisbert, F.O., *François Mitterrand ou la tentation de l'histoire* (Paris: Seuil), 1977.
5. MacShane, D., *François Mitterrand* (London: Quartet), 1981.
6. Bizot, J.F. *et al.*, *Au Parti des socialistes* (Paris: Grasset), 1976.
7. See Hanley, D., *Keeping Left? Ceres and the French Socialist Party* (Manchester: Manchester University Press), 1986.
8. Hamon, H. and Rotman, P., *L'Effet Rocard* (Paris: Stock), 1980.
9. Kergoat, J., *Le PS de la commune à nos jours* (Paris: Syrnos), 1983.
10. Parodi, J.-L. and Perrineau, P., 'François Mitterrand et Michel Rocard: deux ans de concurrence devant l'opinion', *Pouvoirs*, No. 13 (1980), pp. 189–97.
11. Queremonne, J.-L., 'Un Gouvernement présidentiel on un gouvernement partisan?', *Pouvoirs*, No. 20 (1982), pp. 67–86.
12. Christopherson, T.R., *The French Socialists in Power, 1981–1986* (London, Toronto and Newark: Delaware University Press), 1991.
13. Bergounioux, Alain and Grunberg, G., *Le Long remords du pouvoir* (Paris: Fayard), 1992.
14. Cayrol, R., 'La Direction du Parti socialiste: organisation et fonctionnement', *RFSP*, Vol. 28, No. 2 (1978), pp. 201–49.
15. The presidentialisation of French politics and its impact upon the intra-party politics of the socialists is discussed in Gaffney, J., 'The Emergence of a Presidential Party: the Socialist Party'; Cole, A., *French Political Parties in Transition*, (Aldershot: Dartmouth), 1990; and Cole op. cit.
16. Nay, C., *Le Noir et le Rouge* (Paris: Grasset), 1984.
17. Philippe, A. and Hubscher, D., *Enquete à l'intérieur du Parti socialiste* (Paris: Albin Michel), 1991.
18. See ibid., pp. 121ff.
19. Buchard, P., *La Guerre des deux roses* (Paris: Grasset), 1986.
20. See Elgie, R., 'La Méthode Rocard existe-t-elle?', *ASMCF*, January 1991; and Lovecy, Jill, 'Une Majorité à géométrie variable: Government, Parliament and the Parties, June 1988–June 1990', *Modern and Contemporary France*, July 1991.
21. Dupin, E., *L'Après Mitterrand* (Paris: Calmann-Lèvy), 1991.
22. See Hanley op. cit., and CERES publications *ad nauseam*.
23. Makarian, C. and Rey, D., *Un Inconnu nommé Chevènement* (Paris: La Table Ronde), 1986.
24. The full texts of the faction statements were published in *Le Poing et la Rose*, No. 130, January 1990; and see an analysis in Philippe and Hubscher, op. cit., pp. 212ff.
25. For essentially marginal instances of dissent among the rank and file or the parliamentary group, see Elgie, R. and Griggs, S., 'The influence of the Parti Socialiste on public policy since 1981', *Modern and Contemporary France*, October 1991.
26. See Gaffney, op. cit., p. 81.
27. Rey, H. and Subileau, F., *Les Militants socialistes à l'épreuve du pouvoir* (Paris: Presses de la Fondation Nationale des Sciences Politiques), 1991.

7 Conflict and cohesion in the Dutch Labour Party

Philip van Praag Jr

Introduction

The Dutch Partij van de Arbeid (PvdA, Labour Party) is one of western Europe's medium-sized social democratic parties. Its electoral strength has varied between a high of 33.8 per cent of the vote in 1977 and a low of 23.6 per cent in 1967.[1] In countries such as Germany, Britain, Sweden and Spain social democratic parties have a bigger electoral base and have generally had more political influence, but since its foundation in 1946 the history of the PvdA has been determinated by a conflictual relationship with the dominant Dutch religious parties – until the election of 1967 the Catholic Katholieke Volkspartij (KVP) and since 1977 the newly formed Christen Democratisch Appel (CDA). The PvdA has always been convinced that the religious parties have prevented it having more substantial electoral success and its relations with the confessional parties were also often the cause of its internal factional tensions.[2]

This chapter examines the life of the PvdA since 1966 in some detail, charting the slow evolution and maturity of the present identity crisis of the party.[3] The PvdA was from 1966 to 1986 led by Joop den Uyl, and was for a long time dominated by the New Left generation, but was in opposition for three-quarters of this time. The party changed its political and electoral strategy in 1987, without much internal opposition. However, after joining the government in 1989, the party started to loose electoral support and internal confusion and conflict grew steadily. After the summer of 1991 the party moved into profound crisis, and the opinion polls suggested that its electoral support had been almost halved to around 18 per cent.

THE INFLUENCE OF NIEUW LINKS (NEW LEFT), 1966–77[4]

The years 1959–66, before Nieuw Links, were in many ways transitional for the PvdA. This certainly goes for its electoral strategy, its conception about the Dutch parliamentary system and its organisational structure. The PvdA was portrayed in the mid-1960s by Nieuw Links (the New Left movement in the PvdA) as being dull and complacent, but that view must be balanced, because the PvdA was very conscious of the changing relations between political parties and voters and the leadership was convinced that both its platform and its identity needed to be adjusted to the emerging welfare state. The 1963 study by the PvdA's research bureau the Wiardi Beckman Stichting (WBS) entitled *Om de kwaliteit van het bestaan* (*for the Quality of Life*) was a testimony to that awareness. The first part of this study, written by Den Uyl, director of the WBS, was strongly influenced by the views of J.K. Galbraith and Tony Crosland.

The rapid success of Nieuw Links after 1966 can partly be explained by the fact that a large section of the PvdA was already convinced of the necessity for change. In a few years Nieuw Links had gained influence in party branches, had sent its supporters to the party congress and had succeeded in placing its partisans on the party executive (seven out of 21 in 1967, nine out of 25 in 1969). Moreover, by February 1971 A. van der Louw, one of its leading members, had become party chairman, and after 1971 Nieuw Links sympathisers dominated the party Executive and a growing number had become MPs. Yet in May 1971 Nieuw Links decided to dissolve itself. The success of the movement was an important cause of its dissolution. Its leaders held influential positions in the party and believed the continuation of the movement to be superfluous. The lesser figures in the movement were politically too divided and insignificant to continue Nieuw Links, with the result that the attempts between 1971 and 1977 to refound Nieuw Links failed.

During the 1970s a small informal group, the Steenwijkgroep, consisting of 15 former Nieuw Links members and some other leading left-wing party members, retained a strong influence. This group, more a club of friends of a few ministers, under-secretaries, MPs, and members of the National Executive, met regularly and determined the party Executive's policy and strategy to a substantial degree. The group led a discrete occult existence until 1976, but then, just when newspapers discovered it and started to write about its influence, the Steenwijkgroep had begun to lose power.

The influence of Nieuw Links on the domestic party programme was rather limited. Its views on the social-economic order and on the welfare state were similar to the views expounded in 1963 by Den Uyl, although some priorities were promoted, for example the need for income redistribution, and the demand for greater participation and the need for individual well-being was stressed. If it had little domestic impact, Nieuw Links exercised more influence on the foreign policy of the PvdA. During the 1950s the PvdA had been an outspoken anti-communist and pro-Nato party, but by the end of the 1960s the PvdA had become suspicious of both American and Nato intentions. The consensus about the party's foreign policy quickly vanished as a growing minority wanted either to transform Nato into a real peace organisation or to quit. The PvdA also supported anti-colonial movements and gave high priority to increasing aid to developing countries.

Nieuw Links had substantial activist support in the party but some of the older right-wing leadership opposed the new policy and the changing political culture. However, the leaders failed to win sufficient support in the local branches of the party and at the Party Congress of 1969 they were reduced to a small minority. The 'old guard' accused Nieuw Links of 'manipulation' and of undemocratic behaviour and resigned to establish a new party in 1970, Democratic Socialists '70 (DS '70). This was the first right-wing split in the history of Dutch social democracy. In 1971 W. Drees Jr, son of the former popular socialist prime minister, W. Drees (1948–58), became its leader. After the dissolution of Nieuw Links and the departure of a part of the right wing, neither the left-wing opposition nor the right-wing opposition had a formal organisation and informal personal networks were the base for factionalism after 1971.

The organisational reforms Nieuw Links had put in place within a few years were profound, especially those concerning the party's internal operation. Two reforms were important. First, in 1969 the congress decided to decentralise candidate selection: the party Executive was no longer to be responsible for the parliamentary nominations, and regional federations would select candidates for parliament. Second, the number of MPs allowed to have a seat on the Executive was restricted. The Nieuw Links proposals made it far easier for the opposition to gain influence and strengthened the position of regional federations leaders (the middle-level elite) and the party activists.

The party's political strategy was also fundamentally changed during the 1966–71 period. Priority was given to eliminating the power of the religious parties in the hope of creating a bipolar Dutch politics, in which the competition between a progressive bloc, centred around the PvdA, and a conservative bloc would offer voters a clear political choice. This goal was the subject of broad consensus in the PvdA in 1967 although differences of opinion existed about the way in which such a bipolar system could be brought about. If the political leadership wanted to reform the electoral system, a large part of Nieuw Links expected the radicalisation of the PvdA's doctrine and looked to the rejection of a coalition with the KVP to do much to achieve this end. Catholic and Protestant workers were expected to vote PvdA after 'deconfessionalisation' and 'secularisation'.[5] Many people in the PvdA believed that a left-wing parliamentary majority was a real prospect. The new strategy, called 'polarisation strategy', led to cooperation with two newly founded small parties: the Politieke Partij Radikalen (PPR, Radical Progressive Party) and Democraten '66 (D'66). However, the strategy only partially succeeded: although the KVP did lose votes in 1971 and 1972, the PvdA made only modest gains.

Even so, the formation of a government after the parliamentary election of November 1972 took a record time. In the spring of 1973, after 164 days of negotiations, the Den Uyl cabinet was formed, a cabinet of the three progressive parties with the support of the KVP and the Calvinist Anti-Revolutionaire Partij (ARP, Anti-Revolutionary Party). This cabinet, the most left-wing ever to be formed in the Netherlands, was controversial even within the PvdA. A crucial minority of leftist middle-level party leaders had no confidence in the Den Uyl cabinet and this became manifest in May 1973 when a quarter of the party Council voted against the newly formed government.

In reaction a new political strategy was mapped out in the party Executive during 1974. It accepted that the PvdA had become a governing party and that cooperation with the other left-wing parties had faltered. An essential part of the new strategy was to continue the policy of confrontation with the two confessional coalition partners. One important aim was to disrupt the growing cooperation between the three most important religious parties – KVP, ARP and Christelijk Historische Unie (CHU) – and to prevent the merger of these parties into the CDA. This strategy increasingly gained a second importance during 1975: that of convincing the grumbling party activists of the PvdA that cabinet policy was worth defending. The position which the Steenwijkgroep-dominated party Executive took over the government's policies was ambivalent: under strong pressure from party activists it periodically voiced its displeasure at the cabinet's lack of reform.

The elections of 1977 were a great success for the PvdA. After a campaign built up around the popular prime minister Den Uyl, the PvdA gained nine seats and remained the largest party with 53 seats. The newly formed CDA list of the three religious parties won 49 seats. Yet six months of tiring cabinet negotiations between CDA, PvdA and D'66 did not result in a second Den Uyl cabinet. The socialist demand for a majority of the cabinet seats was rejected by the Christian democrats. In the party Executive and in the parliamentary group, the members of the Steenwijkgroep were the most important forces opposing concessions to the CDA in the distribution of cabinet seats. The party Council, dominated by the middle-level elite of the PvdA, rejected a compromise between CDA and PvdA in October 1977. After this traumatic meeting Den Uyl vainly tried for another ten days to form a cabinet, and finally CDA leader Dries van Agt headed a coalition of the CDA and conservative liberals (Volkspartij voor Vrijheid en Democratie, VVD) with a tiny majority.

An important cause of the failure to form a second Den Uyl cabinet can be found in the strategy the PvdA had followed since 1974 to confront the three cooperating religious parties. Priority had been given to preventing their successful cooperation; good relations with the coalition partners were made secondary. A second cause can be found in the internal relations of the PvdA: party activists did not trust the motives of the party elite. The tensions within the party after 1977 were extreme, the PvdA was polarised for a long time and the trauma of 1977 was remembered when the PvdA entered government with unanimous Executive support in 1989.

In the period 1966–77 the core values of the social democracy retained wide support within the party. Nieuw Links undermined neither the broad consensus on the Keynesian welfare state nor the necessity to extend the role of the state. The left wing of the party added new demands, adopted from the women's and ecological movements, and was impatient with the pace of reforms. Only in the mid-1970s did a few prominent members of the small right wing begin to criticise the social-economic policy of the party. One of them was W. Duisenberg, minister of finance in the Den Uyl cabinet.

However, there were two other important sources of conflict. The first was foreign and defence policy. During the Den Uyl cabinet sharp conflicts emerged in the party over Nato and the purchase of combat planes. Second, the political strategy of the party continued to cause tension. The core of this continuing conflict was the question of whether, and under what conditions, the party should cooperate with the confessional parties. The left wing regularly attacked the party leadership over their readiness to deal with confessional parties. Suspicion that the party leaders were too eager to govern was widespread among activists and this was an important contribution to the failure of Den Uyl to form a second cabinet.

The rise of Nieuw Links (and the effect of the organisational reforms) had resulted in a changing configuration of power in the PvdA. There was no longer one central authority in the party; instead there was an unstable equilibrium between different power centres. The Executive, where the left had a strong position, took a more independent role, frequently criticising the party members in parliament and their own ministers in the Den Uyl cabinet. The party Council, dominated by representatives of the regional federations and originally devoted to domestic affairs, became the guardian of the manifesto commitments and policed the party in parliament and the party Executive for signs of backsliding. While the Executive was losing influence in the party, the regional leaders of the PvdA were gaining influence. As a result of their position in the party Council, middle-level leaders played a crucial role in the party's decision-making process and, as regional leaders, they had a decisive influence on the recruitment of MPs and in the selection of members of the Executive. These middle-level leaders played a particularly crucial political role when differences of opinion emerged in the party's top echelons. Although the formal ties with other social democratic organisations had already been partly severed in 1946, the political culture of the PvdA had for a long time the characteristics of a 'solidarity community', based on a unity of party programme, organisational form and social base.[6] The influence of Nieuw Links changed the political culture so that after 1966 the internal life of the party was characterised by distrust and suspicion. Internal conflicts were difficult to solve and lasting and bitter debates could only be resolved by ballot at congress or in Council.

In addition to their rather vague ideology of democratisation and radicalisation, Nieuw Links activists had their social background in common. In general they were students, teachers, university lecturers, journalists or social workers: the educated 'new middle class'. The success of Nieuw Links profoundly changed the class structure of the PvdA membership and by the 1970s almost all the new party members were from the new middle class. The profile of the sympathisers and participants in the 'new social movement', especially the peace movement, clearly resembled the social characteristics of the new generation of PvdA members.

A new cleavage between the PvdA activists and the social democratic electorate slowly emerged. During the 1970s the regional party leaders and party activists were in general more radical than the party members or the party elite.[7] They sustained radical, partly neo-Marxist ideas and partly 'postmaterialist' values such as environmentalism and participatory democracy. Important parts of the middle-level elite preferred expressive activities to instrumental ones so that conflicts that had great symbolic value, such as the PvdA antagonism to religious parties, were more suitable to that end than substantive political problems. On that point also, the attitude of the middle-level leadership of the PvdA was similar to the attitude of activists from 'new social movements' of the 1970s and 1980s.[8]

Internal tensions 1977–82

Being forced into opposition had frustrated the party leadership who were convinced that the middle-level elite was responsible for the failure of Den Uyl to form a second cabinet. In their view the party decision-making process had to be changed, but party activists believed that in order to enter government the party elite had made too many concessions. At that time most of the former members of Nieuw Links and of the Steenwijkgroep were considered to be a part of the moderate party leadership by the activists.

In 1979 the party elite almost unanimously supported the candidature of Wim Meier (former junior minister and member of the Steenwijkgroep) as the new party chair. His bid failed dramatically. Max van den Berg (former member of Nieuw Links and the municipal executive in Groningen) was able to mobilise the party activists against 'The Hague Establishment' within the party. In his view the party needed a clear anti-capitalistic and socialist policy. In 1979 Van den Berg was elected chair by a large congress majority.

Van den Berg was an outspoken representative of the left and under his leadership the party supported the campaign for the closure of the two nuclear power plants in the Netherlands. In the run-up to the elections of 1981 there were serious tensions between Van den Berg and Den Uyl. A conflict arose about the Dutch army's six nuclear war roles within Nato. Taking a lead from the peace movement,[9] the party Executive proposed that nuclear disarmament be written into the election manifesto. Den Uyl refused to accept this proposal, fearing Dutch isolation within Nato and PvdA isolation in Dutch politics. He threatened to resign as political leader if the congress were to accept nuclear disarmament and demanded that two nuclear task forces be kept. Van den Berg accepted this stand-point, and in exchange Den Uyl rejected in principle the deployment of the USA's 572 Cruise missiles in the Netherlands. Den Uyl and Van den Berg agreed, but the party quarrelled over this issue for months. Ultimately the party Congress supported Den Uyl. In the radical peace movement Joop den Uyl was nicknamed 'Joop Atoom'.

The coalition of the CDA and the VVD lost its fragile parliamentary majority in 1981. Although the PvdA lost nine seats and although Van den Berg and the party Executive had originally preferred a left majority coalition, the party entered an unstable coalition cabinet with the CDA and D'66, led by CDA leader Van Agt. During the nine turbulent months of this cabinet, Den Uyl, as minister of social affairs, fought a bitter struggle with the trade unions over sickness benefits. Party activists opposed Den Uyl's policy, and after a dramatic PvdA defeat at the provincial elections, party chairman Van den Berg forced the PvdA ministers to leave the cabinet in the spring of 1982. Den Uyl resisted strong pressure to retire as political leader and led the party to a slight electoral recovery (a gain of three seats) in September 1982. Den Uyl had intended to withdraw as leader before the next parliamentary elections, but Van den Berg, as chair, vetoed Den Uyl's proposal to make Jos van Kemenade (minister of education in the Den Uyl cabinet and again in 1981–82) his successor. Van den Berg preferred Wim Kok as Den Uyl's successor, but Kok was not available. As a result of this internal disagreement Den Uyl was again the political leader of the social democrats for the elections of 1986. It was his seventh election campaign as first candidate.

In the years 1981–86 the social democratic party played an important role in the broad coalition between the peace movement and the left's traditional political organisations. At the first massive peace demonstration in 1981 the PvdA, as a party in office, still defended a vague and ambiguous compromise. However, after the collapse of the CDA–PvdA–D'66 cabinet in May 1982, the PvdA participated enthusiastically in the peace movement and was one of the driving forces in the mass protest against the deployment of Cruise missiles in the Netherlands.[10] Only a few MPs and intellectuals disagreed with the party policy, but in general opponents preferred to keep silent.

During 1982–86 the PvdA fiercely opposed the socio-economic policy of the CDA–VVD coalition cabinet led by Ruud Lubbers (CDA), especially the reduction of public sector salaries by 3 per cent and the cuts in welfare payments. This policy restored PvdA unity for a while, but it was superficial unity; underneath the surface, tensions grew. A part of the parliamentary party, including a number of former members of the left wing, expressed doubts about the correctness of the formal party policy to keep the growing financial problems of the Dutch welfare state out of discussion. However, during the elections of 1986 general harmony appeared to exist. Neither in candidate selection nor in the drafting of the election manifesto was discord manifest between the leaders, middle leaders and members. This was despite the fact that candidates for parliament and members of the Executive were still somewhat more moderate than middle-level leaders and members.[11]

The 1987 change of policy

The 1986 election results were a great disappointment to the social democrats. The media and the party reported a 'victorious defeat': despite gaining five seats to raise their representation to 52 PvdA (33.3 per cent), the outcome fell short of PvdA expectations. For years the opinion polls had indicated a considerably larger number of seats for the PvdA and for quite a while, but not for the first time since 1946, the party had hoped for an electoral breakthrough of about 40 per cent, a breakthrough which was to be achieved at the expense of the CDA. Not only did the party's hope evaporate, at the eleventh hour it was also surpassed by the CDA as the largest party. The two government parties, CDA and VVD, retained their parliamentary majority, ensuring the continuation of their coalition. Frustrations in PvdA circles were high.

Internal discussions following the 'victorious defeat' turned upon three crucial factors: the party's programme and ideology; its electoral and political strategies; and its internal organisation. One of the first changes was the resignation of Den Uyl after twenty years of political leadership and his succession by Wim Kok, former chairman of the largest Dutch trade union, the Federatie Nederlandse Vakbeweging (FNV).

In November 1987 a comprehensive study entitled *Schuivende Panelen* (*Sliding Panels*) was published. Although this study was aimed at renovating the programme of social democracy, it primarily offered a thorough analysis of the increasing individualism of citizens, the (financial) problems of the welfare state, and problems of economic and legal order. While sparking off many discussions in the party and the media, the report failed to produce clear conclusions. In this respect the fall of the second Lubbers cabinet in May 1989 and the subsequent elections came too soon for the PvdA. As for its political strategy, the conclusion was that the PvdA, partly of its own volition, had become politically isolated. The PvdA was said to have lost the 1986 elections to the CDA, as it had been insufficiently attractive to voters in the political centre, particularly middle-class voters. The polarisation strategy was designated the main culprit.

The suggestion that the party's polarisation strategy contributed to its political isolation was correct and should have been seen in 1977. The dramatic failure to enter government in 1977 clearly illustrated that the fight with the CDA for the dominant position in Dutch politics had been lost. In spite of the denominational centre having drastically shrunk (from about 50 per cent to over 30 per cent) over ten years, the confessional coalition was still able to decide whether to form a majority coalition with the liberals or with the social democrats. Moreover, the PvdA had failed to use the electoral losses of the religious parties to any great advantage. The post-1977 polarisation strategy did not tackle the relatively weak position the PvdA still occupied in the Dutch multi-party system and which resulted in its semi-permanent opposition. The 1988 strategy-report *Bewogen Beweging* (*Compassionate Movement*) for the first time recognised rather than challenged the CDA dominance. In the 1989–90 annual report the party secretary, A. Beck, briefly summed up the change in political strategy as 'from polarisation to consensus'. As a political strategy the change of policy was successful. In the autumn of 1989 the PvdA proved to be an acceptable coalition partner, both for leaders, members and voters of the CDA.

The 1987 change of policy also involved a change in electoral strategy. The aim was to appeal more to the centre groups, to show that a PvdA socio-economic policy could indeed be trusted. Electoral analyses indicated that in 1986 the PvdA was regarded as quite left-wing by the electorate, only slightly less so than the radical Pacifistisch Socialistische Partij (PSP, Pacifist-Socialist Party).[12] As the objective was still to reach 40 per cent, support from the political centre was needed, but with hindsight this change in the electoral appeal can be seen as questionable.

It is doubtful whether the party was sufficiently aware of the electoral risks its change of policy implied. A certain loss to the left-wing parties was anticipated but reckoned to be acceptable, since the potential gain among other groups could be much higher. The hope of taking 40 per cent proved to be founded on a miscalculation. At the 1987 Provincial-Council elections the strategy still seemed to work: a slight loss to the left matched by hesitant progress in the centre. In the 1989 parliamentary elections, however, the strategy seemed to backfire. Despite a sound campaign the PvdA lost slightly (1.4 per cent), especially to D66 (the apostrophe was dropped in 1985) and, to a lesser extent, to Groen Links (Green Left), the new alliance of four small left-wing parties.[13] The poor vote from young voters aged 18–24 was alarming because the PvdA now ceased to be the largest party among this group (polling 26 per cent, as against 34 per cent for the CDA and 13 per cent for D66). At the 1991 Provincial-Council elections the governing PvdA had a disastrous result. While the turnout was very low (52.1 per cent), Groen Links progressed slightly while the PvdA suffered heavy losses and took only 20.4 per cent of the vote. D66 improved most, with 15.6 per cent of the vote. A change of policy directed at conquering the political centre paradoxically resulted in boosting the growth of the party traditionally representing the political centre (D66).

Two electoral developments had not been foreseen in this change of policy. First, the response of PvdA's traditional grassroots support had not been sufficiently taken into account within the party and the loyalty of these voters had been taken for granted. The 1987 change of policy rightly did not take into account the possibility that Groen Links might constitute an alternative for these voters and it failed to anticipate that the PvdA's traditional supporters might stay at home or vote for ultra right-wing parties when they could no longer identify with the PvdA.[14]

Until 1987 the expectations of large groups of PvdA voters had been met both by the party's stance on certain issues and its political strategy. The party's confrontation with the CDA, an essential part of the bipolarisation strategy, greatly helped many traditional supporters to recognise the party. A party such as the PvdA did not derive its identity just from its programme. Voters with only a passing interest in politics associate a party primarily with the issues it is prepared to contest with other parties. Conflicts therefore may be highly functional in enhancing a party's identity. Within the limits of the Dutch consensus democracy, the PvdA was always the party least interested in avoiding conflict (even before 1966), but the avoidance of conflicts, especially with the CDA, crippled the party. The blurring of the lines of demarcation with other parties, especially the CDA, is undermining the PvdA's electoral base.

A second unforeseen electoral development was that the PvdA's move towards the political centre, especially its stronger emphasis on issues appealing to middle classes, made it far easier for these groups to vote for D66. Until recently the PvdA had distinguished itself from parties like D66 and CDA with its 'social image'. In the eyes of many voters the PvdA was exemplary in its fight against social injustice and for a substantial sector of the middle-income groups the 'solidarity motive' was an important reason for backing the PvdA. Because of the partial erosion of this distinguishing feature of social solidarity in the past few years, voters have been deprived of an important reason for supporting the PvdA.

One of the considerations underlying the 1987 change of policy was that voters thought the PvdA too leftist, too like the radical socialist PSP and too distant from the political centre. By September 1989 this situation had changed significantly. In the eyes of the voters the PvdA was now clearly positioned to the right of Groen Links and closer to the political centre, while the distance from D66 had been much reduced.[15]

The change of policy in 1987 met little resistance in the party and the new stance towards the CDA was widely accepted. The discussion about the organisational structure, however, did not proceed very smoothly. In 1987 a first critical report was rejected by the party Executive and a second report (the Van Kemenade report) appeared in June 1991. In March 1992 the party congress accepted the Van Kemenade proposals to abolish the party Council (the traditional stronghold of the regional leaders), to reduce the number of congress members and to have the congress meet annually. In December 1992 it decided to make the national party Executive responsible again (after 23 years) for the selection of parliamentary candidates. Over more than ten years the regional elites of the PvdA had successfully defended their power: in 1979 and 1987 the party congress had rejected proposals to change the process of regional candidate selection, but the regional elites had eventually to capitulate. Under the stress of the growing problems of the PvdA they could no longer resist the proposals to modernise and centralise the party organisation, so after an interlude of twenty years, the PvdA again became a centralised party.

Factionalism and the crisis of social democracy after 1989

In the summer of 1991 the PvdA was plunged into a profound crisis. This crisis was a direct consequence of the participation in government in October 1989. The decision to form a coalition government with the CDA was ratified by the party congress by general consent. Party leader Wim Kok became deputy prime minister and minister of finance, and D66 was kept out of the government, particularly at the instigation of the CDA. Yet dissatisfaction with PvdA government policy increased steadily, at first among the voters who inflicted two serious defeats on the party in 1990 (municipal elections) and in 1991 (Provincial-Council elections), and then within the party too. The main dissatisfaction was that the PvdA's return to power had not resulted in a markedly different policy from that of the CDA/ VVD coalition. The PvdA was now paying for the fact that it had raised expectations that it would reverse some social-economic measures, but had failed to come up with any clear ideas about the way in which the Dutch welfare state, subjected to great financial pressure, could be reorganised.

The lack of any credible view about the future of the welfare state is at the core of the ideological and electoral problems of the PvdA. The electoral power base of the PvdA (and of other social democratic parties in north-western Europe) depends on a vulnerable coalition of middle class and lower-income groups. In the past such coalitions were consciously created through a political programme in which the various groups could all see their interests. Esping-Andersen has gone into the reform programme which enabled successful electoral coalitions in the three Scandinavian countries.[16] His postulate is that a precondition for an effective coalition was (and is) that improvements in the material and social position of the lowest-income groups should not be accomplished at the expense of other groups of wage-earners, particularly the 'new middle class'. Hence any programme should benefit the different groups of wage-earners, and should not imply conflicts between the different groups. On the one hand, a conflictual programme (so-called 'zero-sum') would mean that the improvements of the disadvantaged are paid for by the middle class. On the other hand, a successful reform policy benefiting all groups could have a real influence on the electoral position of the party.[17] In the 1945–70 period the social democrats in north-western Europe had such an appealing cross-class programme at their disposal, and the core of that welfare programme was supported by the dominant position of Keynesian economics.

In the 1970s and 1980s the electoral base of the PvdA was founded on just such a class coalition, and the data of the Dutch Parliamentary Election

Studies indicated that the working and middle classes in the PvdA electorate were divided fifty-fifty.[18] The programme underlying the social democratic class compromise ran into difficulties after 1970 because Keynesian theory did not provide an answer to the 'stagflation' problems of the welfare state, and it lost its dominant academic position. Moreover, at the same time, the support for the welfare state among the middle classes was beginning to decline. In the 1970s Esping-Andersen observed the first signs of 'decomposition', the falling apart of the electoral coalition on which the parties were based, in Scandinavia, and particularly in Denmark. In 1985 he was not very optimistic about their future: 'Social-democracy seems, at best, exhausted; at worst dying'.[19] No social-democratic party in Europe had an answer to the increasing criticism of the welfare state.

Being an opposition party, the PvdA managed to defer any serious consideration of these ideological problems until 1989. Although some PvdA politicians were convinced that the welfare state was out of date and increasingly expensive, the party did not say so in its manifesto or in policy statements. Before 1989 non-economic issues hid the growing internal disagreement about the future of the welfare state. In the Netherlands the controversy over the deployment of Cruise missiles temporarily united the various PvdA target groups behind the party and numerous campaigns against the proposed deployment, fully supported by the PvdA between 1982 and 1986, enabled the party to avoid the issues which would cause internal division and discord. The latent PvdA problems became manifest after it entered government in 1989. The party failed to satisfy raised expectations about income and taxation policy. In January 1991 it appeared from an internal survey of the PvdA that its 'social image' was deteriorating. The voters thought the party did too little for the lowest-income groups. There was also some dissatisfaction about environmental policy. While the intentions of the PvdA ministers were valued, their results were seen as disappointing.

Under pressure of budgetary problems and because of the agreement not to raise the burden of taxation, the cabinet in July 1991 took the decision to economise drastically on benefits available to disabled workers under the Wet op de Arbeidsongeschiktheidsverzekering (WAO). Instead of receiving 70 per cent of their wages until the age of 65, all people under 50 entitled to benefit would gradually see their benefits decrease to 70 per cent of the Dutch minimum wage. PvdA activists, members and voters were surprised by this drastic decision by its ministers, especially given Kok's earlier statements that benefit levels would not be cut. In July and August a storm of sometimes very emotional criticism was unleashed both inside and outside the party. Outside criticism was led by the FNV, ideologically close to the PvdA. Internally, senior party officials initially concentrated criticism on party chair, Marjanne Sint, who was taking a six-week holiday in Italy. At the end of August Sint resigned.

In response to this criticism the cabinet somewhat nuanced its decision.

However, criticism continued unabated, and was now also strongly levelled at PvdA leader Kok. At the end of August Kok also contemplated resignation, but eventually decided to convene a special congress to discuss the matter. The representatives to this congress, however, were not given a free choice. Were the congress to reject the WAO cabinet proposals, Kok declared he would stand down as leader. As a result of this threat 80 per cent of the congress representatives supported his policy; without it the policy would probably have been rejected. As a consequence of these problems some 15,000 members (about 17 per cent) left the party during 1991 and 1992, among them were two left-wing MPs and various other prominent people. Relations with the trade unions were seriously disrupted. In contrast to the 1970s, the opposition of middle-level party executives did really express the opinions of large groups of members and voters in this conflict. In the September 1991 polls the party fell to an unprecedented all-time low of 14 per cent.

The congress, which passed off well for party leaded Kok, also decided that a committee would develop proposals for the further reorganisation of the welfare state. The March 1992 congress was to take decisions on this, and also was to appoint a new party chairman. In mid-January 1992 the party committee made quite modest proposals to reform the welfare state: no further cuts in benefits, but a more intensive endeavour to increase labour participation in the Netherlands. Party leader Kok and many others were satisfied, but the response of outsiders was that the party had not established any priorities and had merely contrived a superficial party unity. Meanwhile a group, led by former party chairman Van der Louw (one of the founders of the Nieuw Links in the 1960s and of the Steenwijkgroep in the 1970s), threatened to leave the party and to found a new social-democratic party. Ultimately Van der Louw did not carry out this threat but he did start a caucus to renovate the PvdA and to 'preserve the core values' of social democracy in the Netherlands.[20] Some members of the former Steenwijk-groep supported Van der Louw's effort but after some months it became clear that the support for the Van der Louw group was rather limited and his group plays an inconspicuous role within the party.

At the same time the nomination for the chair took a startling turn. The first serious candidate was Felix Rottenberg (34 years old in 1991), former chair of the Young Socialists, youngest member of the party Executive in the 1970s and 1980s and manager of the Balie cultural centre in Amsterdam for ten years. He was seen by many people as the representative of the inner-party movement striving for a radical break with the past. Some weeks later Ruud Vreeman stood as a candidate, at the request of a number of MPs who mistrusted Rottenberg. Vreeman, as chair of the FNV Transport Union and as an ardent opponent of the cabinet policy on social benefits, was seen as the representative of the more traditional social democratic (union) wing. At the very moment everybody was expecting a fierce struggle, the candidates announced that they would stand on a joint ticket, Rottenberg as chair and

Vreeman as vice-chair, and they were elected by an overwhelming majority at the March 1992 congress. The expectation that they would revitalise the party and modernise its image has been borne out. Organisational problems and old social democratic taboos have been discussed. Rottenberg has introduced a new style of politics and has attracted much media exposure. At the same time recovery in the polls has not been as expected, nor has the restoration of confidence in party policy.

Conclusion: desperately seeking identity

One of the central hypotheses about factionalism is that the public perception of a party as divided can be electorally harmful. The recent history of the PvdA partly refutes this proposition. In the 1970s the party was bitterly divided; during the Den Uyl cabinet there were frequent and intense conflicts within the party. Nevertheless, the social democrats won the elections of 1977. The popularity of Den Uyl and the support for his policy were important causes of the 1977 electoral victory and offset PvdA divisions. In the 1980s the party tried to avoid open conflicts about such issues as security policy and the future of the welfare state. The 1987 change of policy did not lead to conflict within the party, but this remarkable harmony failed to bring about any electoral gains. In 1989 the party congress decided unanimously to enter a coalition government with the CDA. In the first months of 1990 the electoral decline of the party began; the principal cause of this was the disappointment with government policy. During 1991, when the PvdA ministers failed to restore confidence, unrest and political conflict broke out. Discord within the party was more a consequence than a cause of electoral problems.

After 1990 the PvdA sank into disarray. The party had given up some of its political and egalitarian ideals for a more realistic approach to welfare state problems. Although the party still maintains the ideal of social justice, the old means and policy instruments (the dominant economic role of the state) have gone and new ones are lacking. One of the consequences of this development is that the PvdA, as a party in government, has no principles by which to justify its policy and has no specific issues with which to secure the recognisability of its policy. Neither the traditional social democratic voters nor the 'new middle classes' have any reason for supporting the PvdA. (Both rather heterogeneous groups are disappointed with PvdA policy.) The break with the past, and the attempts to change the image of an old-fashioned party into a modern one, have alienated important groups of voters and failed to attract new groups of voters.

Yet one of the astonishing facts is that the policy met no serious opposition. The left wing has partly disappeared and what remains is fragmented. There is no question of organised opposition; even the informal oppositional networks have been in great part dismantled. Only during the summer of 1991, amidst confusion over the proposals to cut benefits for the disabled, was there strong opposition to party leader Kok and other ministers. It seems that the resignation of two leftist MPs (Visser and De Moor) has deprived the opposition of its last leaders.

The women's organisation of the PvdA (de Rode Vrouwen) was in the 1970s an influential internal pressure group but lost a lot of support in the 1980s and changed its internal organisation structure in 1992; it has suffered a partial loss of power and now functions mainly as a discussion network. In the present situation of confusion and non-ideological conflict within the party there are no fixed dimensions of dispute. If there is to be any serious conflict in the near future it will concern the necessity to defend core values of social democracy, but in contrast to the 1970s a greater consensus exists about foreign policy and defence policy.

After the autumn of 1991 the great problems the PvdA faced seemed to bring about unity in adversity. The internal culture of distrust and suspicion was replaced with a confidence in the new chairman Rottenberg. The growing consciousness that the survival of the party as one of the leading political forces of the Netherlands is at stake has forced the middle-level elite to accept organisational measures and points of view which were for a long time unacceptable. During 1992 two important decisions thoroughly changed the organisational structure of the party: the abolition of the party Council and the decision to centralise the selection of the MPs. Both decisions will strengthen the position of the party Executive, especially the position of the new elected chair and vice chair of the party. The regional party leaders will have less opportunity to constrain the party Executive and the party in parliament; MPs will be dependent on the Executive for their re-election and a permanent institution to coordinate the party Executive and the party in parliament has been created.

The dissolution of the small but powerful party Council will have the effect of discouraging internal opposition. The organisation of an influential opposition within the party congress will be more difficult, hence in the near future the management of conflict will not pose serious problems. Traditionally the PvdA has opted for a tolerant approach to conflicts: dissident views were in general not suppressed and the expulsion of dissident members was rare. The desire to seek internal compromise still exists and the election of Rottenberg as chair and Vreeman as vice-chair is a clear example. In the past Den Uyl sometimes threatened to resign on losing a battle, and Kok also adopted this strategy, but it is doubtful whether it can be repeated as his authority as political leader within the party is waning.

The 1994 election will be decisive for the future of the PvdA. The formulation of the 1994 election manifesto will be a serious test of the consensus and homogeneity of the party. If the party fails to secure above 25 per cent of the vote it will lose the influence it has long exercised as one of the two largest parties in Dutch politics. The principal causes of the trials of the PvdA are not a failing leadership, internal discord or incidental factors but the lack of an appealing programme transcending class. The PvdA is desperately seeking a new social democratic identity but the absence of any serious internal opposition is an indication of internal disarray rather than of consensus. The party seems unlikely to resolve its crisis in the foreseeable future.

Postscript

After a successful campaign, built up around Kok as the defender of traditional social democratic values and future prime minister, the PvdA got 24 per cent of the vote (37 seats) in May 1994. The Christian Democrats (CDA) suffered more important losses and got only 22.2 per cent of the vote (34 seats). In spite of a decline from 32 to 24 per cent of the vote, the PvdA is again the largest party.

Notes

1. See Bartolini (1983) for an overall picture of the electoral development of social democratic parties since World War I.
2. For a detailed discussion of the Dutch party system, see Daalder (1987). For an analysis of the development in Dutch politics after 1967 see Daalder and Irwin (1989).
3. See Wolinetz (1977) for a short history of the social democratic party SDAP before 1940 and for the period 1946–66. For a more comprehensive analysis of the SDAP in the 1930s, see Knegtmans (1989).
4. For a more comprehensive analysis of the influence of New Left, see Wolinetz (1977), Kroes (1975), Tromp (1976), Boivin et al. (1978) and Van Praag (1991).
5. 'Deconfessionalisation' is a decrease in loyalty to the religious parties by voters who continue to class themselves as Catholic or Protestant. Secularisation is a process of leaving churches.
6. Padgett and Paterson (1991: 66–67).
7. May (1973).
8. Parkin (1968: 34–40) and Offe (1985).
9. In 1977 the Interdenominational Peace Council (Inter-Kerkelijke Vredesberaad, IKV) launched a campaign against nuclear weapons in general, and against the nuclear task forces of the Dutch army in particular; see Klandermans (1990), Kriesi and van Praag (1987).
10. Kriesi and Van Praag (1987); Klandermans (1990).
11. Hillebrand (1992: ch. 10).
12. Annex I of Bewogen Beweging (Amsterdam: PvdA), 1988, pp. 99–109; Irwin et al. (1987), Van der Eijk and Van Praag (1987: 135–37).
13. At the 1989 elections the radical socialist PSP, the communist CPN, the radical PPR and the small radical Christian EVP presented, for the first time, a joint list under the name Groen Links (Green Left). In 1990 the four parties decided to merge.
14. Electoral research showed a substantial number of supporters of the small racist Centre Party (Centrumpartij) to be potential PvdA voters as well.
15. In a survey by Dutch Parliamentary Election Studies, which used a ten-point left–right scale, the PvdA scored an average of 3.1 (as against 2.7 in 1986), Green Left 2.0 and D66 4.2 (as against 4.7 in 1986).
16. The original article from 1980 was included in A. Przeworski (1985) and elaborated in Przeworski and Sprague (1986). See also Esping-Andersen (1985).

17. Esping-Andersen (1985). In Scandinavia the 'positive sum' was initially related to the coalition of the social democrats with the small farmers; during the building of the welfare state it was increasingly related to the coalition with the new middle classes.
18. More than half (51.8 per cent) of the PvdA voters considered themselves in 1986 to be skilled or unskilled workers. In 1989 this belief was still at a similar level (van Deth *et al.*, 1991).
19. Esping-Andersen (1985: 318).
20. Theses of Van der Louw for the first conference of his group (Rode Hoed Konferentie, Sociaal-demokratie: Hoe nu verder?, Amsterdam, 27 October 1991).

References

Bartolini, S. (1983) 'The European Left Since World War I: The Size, Composition and Patterns of Electoral Development', in: H. Daalder and P. Mair (eds), *Western European Party Systems, Continuity and Change* (London: Sage), pp. 139–75.

Boivin, B. *et al.* (1978) *Een verjongingskuur voor de Partij van de Arbeid: Opkomst, ontwikkeling en betekenis van Nieuw Links* (Deventer: Kluwer).

Daalder, H. (1987) 'The Dutch Party System: From Segmentation to Polarization – and Then?', in H. Daalder (ed.), *Party Systems in Denmark, Austria, Switzerland, The Netherlands and Belgium* (London: Frances Pinter), pp. 193–284.

Daalder, H. and Irwin, G.A. (eds) (1989) *Politics in the Netherlands. How Much Change?* (London: Frank Cass).

Esping-Andersen, G. (1985) *Politics against Markets. The Social Democratic Road to Power* (Princeton, NJ: Princeton University Press).

Esping-Andersen, G. (1990) *The Three Worlds of Welfare Capitalism* (Cambridge: Polity Press).

Hillebrand, R. (1992) *De Antichambre van het Parlement, Kandidaatstelling in Nederlandse politieke partijen* (Leiden: DSWO Press).

Irwin, G.A., Van der Eijk, C., Holsteyn, J.J.M. and Niemöller, B. (1987) 'Verzuiling, issues, kandidaten en ideologie in de verkiezingen van 1986', *Acta Politica*, Vol. 22, pp. 129–79.

Klandermans, B. (1990) 'Linking the "Old" and the "New" Movement Networks in the Netherlands', in R. Dalton and M. Kuechler (eds), *Challenging the Political Order, New Social and Political Movements in Western Democracies* (Cambridge: Polity Press).

Knegtmans, P.J. (1989) *Socialisme en Democratie, De SDAP tussen klasse en natie (1929–1930)* (Amsterdam: Stichting beheer IISG).

Kriesi, H. and Van Praag Jr, Ph. (1987) 'Old and New Politics: The Dutch Peace Movement and Traditional Political Organisations', *European Journal of Political Research*, Vol. 15, pp. 319–46.

Kroes, R. (1975) *New Left, Nieuw Links, New Left: Verzet, beweging en verandering in Amerika, Nederland, Engeland* (Alphen aan de Rijn and Brussels: Samsom).

May, J.D. (1973) 'Opinion Structure of Political Parties: the Special Law of Curvilinear Disparity', *Political Studies*, Vol. 21, pp. 135–51.

Offe, C. (1985) 'New Social Movements: Challenging the Boundaries of Institutional Politics', *Social Research*, 1985, pp. 817–68.

Padgett, S. and Paterson, W.E. (1991) *A History of Social Democracy in Postwar Europe* (London: Longman).

Parkin, F. (1968) *Middle Class Radicalism* (New York: Praeger).

Przeworski, A. (1985) *Capitalism and Social Democracy* (Cambridge: Cambridge University Press).

Przeworski, A. and Sprague, J. (1986) *Paper Stones: A History of Electoral Socialism* (Chicago and London: University of Chicago Press).

Tromp, B. (1976) 'Socialisme, organisatie en democratie', *Socialisme en Democratie*, Vol. 34, pp. 155–72.

Van Deth, J., Leijenaar, M. and Wittebrood, K. (1991) 'Sociaal-economische positie bepaalt kiesgedrag', *Namens*, Vol. 6, No. 4, pp. 19–25.

Van der Eijk, C. and Van Praag Jr, Ph. (eds) (1987) *De strijd om de meerderheid; de verkiezingen van 1986* (Amsterdam: CT-Press).

Van Praag Jr, Ph. (1991) *Strategie en Illusie; Elf jaar intern debat in de PvdA (1966–1977)* (Amsterdam: Het Spinhuis).

Wolinetz, S.B. (1977) 'The Dutch Labour Party: A Social Democratic Party in Transition', in W.E. Paterson and A.H. Thomas (eds), *Social Democratic Parties in Western Europe* (London: Croom Helm), pp. 342–88.

8 Conflict and cohesion in the British Labour Party

Eric Shaw

Labour's civil war, 1979–83

THE SOURCES OF CONFLICT

Social democratic parties face fundamental dilemmas: how to maintain internal political order without smothering dissent and how to balance internal party democracy and electoral appeal. The British Labour Party has had to confront these dilemmas continuously as it has always been prone to disagreements and has occasionally (as in the early 1950s and early 1960s) suffered from severe internal ruptures. But the sheer ferocity and venom of the turbulence which overwhelmed the party after its eviction from office in 1979 and which persisted for almost four years were unprecedented. How can we account for this?

It was precipitated by the loss of the election, for which the leadership was held responsible, but the underlying cause was a profound and pervasive disenchantment with the performance of the outgoing Labour government. For many within the party (and the unions) the acquiescence of the 1974–79 Labour government in what was (at the time) regarded as an intolerably high level of unemployment, its cutbacks in public expenditure and hence the quality of social provision and its pursuit of wage restraint which had eroded working-class living standards represented a betrayal of Labour's most cherished values. This compounded the disappointment many had felt with the record of the earlier Wilson administration: there were no major accomplishments like the NHS of the postwar Labour government in which all might feel a common pride.

The form the left-led assault on the leadership took was the campaign for constitutional reform, a campaign so fiercely fought that for several years it dwarfed all other issues. For years the left had concentrated its efforts on securing party conference majorities for its favoured policies but then found that there were no means by which a Labour government could be persuaded or compelled to implement them. At the tumultuous conference of 1979 rank-and-file frustration erupted, fuelling the drive to alter the balance of power between the Parliamentary Labour Party (PLP) and the wider party through constitutional change.

As it happened, the issue of constitutional reform had been on the agenda for a number of years, largely due to the persistent efforts of the activist-based Campaign for Labour Party Democracy (CLPD, an internal party pressure group established in 1973). After 1979 CLPD spearheaded the campaign (wrongly identified by most of the media with Tony Benn) to achieve three constitutional reforms designed to enhance the power of the mass membership: mandatory reselection of MPs; a broader franchise for electing the leader; and sole National Executive Committee (NEC) control of the manifesto (instead of joint control with the frontbench).[1]

These reforms were bitterly resisted by the right but at the 1980 Annual Conference and the special conference of January 1981 the first two were adopted. Hardly had the smoke cleared from the battlefield than the next round of the civil war erupted. This was sparked by Tony Benn's decision to challenge – under the newly formed electoral college – the incumbent Denis Healey for the deputy leadership of the party. In a most acridly fought contest in 1981, Healey repelled Benn's challenge by a margin of less than 1 per cent.

But there was no mending of fences and within months Labour was embroiled in another phase of the civil war. Since the mid-1970s Labour's right had been clamouring for action to be taken against the Trotskyist Militant Tendency.[2] While under control of the left, the NEC was unwilling to act but as the right recouped its forces from 1981 the initially reluctant party leader, Michael Foot (under massive pressure from the PLP), agreed to back a move against Militant. This eventually culminated in the banning of the Trotskyist body and the expulsion of some of its leaders in early 1983. Foot's line was denounced by the bulk of the left and Labour was locked into a third round of hostilities between left and right which only ceased when the 1983 election was called by Mrs Thatcher.

THE BREAKDOWN OF COHESION: THE CRUMBLING OF CONSENSUS

Conflict between left and right had always existed within the party but from 1979 to 1983 it attained an unprecedented ferocity. In the words of *Tribune*'s then editor, Richard Clements: 'Left, right and centre, the Labour Party seems to be gripped by a collective hysteria . . . [it] is fast beginning to look like the worst example of a sectarian organisation tearing itself to pieces in doctrinal and unfraternal argument'.[3]

To understand why, we must investigate not only the causes of conflict but also the drying up of the traditional sources of cohesion within the party. We shall suggest that, for much of its history, there were three main props which had enabled Labour to weather persistent internal discord: reasonable levels of *ideological, normative* and *procedural* integration. After 1979, each of these disintegrated.

The collapse of ideological integration   Labour has never been a stranger to controversy but in the past a kernel of consensus over a set of core values had helped hold it together: differences over nationalisation and foreign and defence policy were balanced by a shared enthusiasm for improving working-class living standards, extending welfare services and managing full employment. During the late 1970s the consensus dissolved as the 1974–79 Labour government abandoned central tenets of the Keynesian/welfare state strategy while a rapidly growing left concluded that such basic goals as social justice and full employment could now only be secured by more radical means. In other words, the postwar common ground was deserted by both left and right.

The collapse of normative integration   Like societies as a whole, the most effective glue bonding a party together is the possession of a common set of behavioural norms, that is, conventions and expected ways of behaving. As Drucker and Janosik noted, such shared norms were very much part of the fabric of the Labour Party in the postwar decades.[4] These included loyalty to leaders and sentiments of solidarity and fellowship with other members which fostered a sense of community and hence operated as a depressant of internal strife. At an ever-accelerating pace Labour, from around the late 1960s onwards, suffered from progressive normative disintegration. Throughout the 1970s, a new cohort of activists had entered the party. They were predominantly young, educated and employed in public sector white-collar occupations. They were therefore not exposed to the types of socialising experiences that had inculcated traditional labourist norms. They were far more assertive and more rebellious than earlier cohorts and much more impatient of the rules and those who sought to enforce them.

Most dramatically of all, the left's characteristic wariness of leaders now transmuted into a deep and abiding distrust of any form of authority. The right-wing Labour MP, Austin Mitchell, was not far off the mark in his portrayal of left-wingers who thought that: 'To lead was to betray. Leadership itself was an anti-social act, an indictable offence. Leaders would sell out – unless they were stopped.'[5] The old norms of loyalty, respect for authority, fellowship and attachment to the party which had muted the attacks of the rank and file in the past thus lost their restraining influence.

The collapse of procedural integration   A third essential source of consensus for much of Labour's history was procedural integration, that is, agreement over rules and principles defining how decisions should be made and how powers and duties should be apportioned. This was summed up in the theory of internal party democracy: all members had the right to participate in the policy-making process; decisions should reflect the will of the majority (as embodied in conference sovereignty) and be binding upon all; and leaders should be accountable to the rank and file. The theory restricted the power of leaders, but also validated it. In so far as authority was properly exercised, it was obligatory upon all to respect it, and the function of leadership − pursuing the collective interests of the party − was regarded as a valuable, indeed an indispensable one.

For a range of reasons, procedural integration was already disintegrating by the late 1970s. After 1979 it decomposed completely. While the constitutional crisis was obviously a struggle for power it also embodied genuine and fundamental disagreements over the nature of party democracy, the rights and responsibilities of leaders and members and the proper location of authority. Consensus over procedural norms had vanished because the right no longer accepted the notion of conference sovereignty while the left wished to enforce it by installing new and tighter mechanisms of accountability. As the controversy raged, the gap between the two appeared unbridgeable. Austin Mitchell accurately summarised the left's conception of internal party democracy:

Policy would be formulated through the wishes of the activists coming up in resolutions passed by Conference, then welded into a Manifesto, not by the parliamentary party which had abused its independence, but by a National Executive dependent on the Party activists. That Manifesto would then become a binding mandate . . . it would be forced through by the votes of MPs disciplined by reselection making them dependent on the constituency activists rather than on the patronage of leaders.[6]

To the right and the parliamentary leadership, all this represented an unacceptable abridgement of their traditional rights − perhaps even a challenge to the basics of British-style parliamentary democracy. This held that MPs were accountable to the voters not to a narrow party caucus; and that MPs were elected to exercise their judgement and discretion and should not be trammelled by party mandates. Furthermore, the right claimed that party activists were unrepresentative of Labour voters and that MPs were far more sensitive to the currents of public opinion.

THE BREAKDOWN OF COHESION: THE FADING OF CENTRAL CONTROL

Unity may arise less from consent than from conformity, that is, from tight leadership control. The exercise of strong central authority has always been complicated in the Labour Party by its pluralist structure as constitutionally power is diffused through a range of institutions (the leader, the shadow cabinet, the NEC, conference). For most of the party's history this did not in fact impair leadership control because the right dominated all key power centres and because the unions were largely content to operate as leadership supports against challenges from the left.

This structure of leadership control had been under strain since the late 1960s, largely because of the rise of left-wing trade unionism. After 1979 it fell apart. Until 1981 the left controlled the party apparatus through its majority on the NEC: it used this to ease the passage of the constitutional reforms (which might otherwise have been stifled) and of a parcel of left-wing policies. Further, because managerial and disciplinary powers are vested in the NEC and not the parliamentary leadership, the left's command of this body meant that the leadership was stripped of the resources it required to enforce central control.

In addition, the authority of the leader was seriously eroded because James Callaghan had been discredited by the perceived failure of his government and by defeat at the polls; and his successor, Michael Foot, lacked either the power base or the political gifts to stamp his authority on the party. His political standing was battered by a whole range of defeats, including the success of the left in overturning his rash attempt to veto the radical leftist Peter Tatchell as the parliamentary candidate for Bermondsey in 1982, and that of the right in forcing him to backtrack over his wish to replace Eric Varley as employment spokesman by his key lieutenant, Neil Kinnock.

Perhaps most crucial of all, the unions signally failed to perform their traditional role of bulwarks of the leadership against left-wing rebellions. This was for a range of reasons: the strength of left-wing unions sympathetic to the constitutional reforms (most notably the Transport and General Workers' Union (TGWU) and the National Union of Public Employees (NUPE)); the decentralisation of power within several key unions which enhanced the influence of middle-level officials and lay activists unwilling to enact the traditional role expected of union leaders in internal party struggles; widespread disillusion with the record of the 1974–79 Labour government, particularly over pay restraint; and the divisions and political ineptitude of the leadership of right-wing unions (especially the Amalgamated Union of Engineering Workers (AUEW)).[7]

THE ACCOMMODATION OF CONFLICT

Conflict, as we have noted, is an inevitable feature of political parties. Whether it seriously damages party unity is in part a function of the extent to which a party's institutional arrangements are geared to containing differences of interests and views and the nature of its cleavage patterns. The problem with Labour's institutional arrangements was that, far from acting to resolve differences, they exacerbated them. We have noted the division of powers between the leader and shadow cabinet, on the one hand, and the NEC, on the other. This was always a potential source of friction, but rarely realised because the former had effectively controlled the latter. In the mid-1970s, the left gained a majority on the Executive and parliamentary control was lost. Secure in the command of the government apparatus, Wilson and Callaghan simply ignored the NEC, excluding it from any significant input into policy-making. After 1979, the left-held Executive retaliated and it was the turn of frontbenchers and the majority of MPs to feel bitter resentment as the NEC foisted upon them policies in whose determination they played little part. The relationship between the two power centres became one of adversaries rather than partners and the manifold other fractures which rent the party were compounded by a system of institutional antagonism.

The pattern of alignments or cleavages within a party both reflects existing divisions but also reshapes them, because they form the context in which protagonists must operate, influencing their strategy and tactics. In the period 1979–83 cleavage lines within the Labour Party were deep, cumulative and comprehensive. The mass of the party was split into two hostile camps which were locked in combat over an extensive range of issues (constitutional, domestic and external policy, and strategy) and the fault lines were mutually reinforcing. Left and right viewed each other as antagonists adhering to radically different conceptions of the party's role and purposes; as a result attachment at all levels of the party to the rival wings often rivalled that to the party as a whole.

At the same time, Labour experienced an unprecedented degree of factional mobilisation. Those on the left, especially CLPD and the Labour Coordinating Committee (LCC, set up in 1978) were unusually well organised, ably led and achieved a high degree of penetration into all sections of the party. A prominent role in sustaining this mobilising drive was played by Tony Benn. He carried immense prestige as a highly experienced and capable former cabinet minister who (it was widely believed) had battled almost single-handedly for party policies in the last Labour government. And he was one of those rare politicians upon whom the label charismatic could accurately be pinned, with his exceptional ability to communicate his views in a lucid and compelling fashion, to articulate grassroots dissent and to inspire great loyalty and enthusiasm.

In addition, the left displayed in this period a rare ability to work together; thus a whole host of left-wing groups, ranging from the CLPD and the LCC to a medley of Trotskyist sects, worked together in the umbrella Rank and File Mobilising Committee which later became the organising centre of Benn's deputy leadership campaign. This broad coalition was held together not by any common ideology (which did not exist) but by agreement over the pursuit of a limited number of clearly specified goals, especially constitutional ones. The right, too, acted as a block with its counter-offensive spearheaded by the Campaign for Labour Victory, later replaced by Labour Solidarity. But both its cohesion and effectiveness were damaged by the defection of some of its ablest and most energetic leaders to form the Social Democratic

Party (SDP), by demoralisation and by the disorganisation and poor leadership of its trade union allies.

The period of transition, 1983–87

THE SOURCES OF CONFLICT

Labour's new leader, Neil Kinnock, inherited a stunned party in the wake of the Conservative landslide of June 1983. Yet tensions still simmered in the party and scarcely a year had elapsed before Kinnock was embattled with the left on a range of fronts. Despite some sweeping policy changes introduced by Kinnock, including ending opposition to council house sales and European Community membership, and the casting overboard of the left-devised Alternative Economic Strategy, policy was not a major source of internal strife in these years. In fact, it was the actions of the Conservative government, or, more precisely, how Labour should respond to them, that ignited divisions within the party.

In other circumstances, the prolonged and bitter miners' strike of 1984–85 might have afforded a rallying cry for the party as a whole: the strike was all about protecting jobs and communities as well as affording the most determined case of resistance to the Conservative government – all causes close to Labour's heart. But instead the strike caused a year of turmoil within the party. The problem lay in part with the way in which the strike had been called – without a national ballot – and by the way it had been conducted by Arthur Scargill, the militant president of the National Union of Mineworkers (NUM). Kinnock was caught in the cross-fire between the government and most of the media, which demanded that he condemn picketline violence, and the left, which deplored his failure to offer the NUM unstinting support. But it also brought to the fore key issues of political strategy. How could Labour best regain lost ground – by demonstrating its determination to stand shoulder to shoulder with workers locked in struggle, or by conveying an image of moderation and good sense?

The same question was raised by the other major source of discord in 1984–85 – how best to respond to Conservative curbs on local government spending. The most contentious of these was the government's acquisition of the power to 'rate-cap' local authorities, that is, to limit their power to raise revenue by increasing local rates. A number of influential left-wing local authorities urged that the most effective way to thwart the government was through a strategy of 'non-compliance' or refusal to set a rate – an illegal step designed to arouse mass opposition to Conservative policy. Kinnock, in contrast, rejected what he dismissed as 'gesture politics', urging that local authorities do their best to protect services within the bounds of legality – a view which eventually, and after much in-fighting, prevailed.

Both these disputes were in effect manifestations of two utterly divergent conceptions of electoral strategy. The first, embraced by much of the left, held that the route back to power lay through the mass mobilisation of the working class. This entailed full and unequivocal support for all those engaged in struggle with employers and the state: extra-parliamentary mobilisation – whether in the industrial sphere, as with the miners' strike, or in the defence of local jobs and services, as with the rate-capping dispute – was seen as crucial in reactivating sentiments of class solidarity and in energising and maximising mass resistance to the Conservatives. This was totally at odds with the leadership's evolving strategy which aimed to soften the image of the party, to disassociate it from trade union militants and Labour left-wingers, and enlarge its appeal across class boundaries. The longer-term effect of defeat in both the miners' strike and the rate-capping struggle was to strengthen's Kinnock's hand. Large numbers of people at all levels and in all sections of the party lost faith in the viability and value of extra-parliamentary action, the tactic of confrontation and a class-oriented mobilisation strategy. And, as we shall see later, the failure of both helped foment the growing split within the left which eased Kinnock's drive to assert more effective control over the party.

The two other major clashes within the party in this period involved (as in the period of the civil war of 1979–83) its internal rules. In both cases the initiative was taken by the leader and with a similar end – one which he pursued with unflinching determination throughout his leadership – to break the power of the more ardent and intransigent section of the left which came to be labelled the 'hard left'.

The first concerned the perennial problem of reselection procedures. Many within the PLP had never been reconciled to the novelty of reselection and pressed strongly, as a first step, for a move towards transferring the power to deselect MPs from (largely left-wing) constituency General Committees to ordinary party members. In the spring of 1984 Kinnock presented a rather complicated proposal which went some way to meeting this demand. It was opposed by most of the left (though for a variety of reasons) and by a sufficient number of unions (worried that it would undermine their role within the party) to lose narrowly at the 1984 Conference. Kinnock remained convinced that power must be prised from left-wing activists, but he was forced to wait.

The second issue was more pressing – but, ultimately, less divisive. The gnawing problem of Militant had not been removed by the disciplinary measures of 1982–83; indeed, Militant had emerged with its organisation intact and its prestige enhanced. It had also converted Liverpool city council into a flagship of its confrontational strategy with the government. Kinnock was a fiercer opponent of the Trotskyist group than his predecessor, but he carefully waited until the autumn of 1985 when a serious tactical blunder by

Liverpool City Council gave him his opportunity. He seized it with both hands and in his speech to the Labour Party Conference delivered a powerful salvo against the Militant controlled council – to the fury of the hard left but to the delight of most of the rest of the delegates.[8] The die was cast, and a wave of expulsions soon followed. Although press headlines were emblazoned with talk of 'Labour chaos', in fact the really significant feature of this second campaign against Militant was that, unlike the first, it did not provoke much controversy within the party. This was primarily because a large and growing section of the left now agreed that harsh measures against the Trotskyist group were indeed essential.

THE ACCOMMODATION OF CONFLICT: REALIGNMENT OF THE LEFT

As we argued above, cleavage structures within political parties not only reflect existing divisions but also help reshape them. Thus just as a prime cause of Labour's civil war of 1979–83 was its polarisation into two bitterly antagonistic camps, a major factor in the lessening of internal party tensions after 1983 was the process which came to be known as the 'realignment of the left'.[9]

The appearance of left-wing unity prior to 1983 belied growing divisions. These incipient rifts were widened by different reactions to the 1983 election defeat, with one section of the left claiming that the main cause was the leadership's lack of commitment to the party programme while another vigorously urged the case for a thoroughgoing reappraisal of party strategy, organisation and policy. After 1983, sources of friction multiplied, most notably divergent responses to the failure of both the miners' strike and the local councils' challenge to the Thatcher government and – above all – to the expulsion of Militant members.

These intensifying strains reflected, it now became apparent, deep-seated differences in attitudes to the party and the leader. What came to be known as the 'hard left' continued to perceive Labour as riven by a fundamental divide between the socialist left and the reformist right, now once more in the driving seat under the apostate former left-winger Kinnock. The more accommodating section of the left which was prepared to support Kinnock – which came to be known as the 'soft left' – in contrast, no longer viewed the party in these adversarial terms. It believed that a *modus vivendi* between competing wings was essential to Labour's electoral health and was willing to be more flexible over policy. While it shared the objective of loosening the hold of the right it claimed that this could best be achieved by constructing 'a majority centre-left coalition around the Party leader'.[10] By 1985 a distinctive soft left current had emerged. Among activists, it was represented by the LCC, in Parliament by the Tribune Group, in the NEC by a group around David Blunkett, Tom Sawyer and Michael Meacher, and it had the support of the *Tribune* weekly. Within the wider labour movement many senior figures in left-wing unions such as NUPE, TGWU and the National Union of Railwaymen (NUR) now gravitated towards soft rather than hard left positions and for a time it was a significant factor in the internal politics of the party.

THE ACCOMMODATION OF CONFLICT: INSTITUTIONAL CHANGE

The growing accommodation between the soft left and the leadership was facilitated by reforms in the policy-making process. As we have seen, stress within the party had been aggravated by the existence of two separate power centres, the NEC and the shadow cabinet. To remedy this, an important institutional change was introduced in 1983. The old network of NEC policy working groups was replaced by a series of Joint Policy Committees consisting of equal numbers of NEC and shadow cabinet members topped by trade unionists and with outstanding differences ironed out by a Policy Coordinating Committee staffed by senior National Executive members and frontbenchers.

The aim of this system of joint policy determination was to institutionalise cooperation and stimulate the habits of bargaining and compromise between the parliamentary and extra-parliamentary party. With its viability bolstered by the shift in the pattern of internal alignments, the new system proved an effective mechanism for accommodating differences. Perhaps the best example of this was the work of the Jobs and Industry Committee (the two key players here were the right-wing John Smith, frontbench spokesman on industry, and the soft left NEC member David Blunkett) which drafted the NEC's statement on *Social Ownership*. Overarching this new willingness to give and take was an (implied) policy compromise whereby a reluctant right wing continued to swallow the non-nuclear defence policy while much of the left responded flexibly to shifts in domestic policy. But, as we shall see later, it was an unstable compromise.

Institutional changes were further reinforced by the resumption by the unions of their role as stabilisers. The immediate consequence of the left's triumphs of the early 1980s was to provoke a right-wing trade union backlash. An alliance of right-wing unions (whose members included the AUEW and the Electrical, Electronic, Telecommunications and Plumbing Union (EEPTU)) began to operate in a much more organised and effective fashion. Its most notable success was in ousting the left from control of the NEC.[11] Hardliners in the AUEW and the EEPTU wanted to build on this achievement to crush the left. But they were foiled for a variety of reasons, including the continuing strength of the left rooted in its control of two of the biggest unions, the TGWU and NUPE, and, crucially, resistance from senior trade union leaders from traditionally centre-right unions such as John Edmonds of the General and Municipal Workers' Union (GMWU) who preferred to cooperate with leading left-wingers, such as Rodney Bickerstaffe of NUPE and Ron Todd of the TGWU to try to restore consensus within the party.

An end to opposition? 1987-92

THE POLICY REVIEW AND THE WANING OF DISSENT

After Labour's third successive defeat in 1987 the leadership soon concluded that electoral recovery required sweeping changes in policy and ideology and hence instituted the so-called 'Policy Review'. It was the most exhaustive exercise in policy renewal that Labour has ever undertaken and culminated with what the right-wing Labour MP Giles Radice described as 'the biggest shift in the Party's stance and direction for thirty years'.[12] It was the final victory of the revisionist project – but a largely painless one with relatively little in-fighting or opposition.

There were two exceptions to this: defence and industrial relations, both long-standing bones of contention in the party. No issue had stirred passions more fiercely than the question of nuclear weapons. On his own testimony Kinnock had concluded even before the 1987 election that Labour's non-nuclear policy was an electoral handicap. But it took two painful years before the party could be induced to relinquish it. This entailed a series of politically embarrassing twists and turns as Kinnock sought to organise a majority to reverse the policy. From 1983 onwards, most soft leftists, including those holding senior positions in both the party and the unions, had proved accommodating to policy change. But their bottom line was the retention of the non-nuclear policy. This was reiterated by both the giant TGWU and leading soft leftists like Robin Cook and David Blunkett as late as June 1988 when they rebuked Kinnock for appearing to repudiate unilateralism – and the leader felt impelled to stage a humiliating retreat. Yet by 1990 Labour had adopted a position on the deterrent broadly similar to that of the Conservatives. The total renunciation of what was for many on the soft left virtually an article of faith would have precipitated an outburst of outrage within the party only a couple of years previously. In fact it was digested – albeit unhappily – with remarkably little public protest. Why?

One reason was that the international situation was being transformed out of all recognition and the possibility of a nuclear conflagration had all but vanished. This may not have strengthened the case for an 'independent' UK deterrent but it greatly reduced the urgency of the issue. A second was the acceptance by many who remained unilateralists in principle that the policy could never be sold to the electorate. Thirdly (and on a similar theme), the yearning for victory at the polls was so strong that many were extremely loath to risk a resumption of electorally damaging internal strife. Furthermore, by 1990 much of the soft left leadership was so integrated into Labour's ruling coalition that they would rather sink their differences with their former adversaries on the right than make common cause with their erstwhile allies on the hard left.

The same broad pattern unfolded over the thorny question of labour law. Both the unions and the party had fervently condemned successive tranches of Conservative industrial relations legislation and in 1987 Labour was pledged to repeal most of it. But by the conclusion of the Policy Review – and after much heart-searching by left-wing union leaders – this pledge was abandoned: under a Labour government the bulk of Conservative legislation would survive. The path to agreement was smoothed by the availability of a range of consultative mechanisms which ensured that no step was taken without being thoroughly explored and thrashed out behind the scenes in informal meetings between senior frontbenchers and trade union leaders. In addition – once again – virtually all key union leaders were prepared to go to great lengths to accommodate the party leadership on what it regarded as an electorally vital adjustment of policy. As a result, a potentially highly volatile issue was defused.[13]

An additional factor accounting for the muted response to Labour's sharp swing to the right was the eclipse of the hard left as a significant political force. In fact, in 1988, it hastened its political demise by its impetuous decision to challenge Neil Kinnock and Roy Hattersley for the leadership and deputy leadership by fielding Tony Benn and Eric Heffer. Both were trounced and the contest merely highlighted the hard left's dwindling influence in all sections of the party.[14] By the autumn of 1992, no Campaign Group member occupied a position of influence within the PLP and only one – Tony Benn – survived on the NEC. The hard left was reduced to an isolated and helpless rump. It no longer had the capacity to mobilise effective rank-and-file protest against the relentless drift of the party to the right and left-wing activists sank into gloomy acquiescence.

IDEOLOGICAL INTEGRATION

Corresponding with this withering of dissent was a revival of cohesion. The most obvious and most important reason was the common desire for electoral victory. By 1987 the party was shell-shocked by three successive election defeats: the complacency which had fuelled the civil war of 1979–83 had totally evaporated. This zeal for victory at the polls reflected not only a yearning to see Labour back in office, but also a desperation to see an end to Thatcherism. The harsh economic and social policies pursued by the government since 1979 have been a major factor repairing the fractures within Labour's ranks. The mass uprising within the party in the early 1980s was in part a lagged response to the age of consensus and relative afflu-ence. It was still possible for the largely young and middle-class recruits to Labour to regard a consensus-minded social democratic party establishment as the main enemy and the construction of a rather vaguely understood 'socialist society' as the chief goal. Mere 'reformism' could be disparaged. This gradually changed as the relentless Thatcherite squeeze on the public services drove the defence of the welfare state to the top of Labour's agenda; by the same token, it demonstrated that, for the bulk of the party membership what mattered most was not abstract questions of doctrine but tangible issues of health, education and social security.[15] Coupled with this shift to practical reformism was a loss of ideological self-confidence on the left in such traditional socialist planks as public ownership and planning. As a result, once more the mass of opinion within the party could converge on the politics of greater social justice and fairness through improvements in the welfare state.

PROCEDURAL AND NORMATIVE INTEGRATION

In the early 1980s, as we have seen, there was bitter disagreement over organisational principles – how power, rights and duties ought to be apportioned and how decisions should be made. There is some evidence that a slow, halting process of convergence is under way. Thus it appears that there is broad support for the democratisation of conference by reducing the block vote,[16] though significant differences do still remain. Similarly, there were signs that the deep mistrust of authority, so pronounced a part of Labour's political culture in the early 1980s, was now gradually retreating and being replaced by a greater willingness to concede the importance of effective leadership. This was coupled with a strengthening of the sentiment of party loyalty. In the past, strong sentiments of class solidarity helped sustain loyalty to the party and its leadership. Because of the erosion of class solidarity, such sentiments were no longer available to nourish traditional labourist norms. On the other hand, there was a reawakening of a sense of common purpose: the prospect of endless Conservative rule was a very powerful reminder to all party members that, whatever their views, they all shared a common interest in electoral victory.[17]

THE REASSERTION OF CENTRAL CONTROL

Greater consensus is one basis of cohesion; another is tighter central control. From the very inception of his leadership, Kinnock was determined to restore the battered authority of his post and install a firmer regime of party management. This was only achieved after sustained effort on which the support of the unions proved essential. He inherited an NEC which had, since 1981, already shifted to the right but was still not 'reliable'. Indeed, in his earlier years Kinnock experienced considerable difficulty in mustering majorities on key issues and occasionally he was rebuffed. Even less could he anticipate a compliant conference and on a series of issues he was forced into unwanted compromises which still did not always save him from defeat.

But his position gradually strengthened: the fissure within the left and the steady crop of hard left casualties had by the late 1980s delivered to him an NEC over which he wielded a command which no leader had possessed since the early 1960s. The mechanism of the electoral college — by vesting the right to elect the leader in the party as a whole — afforded him a legitimacy to which none of his predecessors could lay claim, and the effect of his landslide victory in 1988 further boosted his leadership by enabling him to assert an overwhelming mandate. Not least, trade union leaders now once more increasingly defined their role as mobilising support for the leadership, and upsets at conference became infrequent.

Against some dissidents — Militant entryists who owed no loyalty to Labour — party discipline could now be used without fear of the consequences. Conference's response to the NEC's further turn of the ratchet in 1991 — the removal of Militant Tendency MPs Terry Fields and Dave Nellist — was illuminating: as Peter Kellner observed, the price of such expulsions a few years ago 'would have been a spectacle of division and blood-letting'. Instead the endorsement of the NEC's action by a majority of nine to one 'demonstrated Labour's near unanimity'.[18] But a firmer hand was also used to restrain loyal dissenters. There was growing pressure on those who uttered public criticisms to get into line and keep quiet. Thus in October 1988 Anne Clwyd, a junior frontbencher, was sacked for voting (along with 34 others) against the government's defence estimates in defiance of a PLP decision.

However, the main instrument employed to curb dissent was adroit media management. Increasing use was made of press briefings (orchestrated by leading party figures) to isolate and discredit those who queried the official line. Victims at various stages included prominent soft leftists such as Michael Meacher, Bryan Gould and John Prescott as they occasionally found themselves at odds with the leadership's thinking over the Policy Review and other issues such as the Gulf war.[19]

A third mechanism of control was — somewhat paradoxically — the extension of democracy. Assuming that the more passive members were less left-wing than party activists on constituency General Committees, Kinnock wanted to extend their rights in order to dilute the left's influence and in this way consolidate leadership control. The principle of 'one member, one vote' was applied to leadership and NEC elections and — to some degree — to parliamentary selection. No research has yet been conducted into the effects of these rule changes, but they do appear to have reduced the influence of the hard left, whose representation on the NEC was by 1993 eliminated with the defeat of Tony Benn.

A fourth method of control was patronage. Although the shadow cabinet was elected by the PLP, the leader has the power to allocate shadow portfolios and to appoint junior members of the frontbench team. Potential rebels could be seduced by the prospect of a frontbench position (several who quit the Campaign Group were so rewarded) while dissidents could be brought into line by threats to their career prospects: such methods became more potent after 1989 when it appeared that shadow jobs could well become real ones.

THE ACCOMMODATION OF CONFLICT: NEW PARTY ALIGNMENTS

A final factor explaining the abatement of conflict after 1987 was the changing constellation of internal party alignments. The soft left had emerged in the mid-1980s as a significant factor in the internal politics of the party but never realised its potential. In the words of one adherent, Chris Smith MP, it was 'unorganised, it lack[ed] direction, it ha[d]n't any coherent definition and it ha[d] precious little influence on Neil'.[20] It was divided over a fundamental strategic issue: should it seek to promote greater left-wing unity or should it align itself fully behind the leadership? Increasingly the latter view prevailed. The Tribune Group – established in 1964 as the organised forum of the parliamentary left – was more and more divided between pragmatists similar in outlook to the traditional right and the soft left. Writing from outside Parliament (though shortly to join it as MP for Neath in 1990), Peter Hain complained that the Group had been converted into 'a forum through which the leadership can pull people into line. Whenever there is a key decision, the payroll vote appears en bloc and stifles the Group's independence and radicalism'. There was, he concluded, 'no longer an identifiably coherent Tribune Left'.[21] In response, left-wing Tribunites (including NEC members and frontbenchers) formed a new group, the so-called 'Supper Club'. However, this merely acted as a loose and informal association of like-minded people who simply discussed matters of common interest. Further, most prominent soft leftists (including Robin Cook, Michael Meacher, John Prescott and Bryan Gould) were on the front bench and preferred to utter their disagreements in private.

All this needs to be placed in a broader context. Old ideological boundaries have become much more blurred and attachments to the various currents within the party have become much looser. Issues which fit uneasily into the left–right spectrum – like the environment, constitutional and electoral reform, and European Union policy – cut across traditional cleavage lines. Thus while much of the right of the party favours the Maastricht Treaty and European integration, a minority (among them Peter Shore and Austin Mitchell) is strongly anti-European. While the left tend to be more critical of Maastricht, this is often due (as in the cases of Ken Livingstone and David Blunkett) more to objections to aspects of the treaty (such as limits on budget deficits, the stress on monetary rather than economic convergence) than to opposition in principle to closer European ties. In other words, the party is differentiated on the issue in complex ways which do not accord with the left–right division.

A TRANQUIL OR TRANQUILLISED PARTY?

The contrast between Labour now and a decade ago is dramatic. Few would query that the end of the rancour and fury of the early 1980s has greatly benefited the party. The debilitating civil war impressed upon the public mind the image of an incessantly brawling and congenitally divided party. The lesson drawn from this by Kinnock and his closest advisers was that cohesion and tight control were indispensable and must be imposed at all costs.

But have order and improved electoral image been achieved at the expense of democracy and tolerance? Certainly, as the leadership's grip on the party tightened and as the 1992 election grew nearer attempts were made to narrow the parameters of acceptable dissent. As one seasoned commentator observed: 'It is one thing to conduct a genuine debate in a civilised manner. It is quite another to forgo the debate altogether.'[22] The temptation to move beyond disabling the hard left to attempting to discourage or suppress all public criticism was not always resisted in the Kinnock-led Labour Party.

Labour demonstrated its new unity and discipline in the measured – perhaps even sluggish – fashion in which it responded to an unprecedented fourth successive election defeat in April 1992. The contest for the leadership (between John Smith and Bryan Gould) and deputy leadership (between Margaret Beckett, John Prescott and again Bryan Gould) which followed shortly after was conducted in a restrained manner: though, significantly, the hard left candidate, Ken Livingstone, was excluded from the contest by a rule which set a high threshold of support (20 per cent) from within the PLP as a condition of entry. Smith easily vanquished his opponent (with his close ally Mrs Beckett joining him as deputy leader) and for the first time since 1976 a politician closely identified with the right of the party assumed the leadership – ironically, with wider support within Labour's ranks than either of his predecessors.

Early indications suggest that Smith is inclined to manage the party with a lighter rein than Kinnock. His task has so far been facilitated by the sharp divisions within the governing Conservative Party (over the European Union, economic policy and the future of the mining industry) and the various disasters which have befallen the government and have over-shadowed disagreements within his own: thus Gould's resignation from the shadow cabinet over policy on Europe made little impact. But whether this new-found unity is rooted in a real and durable consensus over policy, ideology and party rules or whether it was a response to dwindling organisational vitality and ideological exhaustion is a question yet to be answered.

Notes

1. For a full and well-informed account, see Kogan, D. and Kogan, M., *The Battle for the Labour Party* (London: Fontana), 1982.
2. For a detailed discussion, see Shaw, E., *Discipline and Discord in the Labour Party* (Manchester: Manchester University Press), 1988, ch. 11.
3. *Tribune*, 11 December 1981.
4. Drucker, H., *Doctrine and Ethos in the Labour Party* (London: Allen & Unwin), 1979, p. 9; Janosik, E.G., *Constituency Labour Parties in Britain* (London: Pall Mall Press), 1967, pp. 104, 107.
5. Mitchell, A., *Four Years in the Death of the Labour Party* (London: Methuen), 1983, p. 35.
6. Ibid., p. 37.
7. For a full and extremely informative account, see Minkin, L., *The Contentious Alliance: Trade Unions and The Labour Party* (Edinburgh: Edinburgh University Press), 1991, pp. 196–202.
8. For a full account see Shaw, op. cit., ch. 12.
9. For a general account, see Seyd, P., 'Bennism without Benn: Realignment on the Labour Left', *New Socialist*, May 1985.
10. *Tribune*, 4 January 1985.
11. Minkin, op. cit., p. 325.
12. *Independent*, 23 May 1989.
13. Minkin, op. cit., pp. 468–73.
14. In addition, there was a steady drift of Campaign Group members (such as Jo Richardson and Margaret Beckett) to the Tribune Group.
15. While this is largely a matter of altruism it should not be overlooked that nowadays party members are overwhelmingly employed in the public services.
16. Seyd, P. and Whiteley, P., *Labour's Grass Roots* (Oxford: Clarendon Press), 1992, p. 126.
17. These comments are based on interviews with party officials and activists.
18. *Independent*, 4 October 1991.
19. One shadow cabinet member complained: 'We want to talk about policies, but any deviation from the line is interpreted as an attack on the leadership' (*Tribune*, 15 February 1990).
20. *Guardian*, 11 November 1985.
21. After the 1992 election Hain was elected secretary of a revamped Tribune Group but was voted out the following year for being too outspoken.
22. Ian Aitken, *Guardian*, 7 January 1991. One instance of this was Labour's conversion to Economic and Monetary Union, which occurred with virtually no public discussion.

Conclusion
David S. Bell and Eric Shaw

Styles of conflict and dissent within social democratic parties

Socialist parties are old-established parties. Possibly because of the long history of industrial development in Europe and the slow emergence of organised interests which the socialist parties have had to accommodate, most social democratic parties have long-lived and well-structured divisions within them. This longevity and recurrence may be related to a further feature of socialist parties, which is that they also have 'currents of opinion' (trends of thought or outlook like Christian socialism, or pacifism) of some antiquity (relative to the history of western democratic politics, that is). Currents, or identifiable patterns of attitude and outlook, are not organised but can be quite persistent over the same period in most parties. It is possible that 'factions' and 'currents of opinion' in conservative parties may not coincide, but they tend to do so in social democratic parties. However, this tendency for factions to take up stable ideological patterns may also owe something to the importance which has always been given to theory in the socialist parties (on the Continent, particularly Marxism) and the need for groups to situate themselves relative to continuous and intricate theoretical debates. Yet a caveat must be entered because, as our case studies show, not all dissident activity is ideological or theoretical.

If a major point emerges from this overview, it is that the parties do establish limits to activity that can be legitimately carried out within their organisations, although the definition and execution of these limits are not mechanical. The upper limits to toleration are clear, though the putting into practice of prohibitions on 'factions' which have overstepped the mark is not. The existence in parties (or unions) of groups directed by outside parties is regarded as illegitimate. The infiltration of socialist parties by communists and by Trotskyist groups, which are in fact the agents of external (often minuscule) parties, is grounds for expulsion or dissolution of a faction. Most socialist parties have reacted to this constant infiltration by the Leninist extreme left with purges from time to time, and a range of other methods (like lists of prescribed organisations) have been used (how discipline is enforced is discussed below). However, the evidence of factional activity in both the strong and the weak sense is, by the nature of things, difficult to obtain and expulsion can be a messy and destructive business (for any party).

Secondly, the organisation of a 'party within a party' is usually regarded as beyond the pale. However, this is an even more ambiguous and ill-defined limit than infiltration. Social democratic parties are committed to free politics in which minorities can become majorities, but there has to be a limit to debate; parties which descend into internal squabbling will disintegrate. A limit is implicit in the nature of the organisation of parties and in the nature of political competition (and socialist parties, of course, split on a number of occasions) but the tension arises because the culture of the socialist movement puts a high premium on the toleration of minorities.

Western European socialist parties have formally not countenanced overly structured groups, yet organised factions with their own membership subscriptions, journals and offices mimicking the real party structure are frequent. In effect, restrictions on building a 'counter-party' have frequently been breached and the limits of tolerance are more probably determined by political than constitutional considerations. Thus, while an organised group behaving in a 'party-like' manner may be tolerated for some time, when it becomes a crucial element in the wider political struggle (either for power in the party or to the outside political system) it will be disciplined. For example, the French socialist faction CERES was a key element in bringing the then party leader Mitterrand to the leadership. However by the mid-1970s it had become a conduit into the Parti Socialiste (and the leadership) for the views of the communist party (PCF). At a particularly conflictual time in the communist/socialist (PS−PCF) alliance, this Trojan horse had to be moved outside the gates. In 1975 CERES was evicted from the leadership and its organisation partially disbanded. By the same token dissidents can gain greater leeway for their activities by threatening to split and form a new party. This, as Richard Gillespie notes, was what happened in the Spanish PSOE. The left-wing Izquierda faction came under pressure from the PSOE leadership, retaliated by threatening to quit, and saw its grievances accommodated.

Between the tolerant and the intolerant lie a whole variety of factional line-ups which can be accepted depending on how endangered the party feels, what the leadership is like and what the nature of the competition is in national politics. Splitting the opposition is one of the principal features of political manoeuvring, and chronic internal conflicts indicate potential lines of cleavage to political opponents. Disputes must therefore be handled by party leaders within this context of national party rivalry; parties are not isolated and playing up divisions in the parties is one weapon which will be used by opponents. Parties are also coalitions, and office-seeking coalitions at that, which need to attract support from backgrounds as wide and diverse as possible. Hence expelling dissident groups, or disbanding them, is frequently a recognition of failure in socialist party management and a weapon of last resort.

Cleavage patterns in social democracy

In reality the entire range of dissident behaviour has been evident at some time in the western socialist parties. This extends from the organised party (Militant in the British Labour Party) through the structured, ideological quasi-party of the CERES type (in the French Socialist Party of the 1970s) to the personal groupings around powerful individuals (also in the Parti Socialiste of the 1990s). There are single-issue groups and there are 'altruists' (campaigning on Third World issues) as well as 'egoists', and of course the socialist parties have experienced infiltration which (with rare exceptions) centre and right-wing parties have not.

Divisions within parties also follow the old western European socio-political cleavages: between classes, between centre and periphery, between the militant secularists and the religious (on the Continent but not in the UK), and between the rural and urban and, of course, between left and right. The difference is, of course, that these cleavages are imported into the parties themselves, albeit sometimes about different issues and often about very abstruse questions of strategy or organisation, but they almost always interact with and relate to the clashes in society. Social democratic parties are not totalitarian parties which are hermetically sealed off from the 'host' society, they are a part of the society, they express some of that society's values and problems and that was never seen in the past, by them, as a deficiency. There is good reason, given that western European government is predominantly party government, to regard intra-party struggles as sub-systems of the general governmental process in western Europe. At any rate there are many examples of minorities becoming majorities and vice versa – and the struggle for power is perpetual.

It is also possible, according to Duverger, that the country's overall social structure may itself have some bearing on the nature of conflict in the socialist parties.[1] Duverger lays great stress on the middle-class parties in which internal style stems from rivalry between personal cliques. There may in mass parties be a union influence at work in the opposite direction – making for coherence, moderation and discipline. Where there is a strong union link, that is, where there is one major union federation with organic links to the socialist party, then splits tend to be bi-factional (Austria, Sweden, Norway, Britain, Spain, Germany, Denmark, Greece, Iceland and Ireland). Where the unions are split into competing confederations and the party does not have strong organic union links with the dominant federation, then the struggle is multi-factional. In Luxembourg, Portugal, Belgium, Netherlands, Finland, Switzerland, France and Italy, union influence does exist, but is exercised through individual unionists who are members. The socialist parties in the second 'multi-factional' category are, however, also middle class and this sociology too – it has been suggested – is a factor behind the form of activist militancy encountered in them. If it is generally true that 'multi-factionalism' is a feature of southern European parties, this may simply be another way of presenting the data to show how the communist parties have over time taken the 'natural' working-class constituency from the southern socialists. All the same, strip the ideological issues away (as happened in the French Parti Socialiste in 1990) and you find a politics of cliques and of personality. Nobody would accuse the France of 1990 of being a backward society, but the factional position is (as has been said) reminiscent of the factionalism of the stagnant French Third Republic in which the traditions of the party survived but in which there was a concentration on only an exceptionally narrow range of issues.

The social democratic parties' view that argument, debate and conflict are legitimate implies that (unlike communist parties) they were organised to allow factional expression – sometimes to the point of caricature, as in the SFIO in France, which was an amalgam of different socialist parties, and the Parti Socialiste, which recognised as basic givens both factionalism and also the need for a process of a continuing coalition bargaining and positioning on the non-communist left. European social democratic parties have always, however, been more structured than their conservative counterparts on the Continent and there is no equivalent in western Europe to the loose organisation of the American left – the Democrats. However, a distinction has to be made between the left–right cleavage of the British Labour Party and the German SDP and the bewildering kaleidoscope of factionalism in the Italian and French socialist parties.

It is likely that the party organisation has a bearing on these different patterns, and the British and German cases, which support Duverger's bizarre argument, approximate more to Duverger's 'branch parties', and the Italian and French to Duverger's 'caucus parties'. Duverger argued that loosely organised caucus parties which had the prime object of winning elections would be more prone to factionalism and that the factions in them would be less stable.[2] Despite this, the factions in the Italian and French socialist parties are 'stable', and these parties are 'model' multi-factional ones in which fluid alignments are also typical.[3] The attribution of determining weight to organisation alone puts too much explanatory reliance on one variable, and that a technical one.

Internal struggles reflect wider society in some respect. To be sure, the social democrats do have a close relationship with the trade unions, and this is sometimes exceptionally directed and interventionist – as at times in the history of the British Labour Party – even though the unions appear rarely as factional actors themselves. Interest groups in society may be linked to factions but are only rarely in the position of inner-party actors themselves. This probably distinguishes conflict in social democracy from conflict in continental European conservative parties which can be an extension of interest-group politics by other means – farmers, bankers, lawyers and so on (this distinction should probably not be carried too far with the rise of the ideological right and the decline of the socialist left). Within social democracy it is possible to draw parallels between 'altruistic' commitment campaigns (disarmament and Third World issues) and self-interest groups, but the intrusion of factionalism as a form of interest-group representation is difficult to identify in most socialist parties. The role of producer groups such as farmers' groups in the French Gaullist Party or the Confindustria in the old Italian Liberal Party is replicated only rarely in social democracy in western Europe.[4]

Where a party is 'dominant', in the sense that single-party government in free elections has become the norm, then organised groups might be expected to emerge within the party. If Sweden harbours the only social democratic example (the Liberal Party of Japan was, until 1993, a more extreme version of one-party domination) then it is misleading because the party, as a matter of style, incorporated outside groups (and the opposition) as much as possible into elaborate consensus-making processes (sometimes described as 'neo-corporatism'). Single-party government over 40 years in Sweden was possible only because of new ways of achieving political aims. Consultation was inherent in the consensus-seeking 'social democratic approach' and contributed to such governments' longevity (in contrast to the Conservative strategy in Britain, Swedish social democracy was inclusive and not exclusive).

Single-party domination in a region or constituency might be expected to have the same effect as party domination over the society as a whole in encouraging internal party dissent. In the big working-class districts of western Europe domination of the party over, say, coalmining towns might be expected to be offset by lively internal struggles. Faction fighting could be indulged because the opposition had no prospect of power and competition would lessen the potential dictatorial aspect. This pattern does not seem to be a recognisable feature of western socialist parties. On the contrary, the big bastions – the 'one-party districts' – are often the base for factions and faction leaderships extending outward into the party to form coalitions with their supporters in other areas. For example, the working-class Nord-Pas de Calais in France is less faction-prone than many smaller federations and constituencies.

Another aspect of wider society which has an immediate bearing on intra-party conflict is competition within the party system itself. For the massive 'northern European' social democratic parties where there was a negligible communist party this was not an ever-present factor but alliance politics had to be a major concern of the 'southern' European socialist parties. These parties were torn between alliances to the left and to the right: usually these were mutually exclusive and the tactical choice was expressed in intricate strategic debates (baffling to the uninitiated) and invariably violently splitting the parties. There are a multitude of factors at work here. The intensity of debate was directly linked with the cold war and with the communist parties' organisation (and infiltration of socialist parties) and the existence of the Soviet Union as an ideological superpower manipulating a Marxist ideology of great attractive force. The debate was repeated in discussions about strategic alliance with the green parties, but in such circumstances the ideological aspect was somewhat less intense and a coalition with green parties did not exclude other alliances as understandings with communist parties almost invariably did.

Intra-party divisions, it has been argued, will also be affected by the electoral system and by whether there is a primary and a run-off. In particular, the list systems for elections are said to provide an opportunity for the party leaderships to dominate because the voters cannot intervene to change the candidate order. However, some reservations must be made: it depends on the form of proportional representation. List systems controlled by constituencies (not by national leaders) give possibilities to local leaderships and hence factionalism with a strong local base can persist. In Fourth Republic France the SFIO of the 1950s was torn between the Guy Mollet leadership (based on the Nord-Pas de Calais federations) and the Defferre faction (based on the Bouches-du-Rhône federation). Where voters can choose to alter the order of names (preferential voting) a further twist to factionalism can be given (the principal example here is the Italian one). But the effect of the electoral system is in all cases uncertain. Organised groups may arise despite the electoral system − group rivalry is a feature of social democracy across western Europe's diverse electoral systems − and the electoral system may even have been purposely designed to reflect an existing balance of alignments.

The role of ideology

Ideology is a feature of social democracy and its factions, but to what extent is conflict caused by disagreements over matters of ideology and policy, and to what extent are these, in reality, little more than masks concealing the self-interested struggle for power, career advancement and material advantage? In most cases disputes are conducted in the language of ideology, often employing the traditional discourse of left and right. But in practice, this may be operating as a legitimating device for power struggles where the contestants seek to mobilise support (or conceal their real motives) by appealing to a set of verbal symbols embodied in party statutes or hallowed by tradition. Thus in the socialist parties of France and Spain factions are to a greater degree driven by power or material considerations. This is most notably true of the Spanish PSOE. Gillespie writes that 'what appears to be ideological confrontation is often little more than a façade for battles designed to redefine the internal distribution of power between different groups'. The *guerristas*, followers of Alfonso Guerra, the one-time boss of the party machine, exhibited little political consistency. Guerra, having for years acted as the organisational strongman behind González, employing the power of the machine to crack down on left-wing dissidents, moved to an ostensibly more left-wing position criticising the orthodox fiscal policies of Finance Minister Solchaga on the grounds that he feared they would alienate voters. This represented a serious threat to the *guerristas'* power base because, as Gillespie explains, they were 'builders of a clientelistic empire for which electoral success provides further opportunities to expand influence, while electoral decline involves the possible alienation of political clients whose careers are disrupted'.

Although access to patronage opportunities plays its part in the French party too, the struggle for power assumed greater importance in the PS than in the PSOE. The remarkable ideological odyssey of virtually all the French socialist factions over the last decade, as they have travelled from Marxism or self-management – *socialisme autogestionnaire* – to right-wing social democracy undoubtedly in part reflects the sobering experience of government. But it also suggests that, for the PS, as for its predecessor, the SFIO, ideas were at least as much counters to be played in the power game as signifiers of political conviction. The strife which has, with mounting ferocity, overwhelmed the party has largely been over the struggle for the position of candidate for the presidency after Mitterrand's term expires among men (Rocard, Delors, Fabius and others) who have all endorsed the course taken by Mitterrand-dominated administrations since 1983 and none of whom differ significantly over matters of policy.

A pervasive theme in the analysis of left-wing politics for almost two decades has been the crisis of the Keynesian welfare state. Social democratic governments have been under great pressure to cut welfare spending, while restraining wages and switching to less progressive tax regimes and – most dramatic of all – to discard the pursuit of full employment. Even parties in opposition have had to adjust their programmes to prevailing conceptions as to what type of policy is viable, credible and appealing to the electorate – which has often required compromising the basic principles of Keynesian social democracy.

Social democratic governments have responded to these pressures in different ways, and there is no simple conflation between the extent of the shift to the right and internal controversy. The socialist governments in Spain and France largely jettisoned the promotion of equality and solidarity and sacrificed welfare considerations to the pursuit of deflationary economic policies whose predictable results have included high unemployment. Given that influential forces within both parties had subscribed to radical left positions – pouring scorn on the timidity of northern European social democratic parties – it would be reasonable to anticipate strong opposition to policies which placed a higher premium on the strength of the currency than on reducing joblessness. Yet both experienced little internal resistance, offering further evidence that internal cleavages had been in practice animated more by matters of power, patronage and personal advantage than by ideology.

While it would be naive to expect politicians not to be actuated by some personal ambition, it does not follow that ideology always and everywhere conceals a struggle for personal advantage. For the majority of the parties surveyed in this volume dissension has largely been a matter of *genuine* disagreements over policy and ideology.

For example, as Arter shows, the attempts of the Swedish Social Democratic Party, when in government, to impose a degree of austerity provoked serious opposition – on such a scale that Feldt, the finance minister and champion of the view that welfare spending must be scaled down, quit his post in exasperation, though his successor managed to push through a cuts package. Similarly, the decision of Labour ministers in the Dutch cabinet to support cuts in social benefits provoked a wave of criticism within the party, which has proved extremely damaging.

The management and control of conflict

A range of methods is available to party leaders to manage and control dissent. These fall into four broad categories: sanctions, rewards, normative appeals and cooption. All of these means are available to social democratic parties, but they vary, for reasons we shall explore, in the use they make of them.

All social democratic parties are equipped with sanctions to penalise rebellions: indeed, no party, whether democratic or otherwise, could survive as an effective force without the capacity to protect its own institutional integrity. Yet parties vary significantly, both among themselves and over time, in their reliance on disciplinary control.

As Gillespie shows, the PSOE leadership has accumulated an abundant range of disciplinary weapons which it has regularly used to suppress dissent. These have included suspension, removal from the list of parliamentary candidates and from public office and the weeding of dissidents from elected party bodies. Furthermore, as he adds, 'the post-1979 party statutes have imposed great limits on the tolerance of democratic debate and especially public disagreement with the party line' and even these have been interpreted restrictively to inhibit the operation of organised opposition groupings.

In other parties, the resort to discipline has varied over time and according to the ideological and organisational character of dissident groups. Most have been more reluctant than the PSOE to suppress dissent, and expulsions and the disbanding of dissident groups have been relatively rare. In the 1980s the British Labour Party did mount a disciplinary drive against the Trotskyist Militant Tendency, leading to its proscription and the expulsion of its cadres. But here a distinction must be made between 'legitimate' and 'illegitimate' dissent. The former refers to members who disagree with the leadership over a range of questions but owe loyalty to the host party and no other. Organised Trotskyism represents an example of the latter, since Trotskyist bodies – like the Militant Tendency – are independent, separately controlled and disciplined organisations with duly recruited members whose first loyalty is to them and not the host party. In the British case, Militant adopted the tactic of 'entryism', that is, infiltration and subversion from within, in order to gather further recruits and dislocate the Labour Party. (Militant altered its strategy and subsequently operated as a fully-fledged party.)

Two key variables influencing the proclivity of a party to penalise factional activity are its internal balance of power and party norms. Where opposition factions have wide support, are well-organised and firmly entrenched within the party, the use of discipline risks electoral and organisational turmoil. A leader may calculate that a display of ruthlessness may enhance his or her reputation for tough and determined leadership, but the strategy may easily backfire. By the same token, the greater the power of the party establishment, the lower the costs of imposing sanctions and, hence, the greater the likelihood of employing them. However, power structures are fluid so a tough managerial regime which suppresses dissent at one time may actually inflame it at another. Party norms which legitimate the right to free association and open expression of critical views inhibit the use of discipline. Conversely, norms which place a premium on unity and solidarity and discourage the publicising of oppositional views and the formation of factions are conducive to a stringent managerial regime. Other relevant considerations are the vigour of the traditions of party democracy and the existence of a leadership-based factional tradition. Where, as in Spain, the norms and traditions of party democracy are weak and where 'personalist' leadership is ingrained in the wider political culture, conditions are particularly inimical for the flowering of internal dissent. Gillespie notes that the PSOE's political culture was 'resistant to the public airing of disputes, from which rivals may benefit'. In contrast, in France, party norms have traditionally allowed factions to operate freely.[5]

Party culture is, however, mutable and adapts over time to changed circumstances. The Norwegian Labour Party exemplifies this. Between the first and second controversies over EC membership, Heidar notes, the traditional ethos of 'unity and subordination' had been displaced as the prevailing norms shaping the interpretation of the rules by a more liberal attitude. By the time of the second debate over membership in the 1990s, 'what was self-evident party discipline for the old generation was unacceptable oligarchy for the young'. This was a response partly to changes in the wider political culture, partly to the effects of the disciplinarian approach which helped precipitate the split in the party's ranks. In the British Labour Party, in contrast, it can be argued that the ethos is now less permissive than it was a decade ago. This seems to be in large part a response to the destructive effects of the severe in-fighting of the early 1980s and to years of unrelieved Conservative rule. There is nowadays a much heavier accent on unity, entailing more self-restraint in the articulation of disaffection with the leadership or established policies than was the case in the past. This normative shift, in turn, has facilitated a distinct tightening of Labour's managerial regime.

The carrot is often used with the stick. A well-established control technique is to offer rewards in exchange for compliant behaviour, such as jobs in the party or state apparatus, career advancement and other material perquisites. The incidence of patronage politics is determined by matters of supply and demand. Parties occupying government office in countries where objective and meritocratic standards are not always rigorously enforced in the appointments process may control entry to a considerable number of jobs in the civil service and elsewhere. The opportunities for patronage this affords may then be used to control the party. For example, no less than 70 per cent of delegates at PSOE are regularly to be found on the public payroll. Indeed, Gillespie identifies the drive by Guerra, the head of the party machine, to expand his patronage empire as the main cause of the conflict between him and technocratic-minded senior ministers. He concludes that 'the harsh internal regime would not have worked if the rewards for loyalty had not been so great'. In the French Parti Socialiste, the small size of the membership, coupled with the array of public institutions it controlled between 1981 and 1993, resulted in a very high proportion of gratified activists filling an elected or public office. In Italy – an extreme case – the Socialist Party has been transformed into a simple patronage machine and one sunk into a mire of clientelism and corruption. Perhaps more surprising is the fact that the PDS too has succumbed to the temptation of participating, at least to a degree, in patronage and spoils. In these circumstances, maintaining control of government (at national, regional or local level) becomes increasingly an end in itself.

Questions of demand interweave with those of supply. The key variable here is motivation for membership participation. A number of commentators have distinguished between three types of party member: those whose attachment to the party derives respectively from instrumental, solidaristic and purposive considerations.[6] The distribution between types of members is, in turn, a function of the incentive system within the party and the wider political system. Where the political system provides plentiful opportunities for the distribution of jobs, housing, contracts and other material rewards and where the party, as a governing party at national or local level, has some control over disbursements, a patronage-oriented party machine is more likely to develop. The proportion of members drawn to the party by the search for material rewards is likely to swell and the leadership is well placed to use its control over the supply of these rewards to dissident factions. Northern parties operate within political systems which provide markedly fewer opportunities for the exercise of party patronage and within a political culture less willing to sanction such behaviour. Although there are exceptions – for example, within the municipal strongholds of the British Labour Party and the SPD – in general the proportion of materially motivated members appears to be smaller than in southern parties.[7] It follows that material incentives are less effective as compliance-securing mechanisms.

When social democratic parties were predominantly working-class in composition, appeals to class solidarity and unity were an effective means of enforcing organisational discipline. Indeed, such parties were open to a high degree of normative manipulation as leaders often sought to heighten their control by evoking party rituals, symbols and tradition. Solidarity was one of the few weapons available to workers and to the lower-paid in nineteenth-century industrial society and consequently had a strong resonance in union or class-based parties. So convinced was Michels of the significance of this solidarity reflex within socialist parties that he spoke of the 'cult of veneration of the masses' and their 'profound need to prostrate themselves, not simply before great ideals, but also before the individuals who in their eyes incorporate such ideals'.[8] But social democratic parties have lost their early missionary fervour, their members are drawn to a much smaller extent from traditional working-class milieux and rarely exhibit a deep emotional attachment to the party and the cause or feel the need for solidarity. Indeed, in a number of parties, activists are more likely to exhibit suspicion of mistrust of leaders and remain ever on the alert for the 'sell-out'.

Nevertheless, a modernised form of Michels's 'veneration' has survived. Indeed, contemporary methods of communication have stimulated 'the cult of the personality' as television frequently gives disproportionate coverage to the leader, thus encouraging viewers to equate party and leader. In such circumstances, the leader becomes the modern champion who enters the political tournament on behalf of his party. To criticise the leader is to criticise the party and, implicitly, to help the opposition. Where the leader has a considerable personal appeal to both members and voters, he can exploit his indispensability to arouse loyalty and marginalise critics. Felipe González of the PSOE, for example, has continuously used the threat of resignation to outmanoeuvre critics, and his immense personal prestige to consolidate his authority. Mitterrand, too, occasionally used the threat of resignation, but in France, the position of the presidency as the pinnacle of the political system has endowed him since 1981 – like his right-wing predecessor – with a nimbus of dignity and authority which only the inveterate critic dare challenge.

Furthermore, while social democratic party members, and even more activists, may now be largely middle-class and well educated, the appeal to loyalty has not lost its power, though the reason for this is less a matter of solidarity or deference than pragmatic calculation. As the main sources of political communications, the media may be only too eager to publicise evidence of 'splits' either for their news value or through political hostility. The substance of a disagreement may be lost on the average voter who is not interested in the minutiae of internal political conflicts and who therefore may simply be left with an image of a quarrelsome party unable 'to get its act together'. In these circumstances, leaders can make very powerful appeals to dissenters not to rock the boat – and to impugn them as sabotaging the party's electoral prospects if they persist. The outcome, then, is a form of normative control which derives not from internal socialisation but from a pragmatic response to external pressure.

Those who hold, or aspire to hold, party or public office may be animated by a desire to promote ideals or simply by personal ambition, but the desire for self-advancement is a characteristic of the senior echelons of all political parties. This furnishes, as Michels noted, another means by which a party establishment can maintain control: through a process of coopting prominent figures from within the ranks of the dissenters.[9] This was the rather far-sighted management technique adopted by Willy Brandt as chairman of the SPD. He responded to the JUSO-led left challenge by pursuing 'the strategy of integration' — that is encouraging JUSO leaders to involve themselves in the work of the party and inviting them to occupy positions of responsibility. Some of his less astute critics, preferring Chancellor Schmidt's more robust approach, claimed that Brandt was rendering the SPD vulnerable to the far left's long march through the institutions. But Brandt (who had himself been a radical socialist in his youth) had a deeper understanding of political (and psychological) processes and, as former JUSO leaders rose through the party hierarchy, they abandoned much of their leftist fervour, mostly coming to occupy a mildly left-of-centre position (although others quit the party in disillusion to join the Greens). Social democratic parties are replete with examples of leaders who commenced their careers on the left and then progressed steadily to the right.

A similar pattern can be discerned in the Dutch PvdA and British Labour Party. In the Netherlands, as van Praag shows, prominent members of the New Left tended to moderate their stance as they entered the leadership. In the UK, senior figures of the soft left who had once been part of the Bennite camp, secured influential positions in the party hierarchy, usually with Kinnock's approval, and almost invariably moved to the right, thus weakening the voice of the soft left in the constituencies as well as isolating the hard left. However, the examples of all three parties indicate that the tactic has a cost. The impact of cooption has tended to be dialectical, so while left-wingers 'moderated' their politics, so too, under their impetus, did the parties tend to shift somewhat to the left — until, that is, the restored strength of the leadership rendered them superfluous.

Factionalism: force or failure?

Disapproval of factional activity is virtually universal among political (as distinct from academic) commentators. We would suggest that this condemnation is misplaced. Democracy is not about suppressing different viewpoints but accommodating them and seeking to balance diversity and majority rule. Social democratic parties have consistently claimed to be internally democratic consensus-seeking organisations, but it does appear – as Michels had seen – that powerful oligarchical mechanisms operate within social democratic parties. In large voluntary associations, like unions and parties, the leadership enjoys a range of advantages which derive in part from its position within the internal division of labour and in part from its control over the organisation: it has privileged access to sources of information, expertise and internal communication; it holds the initiative in the decision-making process; it controls the disciplinary apparatus and can act much more swiftly and effectively than the rank and file. In these circumstances, power is bound to be concentrated in the hands of the leadership. Lipset *et al.* advanced the hypothesis that oligarchical trends can be countervailed and internal democracy safeguarded 'in organisations where members form organised or structured sub-groups which while maintaining a basic loyalty to the large organisation constitute relatively independent and autonomous centres of power within the organisation'.[10] Where the rank and file is able to organise, it ceases to be an inchoate force. It can orchestrate the activities of the dissatisfied, accumulate political skills, operate its own communication and information channels, respond more swiftly to leadership initiatives, develop its own tactics and strategy and formulate alternative policies.

But for factions to flourish and safeguard a pluralistic structure of power without endangering the institutional integrity and viability of the host party, a range of conditions needs to be in place. Firstly, they must have sources of power independent of the central body, and their power relative to the central body must be considerable enough to resist repression.[11] Secondly, they will only survive in a culture which accepts the legitimacy of factional activity and political conflict, and protects the rights of members to freedom of association and of speech. A pluralist culture which regards the expression of political differences as normal and legitimate will, in addition, be more successful in balancing unity and diversity, since conflict is more likely to be conducted in accordance with established rules of the game. Thirdly, factions themselves should both owe ultimate loyalty to the host party and be motivated by programmatic concerns. Groups which are directed by and under the discipline of outside agencies (like Trotskyist entryist organisations) damage the organisational fabric of the party and perform a disruptive role. Further, the experience of the Spanish and French parties suggests that groups motivated primarily by patronage or power considerations have a more fragmenting effect than programmatic ones while doing little to counter-balance oligarchical tendencies. Finally, conflict between institutionalised groups and the ruling establishment may inflict serious damage on the unity and organisational health of a party, unless it occurs within a framework of consensus which both binds the protagonists to some shared aims and values and facilitates the emergence of effective mechanisms for regulating disagreements.

While our case studies do suggest a relationship between the degree of power centralisation and the existence of well-supported and organised factions (for example, the Netherlands in the 1970s, Britain in the early 1980s, Germany at present) it may be that this perspective overlooks the dysfunctional effects of internal party democracy. Thus, it can be objected that it does not take sufficient account of the electorally detrimental consequences of 'splits'. Indeed, it may be that, for electoral reasons, parties require strong leadership because only where power is centralised will a party have the capacity for swift and effective responses and rapid adjustment in tactics required for effective campaigning and because of public expectation that leaders be strong and in full command of their parties.

This is the position that rational choice analysts, who distinguish between a 'purposive' policy-seeking rank and file and a more instrumental vote-seeking leadership, generally take. Strom, for example, argues that, to motivate activists, leaders may agree to devolve decision-making rights and establish mechanisms of leadership accountability to the rank and file but at the cost of electoral viability. 'If policy-making is decentralised, it will be more difficult to trade policy for votes or office benefits'. The party 'may be saddled with electorally suboptimal policy platforms' with prospects of securing votes and office receding.[12]. But the theory is not entirely convincing. It defines a vote-winning strategy in terms of the capacity of leaders to free themselves from internal party constraints in order to produce the best (electorally most attractive) policy mix, on the assumption that voting behaviour can be understood primarily in terms of demand for desired 'policy goods'. In fact, voters are not solely actuated by policy; the extent of their knowledge of parties' policy positions is often highly imperfect; their preferences are not always compatible; and deciding the right mix of policies to maximise votes is a far more problematic operation than rational choice theorists appear to recognise. Not least, party members may genuinely disagree over what constitutes the 'optimal' electoral strategy. In fact there is no self-evidently optimal electoral strategy, which explains why divergent strategic conceptions are a source of intra-party conflict. As Downs pointed out, 'uncertainty about what ideas are most efficacious in vote-getting permits a diversity of views to exist within a party, just as it permits different party ideologies to exist in society'.[13] Van Praag demonstrates the point well: while the recovery of power by 'vote-seeking' leaders in the PvdA did lead to the adoption of a centrist political strategy in the Netherlands, its results have been dismal. Even more dramatic has been the collapse of the pragmatic, fully 'modernised' and deideologised French Parti Socialiste, pursuing what many commentators would regard as an optimal electoral strategy.

Nevertheless, it does appear that voters dislike parties in which disagreements are openly and freely conducted – that is, more democratic parties. Hence the paradox: the more oligarchical a party, the more it is likely to be seen as possessing the qualities which fit it for the task of government in political systems which value pluralism and political liberty.

Conclusion

In this study we have concentrated on establishing the empirical background essential to the study of factions in social democracy across the continent of Europe. We have brought together comparative case studies and we have been less concerned with taxonomy and definitional boundaries (which bedevil the study of factionalism) or even with the essence of social democracy itself. What we have is a study which might enable future researchers to make comparative judgements about social democracy, Christian democracy, ecological parties, liberal parties and so on. We have not used any particular theoretical framework but we have hoped to provide material support for the theoretical trail-blazers.

Hence the conclusion is less a drawing together of threads, or a conceptual advance, than a number of generalisations from the studies of social democracy presented here. Each party is constrained by national and particular factors, and sceptics may think that these provisional hypotheses go too far, but a study of this sort would be incomplete without some conclusions emerging for a future agenda. We have therefore made some tentative across-the-board generalisations by way of conclusion. These may or may not fit into a more ambitious theory, but the current state of research on the internal politics of social democracy in western Europe hardly permits a more ambitious project.

The generalisations we have made concern the utility of factionalism in social democracy (which we suggest may be more functional than is often allowed), the factors behind cohesion and dissent, the role of ideology, and internal party management. In the conclusion we returned to the question of the disutility of dissidence with a few remarks on the pluralism of party politics and government systems. Social democracy is not alone in facing problems of internal pluralism (though again we lack the empirical material to enable meaningful generalisations) but the intensity of internal debate has often been remarked on. However, we would underline the as yet untested nature of our concluding remarks and their applicability to a narrow range of party life.

Notes

1. Duverger, M., *Political Parties* (New York: Wiley), 1954, pp. 1–3, 17–27.
2. Ibid., pp. 121–22.
3. Zariski, R., 'The Italian Socialist Party: A Case Study in Factional Conflict', *American Political Science Review*, June 1962; and Zariski, R., 'Party Faction and Comparative Politics', *Midwest Journal of Political Science*, 1960, pp. 27–51.
4. The leader of the French farmers' union, F. Guillaume, was made minister of agriculture in the neo-Gaullist Prime Minister Chirac's government of 1986–88.

5. See Cole, A., 'Factionalism, the French Socialist Party and the Fifth Republic', *European Journal of Political Research*, Vol. 17, No. 1, 1989, pp. 77–94.

6. See, for example, Wilson, J.Q., *Political Organisations* (New York: Basic Books), 1973.

7. For the British Labour Party, see Seyd, P. and Whitley, P., *Labour's Grass Roots*, (Oxford: Clarendon Press), 1992.

8. Michels, R., *Political Parties* (London: Free Press), 1961, pp. 93, 96.

9. Ibid., pp. 181–82.

10. Lipset *et al.*, *Union Democracy* (London: Collier-Macmillan), 1956, p. 15.

11. Ibid., p. 80.

12. Strom, K., 'A Behavioural Theory of Competitive Political Parties', *American Journal of Political Science*, Vol. 34, No. 2, 1990.

13. Downs, A., *An Economic Theory of Democracy* (New York: Harper and Row), 1957.

Index